ACCESSORY DESIGN

fb

ACCESSORY DESIGN

Aneta Genova

Parsons The New School for Design

FAIRCHILD BOOKS · NEW YORK

Executive Editor:
Olga T. Kontzias
Senior Associate Acquiring Editor:
Jaclyn Bergeron
Assistant Acquisitions Editor:
Amanda Breccia
Development Editor:
Sylvia L. Weber
Creative Director:
Carolyn Eckert
Assistant Art Director:
Sarah Silberg
Production Director:
Ginger Hillman
Senior Production Editor:
Elizabeth Marotta
Associate Production Editor:
Linda Feldman
Copyeditor:
Nancy Reinhardt
Ancillaries Editor:
Noah Schwartzberg
Executive Director, General Manager:
Michael Schluter
Cover Design:
Carolyn Eckert
Cover Art:
Micca/Dutch Uncle
Text Design:
Carolyn Eckert
Composition:
Tom Helleberg
Illustrations:
Micca/Dutch Uncle
Photo Research:
Avital Aronowitz
Photos:
Courtesy of Aneta Genova

Library of Congress Catalog Card Number: 2010923008
ISBN 13: 978-1-56367-926-1
GST R 133004424
Printed in the United States of America
TP08

CONTENTS

EXTENDED

CONTENTS

PREFACE

THE APPAREL ACCESSORIES MARKET is growing rapidly and has a large share of the overall apparel industry. The booming accessory business requires a large number of new accessory designers, and most fashion colleges and departments are already offering or planning to start a variety of accessory design classes. With this book, I'd like to address the need for a comprehensive accessory design textbook that gives an extensive overview of the actual process for designing accessories from inspiration through design, sketching, and manufacturing. This book traces the steps of the design process for handbags, small leather goods, footwear, and various other accessories as it happens in the industry and will be an invaluable tool to the accessory design instructor.

As an accessory design instructor, I recognize the need for a textbook that gives industry-relevant information and an overview of the process as well as supplies comprehensive visuals from professional sources. In this textbook, I have featured over 200 sketches and photographs from professional designers who are currently working in the industry for prestigious companies around the world. Some sketches have been developed specifically for this book and have never been printed in any other media; others are taken from current or graduating design students, winners of fashion school competitions, and experienced designers. All photographs that feature design processes have been taken in a working factory during the actual design and manufacturing. My main goal throughout this book has been to review the design and manufacturing development as realistically as possible by showing various styles and approaches to the same process.

This book also features individual profiles and interviews with designers who are relevant to each chapter and who show the many sides of this exciting industry. From the President and Executive Creative Director for Coach Reed Krakoff to Marie Havens, the Design Director at MEND, a socially and environmentally responsible nonprofit company, which employs formerly abducted and abused Ugandan women, this book shows a vast array of design paths. All fashion accessory students know they love to design, but not all of them know or see the way of achieving their dreams. With this book, I would like to show how different designers have accomplished their goals and that there are many paths a creative individual can take.

Through my teaching years, I have discovered that there are very limited sources that highlight specifically the history of accessories throughout the centuries in an educational, organized manner geared toward college students. Fashion costume tends to be the leading theme in most books, and accessories are fitted within the larger discussion of apparel. I have scouted through countless sources of historical references in order to separate accessories from general fashion and present them in an educational format in Part One. Chapter 1 takes the reader on a journey through the history of accessories from ancient times to the present and provides highlights of the development of accessories. With that information, I aim to set a solid knowledge of the progression of accessories throughout the centuries so a designer can easily reference and draw inspiration from past experience.

Chapter 2 provides the engaging stories of some of the classic accessory companies, like Louis Vuitton, Hermés, and Coach, followed by profiles of recent successful designers like Jimmy Choo, Kate Spade, and Carlos Falchi in Chapter 3. Such company introductions will help students understand the importance and the process of developing and building a brand and staying true to its identity. Chapter 4 provides an overview of the design processes shared by the designers of the various types of accessories discussed in the remaining parts of the book.

In its entirety, this textbook reviews the following groups of accessories: handbags and small leather goods in Part Two (Chapters 5–8); footwear in Part Three (Chapters 9–13); and a variety of other accessories including hats, gloves, belts, neckwear, and pocket squares in Part Four (Chapter 14). (Jewelry design is not included because the design process is so different from that of other accessories.) Each chapter is followed by a project that relates to the content and is a natural continuation of the obtained knowledge. The projects include:

- A research project, inspired by a time period
- A market research project. This project will teach students the importance of knowing what is happening in the world of accessories and staying current on trends and the competition.
- A trend report-developing project
- Design projects for handbags and for footwear, consisting of the following parts:
  - Concept research
  - Mood-board creation
  - Color and material selection
  - Sketching the design ideas into a cohesive collection
  - Creation of a final presentation

I believe that this book will provide extensive knowledge of the design process of various accessories and aid the instructors with comprehensive tools to teach their accessory design course however specialized it may be. Separate units can be used for a handbag or shoe design courses or the whole book can be used as an overall instructional guide. I am sure each instructor can find a way to adapt the book to his or her own syllabus and course outline, or use the supplied one.

It is with the full understanding that I cannot possibly cover all aspects of design for every single accessory in this vast industry, that I present this textbook. My sincere desire is to merely open the door to a deeper understanding of this vast subject.

ACKNOWLEDGMENTS

THIS BOOK would not have happened without the hard work of a team of people who guided me along the way and the working accessory design professionals who donated their work and time to help bring the real perspective of the accessory design industry today. I want to acknowledge Alan Kannof for his friendship and advice on legal matters, which established a great start for this book. Thanks, too, to Lisa Smilor, associate executive director of the Council of Fashion Designers of America (CFDA), for introducing me to accessory designer members of CFDA who are among the contributors to text, photos, and illustrations.

I would like to acknowledge the contributions of the following accessory design industry professionals who donated some of their design work or prepared sketches specifically for this book and the gracious generosity of those who provided photos or allowed me to photograph their workshops, studios, and factories while they were working: Melinda Albert, freelance accessory designer for Calvin Klein, Replay, Hugo Boss, Ferrari, Pirelli, Rena Lange, and others; Nalini Arora, accessory designer; Amanda Blackwell, accessory designer: Kevin Blow, fashion illustrator; Nancy Boas, VP of Women's Collection Footwear at Ralph Lauren; Steven Broadway, fashion illustrator; Maria Pia Capitano, handbag designer for Fratelli Rosetti; Khirma Eliazov, handbag designer; Carlos Falchi, accessory designer; Alexander Fielden, shoe designer; Nancy Geist, footwear designer and owner of Nancy Geist and Butter shoes; Danilo Giordano, women's shoe designer for Bally, TOD's, Valentino, and senior design director for Ralph Lauren collection footwear, who illustrated countless shoe sketches specifically for this book; Alan Hangad, accessory manufacturer; Marie Havens, accessory designer, photographer, and Director of Design and Product Development for MEND at Invisible Children Inc.; Coleman Horn, freelance accessory designer for athletic brands including Nike and Reebok; Han Josef, men's shoe designer for Cole Haan; Ivy Kirk, accessory designer for kate spade; Reed Krakoff, accessory and fashion designer; Devi Kroell, accessory designer; Judith Lieber, accessory designer; Kerrie Luft, shoe designer; Ann-Marie Mountford-Chu, women's shoe designer and former VP of Footwear Design for American Eagle; Elizabeth Olsen, founder of olsenHaus; Edgardo Osorio, accessory designer for Roberto Cavalli, Rene Caovilla, and Salvatore Ferragamo; Cesare Paciotti, accessory designer; Minna Parikka, accessory designer; Sabato Riccio, accessory designer for Dolce and Gabanna; Fratelli Rosetti, accessory designer and manufacturer; Rafé Totengco, accessory designer; Helene Verin, shoe designer; Stuart Weitzman, accessory designer; and Gabriela Zanzani, women's handbag designer for Celine, Coach, and Ralph Lauren.

Howard Davis, shoe design instructor at Parsons The New School for Design and the following students, past and present, at Parsons kindly shared examples of their work with me: Benyam Assefa, Aimee Kestenberg, Hyeyoung Kim, Fay Leshner, Jovana Mirabile, Frank Nathan, and Clara Yoo. I also thank the following graduates of other design institutions, who shared their student experiences and work with me: Brianna Allen, Yunchieh Chang, Nayany Katayama, and Lina Ladekarl, all graduates of the Academy of Art University, and Kristina Gress, from the Fashion Institute of Technology.

The following reviewers of the proposal and manuscript, selected by the publisher, offered many helpful suggestions: Kathy Bailon, Fashion Institute of Design and Merchandising—Los Angeles; Anne Cecil, Drexel University; Shana Hall, Savannah College of Art and Design; Ellen Lynch, Fashion Institute of Technology; Peggy Quesenberry, Virginia Polytechnic Institute and State University; Melanie Risner, Art Institute of Portland; and Colleen Schindler-Lynch, Ryerson University. Han Josef brought the perspective of an experienced footwear designer for such brands as Reebok and Cole Haan to his review of Part Three.

With enormous gratitude, I'd like to acknowledge Jaclyn Bergeron, acquisitions editor, who believed in me from the very beginning; my irreplaceable development editor, Sylvia Weber, who spent countless hours bettering the manuscript and turning it into a real textbook; the photo editor, Avital Aronowitz, who persevered in finding the perfect images; Elizabeth Marotta, who guided the book expertly through production; Carolyn Eckert, who oversaw the design of the text; Jennifer Crane, director of editorial development, who offered her support at all stages; and Noah Schwartzberg, ancillaries editor, who provided invaluable aid in preparing instructor's resources that will help bring readers into the exciting business of accessory design.

To my loving husband Luis, who endured through all the late nights when I was working on this book, thank you for your patience, love, and support!

ACCESSORY DESIGN

A HISTORY AND OVERVIEW

of Accessory Design

Part One

1

HIGHLIGHTS IN THE HISTORY OF ACCESSORIES

From Ancient Times to the Present

CHAPTER ONE traces the history of accessories as they developed in the Western world from ancient Egypt through the twentieth century. After reading this chapter, you will be able to identify and describe features of accessory design throughout history that can inspire your own designs.

ACCESSORIES HAVE DEVELOPED THROUGH THE AGES as functional items as well as important symbols of social standing or rank in society. They have gone through many transformations, some ridiculous, some practical, and have endured through the centuries as items that are important in any wardrobe. They can complement a garment, create a statement, or be purely utilitarian. Many accessories like handbags, hats, gloves, and purpose-specific shoes have a more functional use beyond that of style. They were first and foremost created to protect the face, feet, hands, and head from nature's harsh conditions. Shoes are used to cover the feet when they cannot withstand extreme cold, hot, or wet conditions. Belts help to support trousers on the body or can gather a loose dress to create a thinner waistline and add a bit of color and style. There are many uses of accessories throughout history that signify belonging to a particular group, through wearing uniforms, insignia, or even tattoos that have a tribal significance.

Whatever the use, accessories have been and always will be an important element of an outfit for men and women. This chapter takes a look into the development of accessories from ancient times to the present, highlighting the handbag and its precursors, footwear, headwear, belts, gloves, and neckwear. Carefully constructed current illustrations depict some of the most significant styles for each historic period, styles that can serve as references for your own accessory designs. This chapter provides a guideline to give you a solid foundation of the most important styles leading fashion trends in Western civilization through the ages.

Ancient Times
The forebears of Western accessory design date back to the civilizations of ancient Egypt, Greece, and Rome.

Egypt
Most Egyptian accessories or art depicting them have been preserved in pyramids and the tomb burials of mummies. While tombs of pharaohs contain various sandals, headdresses, and other objects, many of these accessories might have been ceremonial or special burial pieces in addition to ones from the actual wardrobes of their times, and they show mostly the symbols of wealth and privilege. In order to discover the accessories worn by common people, you should look at art depicting everyday scenes involving diverse people. What has been uncovered points out that the workmanship of Egyptian artisans was exceptional and

accessories created during that period were of the highest quality and very functional. Here are some of the most significant styles.

HEADWEAR

The common Egyptians did not wear any headdresses, caps, or hats apart from headbands. They just covered their hair or shaved heads with wigs. The pharaohs and their families, on the other hand, were rarely depicted with uncovered heads. They wore crowns, diadems, metal headbands or **nemes**, a striped headcloth, extending low down the back. The crowns, like the sceptres, were symbols of power.

BLUE CROWN/ WAR CROWN

NEMES

BELTS

Bejeweled belts often added color to the plain white garments of the Egyptians. They were constructed of woven designs or decorated with appliqué, leather, or beads.

FOOTWEAR

The footwear of this ancient civilization was a very simple thong sandal. The sandals developed for protection from the hot sand and pavement in this dry and warm climate do not even appear to have been worn indoors. Most people, especially children, usually went barefoot. Historians seem to agree that wearing shoes was a privilege reserved for nobility, priests, and warriors. For those who could afford them, shoes were made

ROYAL SANDAL

SOLDIER'S SANDAL

of interlaced strips of flax, straw, palm, papyrus stalk, reeds, or wood and were shaped to the left and right foot. Shoemakers wove the straw into the desired shape with a strap between the toes that joined the sides. The outsoles were built to have three or four thicknesses. Wealthier people had sandals soled or entirely made out of leather. Rawhide or untanned cattle or buffalo skins were used, as well as vegetable tanned leathers. Naturally fine leathers were reserved for the rulers and heavy leather for soldiers. Priests wore sandals made of papyrus only, refusing to have contact with dead animals. The kings were also often depicted barefoot, just like their gods, but wore very elaborately decorated sandals for ceremonies. Among the belongings discovered in the tomb of Tutankhamen were 93 pieces of footwear, including wooden sandals with depictions of enemies on their soles, so he could step on them as he walked.

Sandals symbolized prosperity and authority during those times and ones made out of gold have been found, although it is not clear if they have been worn or used for decoration. The only people who increasingly started developing a need for sandals were soldiers and travelers.

Ancient Greece

Ancient Greece had its golden age approximately 500–323 BC, which marked incredible creativity in architecture, writing, philosophy and the arts. Philosophers pondered on the meaning of life and the nature of the universe and Greek sculptures glorified the body. Sculpture and vase painting provide some evidence for dress and accessories even though it was highly stylized. Marble statues offer much more realistic representation of shoes and headwear although the color has worn off the statues over the passage of centuries. Spinning and weaving were occupations that were fit even for queens and goddesses, and embroidery skills were quite evident on some shoe styles.

HEADWEAR

Hats for men often shown in Greek art include fitted caps and the **petasos**, a closely fitted cap with a wide brim, as well as **Phrygian bonnets**, high brimless caps with the peak folding towards the front. Both men and women wore a **pilos**, another brimless or very narrow brimmed cap with a pointy crown. Fillets, ribbons, and scarves were often used to create the layered curl looks for Greek women. Some paintings also depict veils worn over the head or pulled across the face.

PHRYGIAN
BONNET

FOOTWEAR

Men and women wore sandals, often with multiple straps that secured the sole to the foot. The styles vary from simpler ones with leather straps to complicated designs with metal ornaments, embroidery and decorated turned-down cuffs. Men also wore closely fitted ankle-

KREPIS WITH
SOLE SHAPED
TO TOE

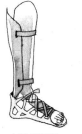

MILITARY
KREPIS

KREPIS
WITH
THONG

high shoes or midcalf length boots with front lacing and decorative trims. Military shoes and leather boots even had spikes or spurs. The soles could be hobnailed to increase the durability, and some were shaped to the form of the toes.

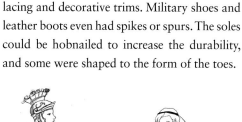

Roman Empire

Romans were citizens of a wealthy society and believed in order, civil service, and customs duties. Their clothing included simple tunics and togas and, for women, scarves and veils. Accessories used throughout this period were symbolic of status and occupation in Roman society and were often intricate and elaborate.

HEADWEAR

Roman women wore their hair up, in carefully arranged styles held with jeweled hairpins, or curled in ringlets and spirals rather than wearing hats. In addition to hairpins their complicated hairstyles were often decorated with elaborate diadems or hairnets made of finely woven gold wires. For Roman matrons, intricate hairdos were also bound by a woolen band called a **vita** or covered with a veil.

Headwear was very important for the Roman soldiers. Their protective helmets, called **galea**, were made by hand. The design of the helmet varied according to army unit types and individual examples and had various cheek guards. Most had a crest of the soldier's legion made of plumes or horse hair.

BELTS

A military belt, called a **balteus** or **cingulum,** was made in army workshops and was a valuable personal possession. It was used to gather and tuck the clothing and to carry a sword or a dagger. These belts were usually custom-made according to one's personal budget and wealth. A soldier could carry a single belt or two crossed over each other. They were made from leather and covered with ornate cast or stamped plates of tin or bronze or were cast entirely out of metal and typically had a decorative apron with four to eight leather apron straps ¾–inch to 1 inch wide, decorated with iron or bronze studs or plates, with dangling ends.

FOOTWEAR

Sandals, boots, and shoes were very common, and virtually all men and most women wore them. Both men and women wore sandals (called **solae** in Latin or **sandalis**), boots, and slipperlike shoes reaching to the ankle, called **soccus.** The variety of footwear though defined a person's position in society. Women wore closed shoes in white, green, or yellow. Patrician men wore red sandals with an ornament at the back. Senators wore brown footwear with black straps, which wound round the leg to midcalf, where the straps were tied. Consuls wore white shoes, and soldiers, heavy boots.

Caligae sandals were the classic Roman military army boots. The uppers and soles were cut from pigskin and were heavily soled. Iron "hobnails" protected the bottom of the boots and secured the uppers to the soles. A softer lining was used inside for comfort, but the shoes were overall very heavy and sturdy, built to last in battle.

CREPIDA WITH EAGLE
EMBROIDERED ON
LUNULA

The Byzantine Empire and Medieval Europe

The Byzantine Empire (339–1453) was technically the late Roman Empire and is a link between the Classical and Medieval periods, extending in the eastern Mediterranean area though the end of the Middle Ages. In Western Europe, the most noteworthy developments in fashion and accessory design occurred during the tenth through the early fifteenth centuries. The predominant religion in Byzantium and Medieval Western Europe was Christianity.

The Byzantine Empire

Naturally, clothing and accessories of the Byzantine Empire derived from the Roman designs, but the body was more covered because of the religious beliefs and practices. The Byzantines were very fond of vibrant, bright colors, reserving royal purple for the emperor and empress, and textiles were rich in ornaments and embroideries. Some of the best examples still survive in the Christian Orthodox churches as painted icons and mosaics, the best known of which are the sixth-century group of mosaics in Ravenna. They portray Emperor Justinian, his wife, Empress Theodora, his bishops, priests, and other dignitaries.

HEADWEAR

Hats were mostly limited to royalty, with ladies choosing to wear elaborate hairstyles with soft curls. Most men went bareheaded, except for some large hats that were worn by officials towards the end of the Byzantine period. The few women's hats portrayed during these times were turbanlike and evolved into caps with rolls around them. Empresses set their heavily jeweled crowns or diadems on top of those hats until late in the fifteenth century. Some pleated fillets and a variety of veils were also worn by most ladies as well as jeweled hairnets. Veils were worn in the street by upper-class women, a practice later adopted in much of the Islamic world.

BELTS

Discs or coins were mounted on simple frames to form **girdles** (a term used synonymously with belts by fashion historians), which were worn around the waist to secure garments. Alternatively, they could be worn in the manner of a necklace. Gold pieces mounted in this way could be bestowed as gifts to high-ranking officials and nobles or as rewards for military or other services.

FOOTWEAR

Shoes had a soft, socklike construction and were made out of leather or cloth, including silk. Most were heavily ornamented with self material, stones, pearls, gems, embroidery, and appliqué work and ended below the knee. Red shoes marked the Emperor (a mosaic of the Empress Theodora shows her wearing red, slipperlike

SOFT LEATHER BOOT

shoes); blue shoes were reserved for members of the imperial family; and green shoes for generals, ambassadors, and other appointed officials.

Soldiers wore sandals tied around the calf or strips of cloth wrapped round the leg to the calf. There are examples of knee high boots, also lavishly decorated in gems and pearls. Closed-toe military boots came later in the period and were worn only by men.

12TH C.   14TH C.

Middle Ages

By the tenth to thirteenth centuries, Europe grew more prosperous, the urban middle classes began to wear more complex clothes and accessories, which followed, at a distance, the fashions set by the elites. Increased production of quality textiles and import of goods gained an economic importance. Wealthy merchants traded fabrics and lavishly decorated accessories. Nobles were willing to spend great amounts of money on their look, in order to gain status.

Fashion in fourteenth century Europe (the Late Middle Ages) was marked by the beginning of a period of experimentation with different forms of clothing and accessories and from this century onward, Western fashion started changing at a much faster pace. Northern Europe, and especially the French court, became the main innovator in fashion and accessories.

HEADWEAR

Married and older women covered their hair with veils, pulled around their face and under the chin or hanging loose to the chest area. Some of the developments in women's headwear during the twelfth century were the barbette, the fillet, and the wimple. The **barbette** was a linen band which passed from temple to temple under the chin and was worn with a **fillet**, a standing linen band, much like a crown over which a veil was often draped. The **wimple** was a fine white linen or silk scarf that covered the neck, with ends pulled and tied above the ears or temples. It was usually worn with a veil and became a part of the dress for many orders of the Roman Catholic nuns until the 1960s.

The most important head covers during the thirteenth century were the **coif** and the hood. The coif is a close-fitting cap made of a light fabric, usually white or natural-colored linen (or silk, for the nobility), which was worn by men and women for warmth and protection from the elements, and to keep hair out of the face. Hoods fitted the head very closely, and some of them were not attached to capes. They were made with long tubes of fabric, which hung low in the back. In the second part of the fourteenth century, hoods started to be transformed into turbanlike styles, and a variety of hats were created from colorful brocades, trimmed with colored bands.

BARBETTE AND FILLET

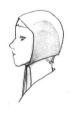

COIF

A tremendous variety of hats and headdresses were worn in Europe during the fifteenth century. There were styles that were draped, folded, padded, pinned, jeweled, and feathered in countless ways. Here are some of them:

- The **caul** was a netting, sometimes lined in silk, that covered the pinned up hair.
- The **bourrelet** was a padded, crownlike, internally supported roll that was worn by men and women on top of the head.
- Women wore veils of different lengths, draped over the hair, layering over the ears, and draping above the forehead. These veils were often supported by wire frames that exaggerated the shape and were variously draped from the back of the headdress or covered the forehead.

- The **hennin** was one of the most extravagant hats worn during this century. It was in the shape of a cone or a steeple and often had a veil hanging from the top. These hats were worn throughout Burgundy and France and in Northern Europe. They were rarely seen in Italy or England.
- The **snood** was a type of a close fitting hood or hairnet worn over long hair by women. It was revived centuries later in the 1860s and again in the 1940s.

BOURRELLET

SNOOD

- The **crespine** of Northern Europe, originally a thick hairnet or snood, evolved into a mesh of jeweler's work that confined the hair on the sides of the head.
- The **chaperon** started as a form of hood with a short cape and later evolved into a highly versatile hat worn in all parts of Western Europe in the Middle Ages. It was especially fashionable in mid-fifteenth-century Burgundy, before gradually falling out of fashion in the late fifteenth century and returning to its utilitarian status. It is the most commonly worn male headgear in Early Netherlandish painting. Chaperons were used in France and Burgundy to denote, by their color, allegiance to a political faction. Women also wore the chaperon, a draped hat based on the hood and **liripipe** (a long tail), and a variety of related draped and wrapped turbans.

CRESPINE

CHAPERON

GLOVES

Gloves were popular among all classes, with simpler styles for the less privileged and elaborately decorated ones for the upper class.

BELTS

Jeweled girdles made out of gold coins were often worn as belts or neckbands. Men wore metal or leather belts with plates to which they attached daggers and pouches for carrying money and valuables.

LATE 14TH OR
EARLY 15TH C.
MAN'S BELT

12TH C.
DRAWSTRING
POUCH

POUCHES

Both men and women attached drawstring pouches to their girdles on a long cord, according to the fashion, personal status, and lifestyle of the wearer. Pockets were not invented yet, so people attached most valuables, such as a rosary, Book of Hours, pomanders (scented oranges), **chatelaine** (a clasp or chain to suspend keys, etc.), and even daggers. Women particularly favored ornate drawstring purses which were known as **hamondeys** or **tasques**. Some simple purses in rectangular shapes were seen richly decorated with embroideries.

FOOTWEAR

Women's and men's shoes were mostly open-toe slippers with bands across the ankles. Soft foot coverings for the wealthy class were made from soft leather or luxurious fabrics like velvet and silk, adorned with elaborate embroideries and pearls. A favorite color for noblemen was red, darker more somber tones for people with less means, and untanned hides for poor people, who often couldn't afford any shoes. Some gentlemen also wore plain black shoes and slippers.

Some elongated toe-points started to appear in the twelfth century and remained popular into the fifteenth century until they were banished by Edward IV of England in 1463 and by 1470 in France. Some of them curled up, and some curled down; they were usually stuffed with moss, wool, or other soft material and sometimes shaped with whalebone. By the fourteenth century, these shoes reached fantastical lengths of 12 inches past the feet. Dandies sometimes had the toes held up with strings or chains attached to garters at the knees and even added bells to them. These extreme shoe styles were called **poulaines** or **crackowes**, named after Poland and the Polish capital city of Krakow, where this style originated. By 1480, the shoes had disappeared, and the opposite extreme of shoes with blunt wide toes started appearing.

Sensible people wore shoes with normal length pointed or round toes. Loose or fitted boots from ankle to calf length were worn for everyday and were extended to the thighs for riding styles. Nobles, soldiers, and peasants all wore thigh high boots made of brown cowhide. They were created for the left and right foot and had the vamp cut separately from the leg.

Pattens, thick-soled overshoes, were worn over the thin-soled soft shoes of the day for outdoors. Pattens had wooden soles, held

11TH C.

11TH–12TH C.

POULAINE

13TH C.

SHOE WITH PATTEN

SABOT

on the foot by leather or cloth bands, and were worn by both men and women to lift the wearer above the mud or snow. For women, they continued to be worn in muddy conditions until the nineteenth or even early twentieth century. The **sabot**, a shoe shaped from a single block of wood, was worn by the peasants of France and the Low Countries to keep their feet dry.

Renaissance Europe

By the sixteenth century, the Renaissance was pervasive throughout Europe. The rebirth that the name of the era refers to is a renewed interest in the art and culture of the classical period. Renaissance intellectuals and artists contrasted the focus on religion during the Middle Ages with their own interest in the world around them though the church was still a dominant institution. One aspect of Renaissance worldliness was increased contact with faraway lands and cultures, which had an influence on clothing and accessories. Silks from the Orient and turbans from the Ottoman Empire became quite fashionable because of the trading relationship with Turkey.

Women's Headwear

In France, England, and the Low Countries, black hoods with veils at the back were worn over linen under-caps that allowed the front hair (parted in the middle) to show. These

hoods became more complex and structured over time. Unique to England was the **gable hood**, a wired headdress shaped like the gable of a house. In the 1500s gable headdress had long embroidered lappets framing the face and a loose veil behind. Later the gable hood was worn over several layers that completely concealed the hair, and the lappets and veil were pinned up in a variety of ways.

The simple rounded hood of the early years of the century evolved into the French hood, popular in both France and England; its arched shape sat farther back on the head and displayed the front hair, which was parted in the center and pinned up in braids or twists under the veil.

German women adopted hats like fashionable men's berets early in the century; these were worn over caps or cauls (**colettes**) made of netted cord over a silk lining. Hats became fashionable in England as an alternative to the hood toward the 1540s. Close fitting caps of fur were worn in cold climates.

Linen coifs were worn under the fur cap, hood, or hat. Their most important functions during Elizabethan times were to confer respectability upon a woman, and for more affluent people, for decoration. The coif, in one variation or another, was one of the most common pieces of headwear worn by women, and sometimes by men, throughout the sixteenth century. It is quite likely that a coif or close-fitting cap of some sort was worn underneath the heavy and concealing veils and the English gable hoods of the 1520s and 1530s and the lighter French hoods that followed them, but all that would show of a coif worn underneath a hood or veil would be the front edge.

Men's Headwear

Through the 1570s, a soft fabric hat with a gathered crown was most popular, and over time the hat became stiffer and the crown became taller. Later, a conical felt hat with a rounded crown called a **capotain** or **copotain** became

fashionable. These became very tall toward the end of the century. Hats were decorated with a jewel or feather, and were worn indoors and out. Close-fitting coifs or **biggins**, covering the ears and tied under the chin, continued to be worn by children and older men under their hats or alone indoors; men's coifs were usually black. A conical cap of linen with a turned up brim called a nightcap was worn informally indoors; these were often embroidered.

Belts

Belts were worn as an accessory over the high-waisted dresses. They were richly embroidered or intricately constructed of chainmail. In the late 1500s, women wore a bum roll at the waist. Worn below the natural waist, it provided support for the skirts, added an illusion of wearing many layers, and enhanced the silhouette of the figure.

Elizabethan men and women wore belts; costume scholars also use the term **girdles** for women's belts. Belts often matched the style of the chain worn at the neck, or the billiment sewn to the neckline. Clusters of pearls, decorative gold links, and set jewels could be combined to make a girdle. Some girdles were long sashes of silk with jewels set on them. Girdles attached around the waist and often hung down two or more feet. Pomanders, tablets, pendants, or girdle books could be attached to the end. Fans, gold-leafed cameos, girdle books, purses, needle cases, scissors, and a variety of other items could be attached to the girdle itself.

Bags and Pockets

During the Elizabethan era, women's skirts expanded to enormous proportions and women began to wear small pouches under their skirts. Men wore pockets (called **bagges**) made of leather inside their breeches. Peasants and travelers carried large satchel-like leather or cloth bags or wore them diagonally across the body.

Footwear

Shoes for men and women in the first 50 years of the sixteenth century were flat with a one-piece sole, and often slashed and fastened with a strap across the instep. Rounded toes were in fashion early on and later were replaced by broad, squared toes in the 1530s. Toward the middle of the century, shoes became narrower and were shaped naturally to the foot. Later shoes tied with a ribbon over the instep. Soft boots for riding fitted to midcalf. Wooden or cork-soled thick-soled pattens were worn over delicate indoor shoes to protect them from the muck of the streets, and men wore boots for riding. A variation of the patten popular in Venice was the **chopine**, a platform-soled mule that raised the wearer sometimes as high as two feet off the ground. Lifting up the feet away from the ground on some kind of platform heels or clogs was not a new idea, but the modern heel as we know it today originated from a cork wedge placed between the leather sole and the upper, higher at the heel. These heels changed the overall idea of shoe-making. Pumps were mentioned for the first time during the Elizabethan era, and in this age of exploration and discovery, women's footwear became more beautiful and extravagant than ever.

SCARPINE   CHOPINE

Boots during the sixteenth century were mostly made from leather and were used for hunting, long travels, and by the military. They were mostly wider at the top and were fastened by buckles, laces, and buttons. The tops were sometimes scalloped or turned down, revealing a colored lining. Some fabric boots made from velvet were still worn in court. Common people continued to wear a wooden sabot or leather galosh in a low shoe or boot shape. The sabot was painted in bright colors for dressy occasions.

Seventeenth-Century Europe

The Renaissance was followed by a period called the Baroque, roughly corresponding to the seventeenth century. Art, architecture, and music became more elaborate and ornate, in contrast to the revival of classical styles in the Renaissance. By the seventeenth century, fashion and accessories had become more complicated because of the clear divisions among Europeans in their religious, national, and class differences. For example, members of various conservative sects of Protestantism in this period developed "plain dress" as a form of anti-fashion (a style that has been modified but is still worn by Amish people today). Conservative Catholics at the Spanish court, on the other hand, keep wearing fashions from the previous century well into the seventeenth century.

Headwear

Throughout the century there were a variety of hats from small, embroidered caps with lace and capotains, to beaver felt hats with feathers, velvet ribbons, and jeweled brooches and broad-brimmed hat with plumes. Hats were somewhat useless for the large scale wigs and were sometimes carried under the arm rather than worn. There were some flat hats with brims which turned up at three points.

Women's hair was built up high on top of the head with long curls on the sides and back, and a silk gauze handkerchief was sometimes pinned on top of the hairdo for street wear. Toward the end of the century, around the 1680s, women adopted a headdress known as the **fontange** to further heighten and elongate the silhouette. This style evolved from a small bow tying up the hair to an elaborate layered structure and was in fashion into the first decade of the next century. The fontange is a frilly lace cap, wired to stand in vertical tiers with streamers to either side. It was named after Duchess de Fontanges, a mistress of King Louis XIV of France. It is said that she tied her hair up with a ribbon after losing her cap while horseback riding. The king liked the look, and it soon became fashionable.

For men, until about 1620, the fashionable hat was the **capotain**, with a tall conical crown rounded at the top and a narrow brim. By the 1630s, the crown was shorter and the brim was wider, often worn cocked or pinned up on one side and decorated with long ostrich feathers. Cavalier wide brimmed hats with large feathers and ribbons were very popular. Coifs or biggins were

FONTANGE

CAPOTAIN

worn under the capotain or on their own and were used by all classes in England and Scotland from the Middle Ages to the early seventeenth century. Later on they were worn only by young children and old men under their hats or alone indoors.

Toddlers who were just learning to walk often wore a protective head covering called a **pudding hat**. It was open on top and consisted of a roll around the crown of the head, fastened with ties under the chin.

PUDDING HAT

Neckwear

The **cravat** is the grandfather of the current tie. It was first worn in the end of the sixteenth century as a band around the neck. The neck-cloth, or cravat, had been worn by German troops as early as 1640, and soon after the beginning of the new century, began to replace the lace collar in general use. It consisted of a strip of white material about a foot wide and a yard long, twisted round the neck, and knotted in front. Considerable variety was practiced in the manner of tying it, and each variety had a special name.

A **Steinkerk** was a lace cravat tied very loosely, with the ends passed through a buttonhole in the coat. It was so called after the Battle of Steinkerk in 1692, where the French officers went into action so hurriedly that they had not time to tie their cravats properly; and the fashion was popular in England in spite of the fact that Steinkerk was an English defeat.

Belts

Girdles can be seen on some portraits of this century, too. As in the sixteenth century, they often matched the style of the chain worn at the neck, or the billiment sewn to the neckline. Some girdles were long sashes of silk with jewels set on them.

Purses and Pockets

Both men and women in the seventeenth century didn't wear obvious bags and hung long embroidered drawstring purses under their skirts and breeches. Purses were functional and usually used as decorative containers for small belongings like gifts, money, perfume, or jewels. Toward the end of the century, purses became increasingly sophisticated, moving from a simple drawstring design to more complex shapes and materials.

Footwear

This is the century in which the art of shoemaking began in the New World as **cordwainers** (shoemakers) and tanners settled in America from Europe. The ordinary shoe was fashioned straight without a left or right designation, but the wealthier colonists had shoes made to order or had them imported from Europe. Moccasins also became popular among the new Americans.

Men and women generally wore shoes and mules with a square toe and high heels, often blocked and domed. Flat shoes were worn to around 1610, when a low heel became popular. The ribbon tie over the instep that had appeared on late-sixteenth-century shoes grew into an elaborate lace or ribbon rosettes called **shoe roses** that were worn by the most fashionable men and women. By the 1620s, heeled boots came into fashion for indoor as well as outdoor wear for men. The top part of the boot was usually turned down below the knee. Boot tops became wider and wider until

the "bucket-top" boot appeared in the 1630s. These soft shaped high-topped boots are what most people associate with *The Three Musketeers* and Edmond Rostand's *Cyrano de Bergerac*. Light colors were very popular for these boots with beige, yellow, pale blue, and even white as top choices. The top part of some of these boots was adorned with large bows and rich laces, but by 1660, this frilly footwear started to disappear.

An important innovation in 1660 was the buckle to fasten a shoe. Samuel Pepys writes in his diary of January 22, 1660, "This day I began to put on buckles to my shoes." Buckles were first more popular for men but women started wearing them too.

Eighteenth Century in European and European-Influenced Countries

From approximately 1720 through 1770, the ornate Baroque style evolved into the Rococo. Ornate, curvilinear forms were still prevalent in the visual arts but were more delicate, and pastel colors added to the feeling of lightness and airiness. These trends were also apparent in the fashions of the times.

Headwear

Hats during this period were quite elaborate and decorated. Women wore wide brim hats with a lot of flowers and ribbons outside during summer days. Smaller hats were worn inside or for special occasions, usually matching the color of the gown. Both men and women wore tricorne hats for riding and hunting and sometimes even indoors.

Bonnets or "house bonnets" were worn in the mid-eighteenth century as well as a folding hood called a **calash**. It was just a brimless head covering tied under the chin.

Wigs in a variety of styles were worn for every occasion by virtually everyone almost until the end of the eighteenth century and some of them expanded to ridiculous sizes. Towering structures and arrangements with tiny hats, jewels, ribbons, flowers, fake birds, and toy ships were perched as much as a foot high on top of the head. For men one of the main headwear pieces was the wig bag. Charles II used to wear a voluminous black wig, and throughout his reign it kept falling on each side of his face with the ends drooping onto the chest. This proved so inconvenient, especially for soldiers that he started tying the hair back with a ribbon, and enclosing it in a silk bag at the back of his neck. Thus the use of these silk bags became quite popular.

Gloves

Gloves were quite popular outside the house. If they were worn inside on formal occasions or a ball, they were removed when dining. Gloves were long—above the elbow—and fastened with ribbons or worn loose and the arm was partially displayed.

Handbags

The eighteenth-century women's garments had numerous pouches hanging from a ribbon tied around their waist. The women reached into them through slits under all the skirts and hoops. Women carried everything they needed hanging from their belts or in delicate pouches through the 1760s, when actual pockets were sewn onto the garments and some small bags appeared as separate accessories.

Footwear

In the eighteenth century, women's shoes reflected the elaborate patterns of their dresses and had similar embroidery and trimming, and the most fashionable footwear featured the Louis XIV heels. Bands of metallic braid were popular as decoration on shoes and the silver or gold braids were transferred from one pair of shoes to another. Other characteristics included pointed toes; ribbon and buckle **latchet ties**, white kid leather rounds between the shoe sole and upper; and high covered wooden heel. Mules and, in the late 1780s, Asian-inspired slippers with low heels and turned up toes were very popular. They were made from kidskin in all colors or fabrics like velvet, brocade, damask, or satin. In France, buckles were fashioned of gold, silver, or bronze and were engraved, enameled,

and encrusted with precious stones or pearls, according to the wealth of the wearer.

Clogs and pattens were still a necessity to walk the filthy streets. Dressy slippers had pattens with matching fabric straps and wooden or thick leather soles.

By the end of the 1760s, thick heels began to thin down and the top became wider and more wedged, producing, in the 1770s, the "Italian heel" for women's shoes. Towards the end of the eighteenth century and beginning of the nineteenth century, women's shoes became lower cut, and heels became lower until they disappear altogether and the pointed toe was replaced by a narrow oval toe and then square toes. Shoes made from satin and silks became so dainty that ribbon ties were added to keep the shoe on the foot.

During the last decade men's shoes became quite plain, made of black leather with pointed toes and small, low heels. They fastened with large buckles and were worn with silk or woolen stockings.

For most of the eighteenth century, boots were reserved for soldiers and sportsmen. A heavy jack boot was used as protective riding gear of post men, while a more elegant version was used for the military. During the seventies, the boot became more acceptable for general wear because of a general desire for simpler living. The hussar boot was first introduced to the European armies during the seventeenth century, but reentered England in 1770 and eventually became known as the **Hessian boot**. By the end of the century, it was one of the most fashionable boots, worn over tight fitting pantaloons. It was made of shiny black leather with the top finished with gold or silver braid and a silk tassel hanging from center front.

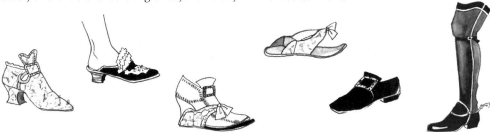

Nineteenth Century in European and European-Influenced Countries

In the beginning of the nineteenth century, after the extremes of the eighteenth century, fashion in European countries became much more informal and classic. That sentiment translated into accessories and made them a bit more relaxed and practical. The invention of the sewing machine at the end of the eighteenth century completely revolutionized most handicrafts including shoe making and made them more accessible for the masses. Machinery allowed for faster production and the newly build and ever-expanding railways moved goods faster than horse-drawn wagons. European and European-influenced countries started seeing frequent changes in the overall fashion silhouette and accessories.

Headwear

Bonnets were the most common types of headwear for women throughout most of the nineteenth century. Bonnets were shaped with the help of wire and were covered with the most fashionable fabrics of the time. Silk bonnets, elaborately pleated and ruched, were worn outdoors and during visits to friends. The outdoor bonnets had small brims that revealed the face. During spring and summer, bonnets were made of straw, woven horsehair,

or net. During the winter bonnets were made of heavier fabrics like velvet. They were trimmed according to the individual. A bonnet usually had two sets of ties: one set of thin ties to hold it down and a set of wide fancy ones to be tied in a large bow and show off the rich material. By midcentury, **spoon bonnets** were in fashion, which had increasingly high brims and more elaborate trimmings. Toward the end of the century, bonnets eventually fell out of fashion in favor of small hats. Some flat straw **boater hats** were worn by women for yachting and other nautical adventures.

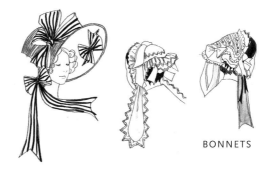

BONNETS

In the beginning of the century, men still wore tricorne and bicorne hats, but the most fashionable hat was the tall and conical one, which eventually evolved into the top hat. It became the only hat for formal occasions. It grew taller and taller into a stovepipe shape. The brim crown became quite curvy around the 1820s and flared towards the top. The **bowler** hat was invented in 1850 but remained a working-class accessory. It was a nice compromise between a formal hat and a casual softer hat, but it was worn mostly by the lower class. The homburg and fedora, which appeared in the nineteenth century, continues to be worn up to the present.

TOP HAT

BOWLER   FEDORA

Neckwear

Men's shirts were worn with stocks or cravats tied in a soft bow in various ways. Cravats were worn in white as well as dark colors and various patterns. Around the 1850s, the popular necktie was the **four-in-hand necktie**, which is simply a rectangular cloth. Also fashionable was the Ascot tie, made up as a neckband with wide wings attached and worn with a stickpin. Narrow ribbon ties were tied in a bow, and a white bowtie was the proper attire for formal evening wear.

FOUR-IN-HAND
CRAVAT
ASCOT

Shawls

Shawls were very popular, worn over evening gowns with short sleeves. They were considered one of the most useful and attractive accessories and were made out of cashmere, silk, and muslin depending on the season and the occasion, with paisley patterns being the most popular.

Belts

An already small woman's waist was accentuated with a wide belt and a decorated buckle. Towards the end of the century, after the 1870s, dresses were mostly worn unbelted. For men in the military in the latter half of the nineteenth century until the First World War, the belt was mostly a decorative part of the uniform. It was common for officers to wear extremely tight, wide belts around the waist, on the outside of the uniform. They gave the wearer a trim physique, emphasizing wide shoulders and a large chest. Very often the man's actual waist was made smaller by a corset worn under the uniform, and the belt just accentuated it.

Gloves

Gloves were a favorite accessory and were always worn outside the house. If a lady wore them inside at a social visit they were removed for dinner. Opera length gloves worn with sleeveless gowns reached the elbow and above it.

Handbags

After using their pockets to carry small things throughout the eighteenth century, women started carrying a small simple bag called a **reticule** in the nineteenth century. The purse had ribbon or cord drawstrings and was intricately decorated with embroidery or feather trims and wrapped in mesh or trimmed with a fringe. By midcentury the small purses became proper handbags made of soft or hard leather with metal buckles. As more people traveled by train and women became more mobile, professional luggage makers started creating not just trunks but also true hand-held bags for all traveling. Companies like Hermès and Louis Vuitton (see Chapter 2) were first to create sturdy styles for these needs as opposed to the soft and pretty purses and pouches, previously made by dressmakers.

Footwear

In the beginning of the nineteenth century, the most fashionable shoes were flat slippers or very low heeled shoes. They were made of silk, velvet, or leather and usually decorated with a ribbon, bow, or buckle. A leather toe cap was sometimes added to cloth shoes. Pattens were still used for fine shoes in order to protect them from rain or mud on the streets. Towards the end of the century, the heel reappeared on slippers, shoes, and boots again. Footwear was decorated again with bows, brooches, silk cords, and laces, imitating natural leaves and flowers. Boots with buttons to one side or in the center front were widely used during carriage rides. New leathers from reptiles and alligators appeared in the eighties and were tanned specifically for footwear.

The process of rubber vulcanization was discovered in 1839 by Charles Goodyear and had a tremendous impact on footwear from that point on. The resulting rubber shoes and outsoles created a whole industry for manufacturing them, which is still thriving today.

Hessian boots became the latest fashion after the Duke of Wellington defeated Napoleon at Waterloo in 1815. **Wellington boots**, a modification of the Hessian boot, became fashionable during the nineteenth century. The new boot was made out of soft calfskin leather, cut close around the leg with low heels. Hiram Hutchinson bought the patent for the vulcanization process to manufacture footwear, moved to France and started making rubber "Wellies." The rubber boot

WELLINGTON BOOTS

became an immediate success, since it kept farmers' feet dry and mud-free. It remains a popular style of protective footwear for both men and women.

Boots and shoes with cemented soles saw its first attempts in the 1850s although successful manufacturing didn't appear until the 1920s.

Sports became popular during the second part of the century and prompted development of sport specific shoes with rubber soles for croquet, archery, tennis, polo, baseball, football, and bicycling.

Accessories of the First Two Decades of the Twentieth Century

Fashion changed more rapidly in the twentieth century than in earlier times, and of course, more examples of apparel and accessories from the decades of that century have survived for designers to study and use as a source of inspiration in the twenty-first century. We begin our survey of twentieth century accessories with the first two decades.

Headwear

In the beginning of the century, women wore large brimmed hats decorated with lots of feathers, wide ribbons, artificial flowers, and stuffed birds. By the end of the first decade, hats became smaller, with small drooping brims and deep crowns.

Summer hats were woven of natural straw and wreathed with roses and leaves and could be edged with velvet. Hats were designed with a specific purpose. The hunting hat was different in shape and decoration from the hat worn at the racetrack or for outdoor activities.

Men of upper class wore tall hats, especially for evening. During the day a softer felt hat like the **homburg** was more popular. The elegantly dressed gentleman also wore ascot ties and shined leather shoes and carried a walking stick. Bowler hats were also worn during the day or by working class men.

Neckwear

At the beginning of the century, men continued to wear the narrow four-in-hand neckties. For formal day attire they used an ascot tie and for formal evening dress a white bow tie. Women also wore various ties around the neck of a shirt or a dress. Those ties had intricate embroideries, trim, and lace details and ranged from one color to bright and colorful prints.

Gloves

Gloves were worn outdoors both by men and women. Muffs made from real fur were used during the colder months of the year.

Handbags

Bags in the early twentieth century became more than just luggage. Women could choose from small reticules or leather bags with attached opera glasses or fans to larger handbags for shopping and even briefcases with pockets. Leather and exotic skin bags became more popular and often had rigid structure with a short handle. Evening bags were heavily beaded and decorated and had ornate motifs on the hardware.

Footwear

The manufacturing of footwear during the new century attained a high volume never seen before. The revolutionized process of cordwainery now had a scientific method for every step from tanning the leather to cementing rubber soles and heels. For the first time in history, ready-to-wear models for riding, hunting, or even the military could be purchased from shops. The United States became the largest producer as well as the largest consumer of footwear.

For the first two decades, men adhered to a leather high boot for winter and a low shoe for summer, usually an oxford, brogue, or buttoned style. Within the second decade, men started wearing various low shoe styles all year round adding **gaiters** or **spats**, cloth or leather accessories for shoes, designed to cover the instep and the ankle and protect during the winter or bad weather.

SHOE WITH
GAITER (SPAT)

For women one of the most exciting changes was the increasing number of different shoe leathers. Skins were tanned from box calf, lamb, kid, buck, antelope, reversed calf with the suede finish on the outside, and patent leather. Predominant fashionable colors were: beige, bronze, taupe, brown, and shades of gray. Women wore oxford and brogue styles for sportswear and a pump style for a carriage ride or a stroll along the street. For evening parties or dancing at night, the most popular styles were bejeweled slippers, decorated with ribbon ties or buckles from cut-jet, marcasite, or even silver and gold. To protect their shoes in the winter, women wore carriage boots of velveteen or satin edged with fur.

1920s Fashion Accessories

The 1920s marked the beginning of modern life and liberation. Women gained confidence and started wearing comfortable clothes and cut their hair short in order to break from tradition. Jazz music was growing fast and the flapper fashion was part of the Roaring Twenties. Women started wearing more androgynous clothes and accessories.

Headwear

The **cloche**, a small, round hat with a very short soft brim was the most popular women's hat during the twenties. It was a very close fitting hat, resembling a helmet and was worn over the popular short bob haircut. It was pulled over the eyes and required a particular body posture and head angle so that one could see.

CLOCHE HATS

Men wore mostly hard felt hats with a wide band as business attire. They were made in a variety of tan, brown, and black colors with colorful or black ribbon. Berets in woven menswear fabrics were also worn as a more casual alternative. Boater hats with multicolored ribbons were very fashionable and were worn with suits and ties.

Women's Scarves

Long skinny scarves were widely used in women's outfits. They were tied around the neck in various ways, hung out of a pocket of a suit jacket or coat, tied or pinned to a dress, or just held around the arms like a shawl.

Men's Ties and Pocket Squares

Ascots, bowties, and neckties were worn with suits and dressy shirts and usually came pre-tied with a closure in the back. They often featured bright colors and small-scale geometric patterns like dots and stripes. Colorful pocket squares were an important accessory for a man's dressy suit. They came in a variety of bright colors and patterns.

Handbags

The Art Deco period had a great influence on the bags designed during the twenties. Reflecting the architecture they often had geometric patterns, created with beading and fringe. Intricate, realistic, or stylized, geometric floral patterns were also extremely popular. Bags were overall elegant, functional, and considered an ultramodern accessory. Leather was used for travel bags and trunks, and exotic skins like alligator, lizard, or ostrich were used for day handbags. One of the important developments during this period was the **pochette**, a type of handle-less small clutch, usually decorated with dazzling geometric and jazz motifs.

Footwear

Because dresses were shorter during this era shoes were more visible and became a much more important accessory. Heels were just over 2 inches high and Mary Janes with ankle straps or with a T-bar were the most popular styles. They were often decorated with embroidery, sequin, rhinestones, or multi-straps, forming a decorative pattern. Lace-up boots in leather with about a 2-inch heel were also a popular choice. Boot-tops were worn over shoes to protect them from the mud on the streets. They were strapped on with side closures or buttons and came in a variety of colors.

For men, black patent-leather shoes were popular during this era and often appeared with formal evening wear. Fashionable men chose some of the newest colors of mahogany, rust, and other shades of red-brown. Casual clothing demanded two-tone shoes in white and tan, or white and black. Fringed tongues on oxfords and brogues were seen frequently. Lace-up style shoes were most in demand. Sport-oriented shoes for an active lifestyle were also emerging. Men's riding boots in a knee height or just above the ankle were beautifully crafted from quality leather and were created as walking boots.

Spats were made out of stiff fabric and covered the top of the shoe and part of the lower leg. They were also a part of the formal attire for social events and weddings. They came in white, tan, and black. White boot spats were usually worn over highly-polished shoes and were a sign of wealth as common people couldn't afford to have them changed very often or wash them every day.

1930s Fashion Accessories

The most important economic event of the 1930s was the great Wall Street Crash of October 24, 1929, leading to the Great Depression. Fashion was largely influenced by it, and women started sewing and mending the clothes instead of buying new ones. During the Depression, accessories were easier to buy than clothing because they were cheaper, and so they were widely used. Movies were viewed as an escape from the economic crisis, and movie stars endorsed accessories and style in general.

Headwear

Women's hats in the thirties were again more feminine and elegant and often worn tilted at an angle. The small, fitted cloche hats started evolving into hats with larger, flatter brims, and the crowns started getting lower. Turbanlike hats with a feather, contrast trims, or multiple folds were also very popular. The opposite trend of tall hats with extra feathers emerged toward the end of the 1930s.

Men's hats featured fedoras in muted and very bright colors, berets, and straw and Panama hats.

Elsa Schiaparelli was one of the most influential and innovative fashion designers of the 1930s. She loved art and often worked with artists and close friends Christian Berard, and surrealists Jean Cocteau, and Salvador Dalí, who designed fabrics, patterns, and embroideries for her. One of her most famous designs is the shoe-shaped hat.

Neckwear

Men's neckties and bows continued to feature bright geometric patterns during the 1930s.

Gloves

Gloves during the 1930s featured multiple decorative seams and lots of surface treatments like decorative stitching, and closures and straps with interesting buckles.

Belts

Belts for men were quite conservative, made from leather with a simple rectangular buckle or small plate buckles featuring an inlay or embossed design. Women's belts were a bit wider and more ornamental in design.

Handbags

By the 1930s, most of the modern handbag styles and constructions were already invented, including the satchel, the shoulder bag, and the modern clutch, as well as various metal clasp frames. Handbags of the early thirties were still inspired by Art Deco, with abstract patterns and industrial materials, including plastic. Beaded bags were still abundant, as well as enameled mesh bags. During the later part of the decade, leather became more used than fabric. Three-pocket leather clutches with a generous flap over the front and the owner's initials were especially popular.

The luxury goods manufacturer Hermès popularized the zip as a closure for handbags in the early thirties and introduced one of the most popular accessories, the Kelly Bag, in 1935.

Footwear

In the 1930s, women's shoes were a little heavier with wide, thick heels. The toes were less pointy, more rounded, or square. Pumps and flat shoes were available, as well as styles with moderate heels under 2 inches high. The **spectator shoe**, a two-tone shoe in styles for

both women and men, appeared in the early thirties. Slip-on styles, lace-up shoes, and buckle shoes were all in fashion at one time or another for both men and women. In 1936, the Italian shoe designer Ferragamo made the first wedge heels, which paved the way for chunkier, clunkier soles.

1940s Fashion Accessories

During the 1940s, World War II had a tremendous impact on fashion and accessories. Accessories like hats, caps, suspenders, and garters were widely used because they were not rationed. Ribbons, lace, lace net, and other trim less than 3 inches wide were not rationed either, and so they were utilized to decorate accessories or entire outfits. The food and gas rationing did not stop people from going out and having a good time at nightclubs and restaurants. Movies and music were escapes from the war, and the glamorous looks of movie stars could be duplicated through accessories.

One of the most famous American ladies' handbags company, Coach was founded in 1941. Bonnie Cashin flourished as a designer during the forties and transformed boots into a major fashion accessory (see Chapter 2). The New Look by couturier Christian Dior appeared in 1947 and had tremendous impact on fashion and accessories until the late fifties. With the end of rationing came more lavish apparel designs and the accessories to enhance the post-war look.

Headwear

Hats of all kinds and shapes were popular for women, but turbans seemed to dominate for a while. The turban was one of the significant trends in headwear. It began as a simple head-cover to prevent the wearer's hair entangling in factory machinery and became extremely popular in the forties. It ended up being a cover-up for women's hair since they were so busy running homes and working and had less time to attend to their hairdos.

Hairnets were also widely used because they were not rationed. The net kept the hair tidy and in place and was worn in the factories where women operated machinery as part of the war effort. The hairnets worn for dress were usually decorated with flowers and ribbons. All kinds of mesh were also used as part of a hat decoration because mesh wasn't rationed.

The New Look brought "real hats" back in fashion. After years of casual headwear, heads were adorned with carefully constructed chic hats, often pinned to one side of an updo.

Men wore hats with every outfit. A hard felt hat with a wide ribbon was worn for a dressier look. All kinds of caps were worn for more casual occasions. Hugger caps, as well as berets in wool or cotton, were some of the most popular styles.

Neckwear

The end of the war and rationing brought a dramatic change in men's neckwear fashion. Hand-painted wide ties, featuring exotic locations and foliage, limousines, rodeos, Tahitian sunsets, and even pin-up girls were most popular.

Handbags

Large, functional bags made of leather or fabric were in vogue in the beginning of the 1940s, as were smaller, jeweled, precious bags for evening.

Handbags made after the New Look became tailored, elegant, and even extravagant, usually made in leather or fancy fabrics. Evening bags were created out of satin, brocade, or tapestry, often with embroidery or beading and matching the outfit. One of the interesting features of 1940s bag is the dominance of wrist-strap bags in all shapes and sizes from pouches to box shapes.

BELT BAG   BAG WITH UMBRELLA

Footwear

Shoes in the 1940s were rationed to two pairs of new shoes a year. Women's shoes ranged from low heel to high heel with a limited range of leathers. The high heels were sturdy, stable, and sensible. Wedge sole shoes became popular. The surface of the shoes was usually textured or decorated with bows or studs or seamed into different designs. Soles and heels for sports shoes were to be made only from plastic or reclaimed rubber, and manufacturers made great efforts to find substitutes. Some of the inventions as a result of it were synthetic rubber cement and synthetic waterproof soles.

Men's footwear was conservative compared to styles of earlier centuries. The popular styles included leather lace up shoes and boots with a low heel. There were some designs featuring multicolor leather and woven leather patterns but the heel remained lower than 1 inch.

1950s Fashion Accessories

The New Look by Christian Dior continued to exert great influence on the fashion and accessories of the fifties, adding an extra touch of elegance.

Headwear

Hats continued to be extremely important for men's and women's outfits. They were designed specifically for every occasion each season. Women wore various hat shapes, decorated with feathers, flowers, acorns, leaves, and fruits like cherries. Toll hats rose to unusual heights again, and domelike shapes appeared in the midfifties as well as knitted or felt berets. Quite a few hats had complicated design made out of softer fabric, tied or twisted with bows or self extensions.

Men's hats continued to follow the classic shapes of fedora, bowler, and helmetlike hats, made from felt and trimmed with contrast ribbon or matching fabric trim. Berets made from tweed or cotton fabrics came in various patterns like herringbone and plaid.

Neckwear

Men's ties in the fifties continued to feature bright colors and exotic hand-painted geometric forms, flowers and leaves, musical instruments, butterflies and all sorts of animals, as well as sunsets and even pin-up girls.

Gloves

With coat sleeves getting shorter, gloves became an extremely important accessory. From short to almost shoulder length they were worn every season and were made of leather or woven fabric or were crocheted. White or cream colored gloves were a sign of a real lady. Colored gloves made in cotton were an easy and affordable purchase as they could be washed often and looked great. Women not only bought gloves but also made them from patterns.

Belts

Wide belts with decorative buckles, made out of leather or fabric in contrast colors were used to synch the waist and emphasize the figure curves. Simpler fabric belts without buckles in a matching or contrast texture were just tied to accentuate the waistline.

CUMMERBUND

Handbags

The postwar economic boom of the 1950s allowed bags to flourish. A bag color-coordinated to the shoes or outfit became a must for any fashionable woman. Major design houses creating accessories, such as Chanel, Louis Vuitton, and Hermès acquired a cult following by loyal ladies willing to spend money on status objects (see Chapter 2). Christian Dior's New Look emphasized femininity with very small bags as symbols of beauty and sophistication. Even these small bags were designed with practical pockets and rings to hold gloves and hide flat shoes. Larger handbags and luggage were still designed for travel needs.

Footwear

Some of the major innovations for women's shoes in the fifties were found in the design and decoration of the heels. High and slender stilettos appeared as well as low and square, bobbin, facet comma, and polygonal shapes. They incorporated ornate rhinestones, plastic, wood, metal, and ceramic elements. The most popular shoe of the fifties must have been the pointy stiletto shoe. Dior had them first on his runway show in 1952, and they caught on quickly, with heels up to 5 inches high. They usually had metal tips instead of rubber. Steel lasted much longer than rubber, but the drawbacks were that these shoes were quite noisy and ruined many wood floors. Many buildings banned the metal-tipped shoes, and women used to carry a pair of flat shoes in their bag so they could change.

Men's shoes became a bit more interesting during the fifties, with two-tone designs, variety of textures, perforated leather, and stitch details added to the overall design of the shoes. Comfortable casual shoes also started making their way as everyday styles.

1960s Fashion Accessories

The sixties was a decade that reflected social movements and offered many exciting trends in accessories. Youth culture and fashion blossomed. Twiggy, with her boyish young look and stick-thin figure emerged as the number one model. Unisex was an acceptable style. The swinging sixties reflected the Space-Age mood, and Mod fashions dominated in the beginning of the decade.

By 1965, hippies were an established social group, and their influence is still an inspiration. Sexual liberation and psychedelic drugs expanded the mind and produced great music and music stars who dictated fashion trends. There was an urge to

decorate clothing and accessories like shoes and bags with political slogans. Symbols and flowers were hand painted as a sign of flower power and were widely used in clothing and accessories. Bright colors and tie-dyed clothing and bags were popular. Peasant motifs as well as Native American, African, and Latin American designs dominated the American market.

Jackie Kennedy became an icon for simple elegance and overall style in more traditional dress and accessories.

Headwear

Pop-art and op-art had a great influence on all accessories including hats. Prints in black-and-white check variations were developed to be used in everything from dresses to socks and hats. Jacqueline Kennedy was often seen in a **pillbox hat** and so kept it in fashion throughout the sixties. Men's hats went out of style toward the end of the decade. Tie-dyed and brightly colored bandanas over loose long hair were the choice of hippies.

PILLBOX HAT

Handbags

Handbags and luggage became bright and fun. High-shine materials like vinyl or patent leather in all colors of the rainbow were widely used. Large closures and flower details were common basic accents. The narrow long clutch was a very popular style because it gave a youthful informal look, so suitable for this decade. Another style that kept up with the fun childlike qualities of the miniskirt was the small shoulder bag with long chains or thin straps.

CLUTCH

Footwear

Shoes during the sixties started to vary considerably from high heel stilettos to fun and colorful low heels, flats, or fantastical high go-go boots. They were often worn with contrasting color socks. Toward the end of the era, gold and silver metallic shoes also started to appear. Men's casual shoes during the sixties came in a variety of bright colors.

GO-GO BOOT

1970s Fashion Accessories

The hippie look with its tie-dye fabrics, embroidered peasant looking leather shoes, and embroidered and fringed bags was still popular in the beginning of the seventies.

Punk as an influence appeared in the seventies with Vivienne Westwood and Malcolm McLaren dressing bands like the Sex Pistols.

Safety pins and tape appeared as accessories, holding together the ripped jeans and other clothing. Fishnet stockings were a staple of the punk girl, as well as big clunky boots.

Handbags

Individual expression with an ethnic look became popular during the seventies and psychedelic patterns and later "flower power" introduced a romantic feeling to accessories and handbags. Larger satchels and fabric shoulder bags became popular after young people started traveling to India in the late 1960s. Handmade patchwork shoulder bags or recycled army bags with hand embroidery were in fashion as opposed to machine-made goods.

Footwear

Platform shoes with soles up to 4 inches became popular for both men and women. Some of them were covered in sequins and had quite outrageous designs, like clear plastic heels with fish swimming inside.

Women's shoes in the late seventies began to echo the 1940s, with high-heeled lower-platform mules, "Candies" made of molded

plastic with a single leather strap over the ball of the foot, or "Bare Traps" made of wood. Wooden clogs with rivets and studs and colorful or perforated leather uppers were designed like Dutch shoes and became very popular. Disco years brought even more fabulous and sparkly designs with thick soles and high heels, kept in place with thin straps for hours of dancing at night.

1980s Fashion Accessories

Affluence was socially acceptable during the 1980s, and lavish clothing and accessories from couture houses flourished. A variety of fashion accessories were offered seasonally from a variety of designers and design houses as well as accessory brands. Vintage stores became popular for purchasing shoes and handbags, especially when grunge appeared in the late eighties.

Headwear

Wide brimmed hats with large ribbons were very popular among women for special occasions and sunny days. Straw in different weights and felt were the most popular materials respectively for summer and winter dressy hats. Flowers, bows,

and netting were some of the most popular trims. Fedoras in felt or straw were the most popular style for men, but men's hats did not have the importance of earlier decades.

Gloves

Gloves were still used as a functional item during the cold months of the year, but colorful mesh gloves and black lace ones experienced a great demand as a fashion item, popularized by the pop icon Madonna.

Belts

Belts became wide, with bold buckles and came in bright primary or neon colors. Chunky artistic trims, like colorful stones or geometric shapes often adorned the buckles. The wide elastic belt was often used to accentuate the waist.

Handbags

The Chanel quilted bag with a chain handle was one of the most popular bags, copied by endless manufacturers. Handbags covered with the logos of the most desirable luxury companies like Gucci, Louis Vuitton, Fendi, and Chanel became extremely popular, proving that excess was embraced as a virtue in the eighties. Other bags featured big, bold contrast color geometric patterns.

CHANEL BAG

LOUIS VUITTON BAG

Footwear

Business shoes with pointed toes and spiked heels were popular and were often custom dyed to the customer's preferred color. The most popular shoes among young women were bright-colored high heels, often featuring geometric patterns in contrasting colors. This decade also marks the emerging popularity of **Jellies**, the colorful, transparent plastic flats.

Men's shoes stayed a bit more conservative than women's in terms of colors and patterns. Athletic shoes from Adidas and Nike in bright colors were popular and widely used for street wear.

1990–2000 Fashion Accessories

Fashion in the 1990s was characterized by minimalism and even "anti-fashion." Nineties fashion and accessories were very casual with little color. Retro was popular, leading to minimalist takes on styles from previous decades. Fashion and accessories inspired by sports clothing were also popular during the 1990s.

Handbags

Handbags during the nineties featured a more somber look than in the eighties. Darker colors and conservative styles prevailed. They were made in an endless array of styles and materials, from plain canvas to leather and faux versions of every exotic skin imaginable. Lighter materials like nylon and cotton canvas were used in luxury handbags with leather trim.

Footwear

Shoes followed the trend of "less is more" during the nineties. After the excess of the eighties, the beginning of this decade marked a somber palette of colors like grey and black and more functional styles with lower heels and outdoors styles. Athletic shoes developed tremendously and became a staple in any wardrobe. By the end of the century color and creativity made its way back into the footwear world with exciting creations.

Development of Accessories in the Twenty-First Century

The end of the twentieth century marked a rapid rise in development of technology, and the effects can be seen in today's accessory design. Functional accessories like sneakers and other sport-specific shoes are the ones that benefited most from the technological advances. We examine these styles in Chapter 9.

The most significant change in accessory design is that trends change globally, and new styles are developed every season. Workmanship and quality are still highly valued, but cheap labor allows for development and global distribution of low-priced items. The evolution of technology allows for instant exchange of information, so accessory styles seen on the runway today can be easily duplicated around the world by any manufacturer. With the benefits of instant e-mails and video uploads on the Internet comes the problem of fighting counterfeiters. Major companies like Louis Vuitton and Prada, which are so popular and so expensive, face the constant problem of battling countless counterfeiters around the world.

On the other hand, the benefits of globalization are undeniable when it comes to manufacturing and distribution. A company in any part of the world can participate in the global market of accessories in any part of the cycle.

Handbags

Handbag styles have crossed over genders, and men and women wear similar functional bags like backpacks, tote bags, messenger bags, or laptop bags. Variety and functionality are main features of today's bags.

We are inseparable from our cell phones, PDAs, and computer gadgets, and accessories have evolved to accommodate those needs. Handbags now come with extra pockets and compartments, specifically designed to house our electronic friends, and a whole new section of holders and cases has appeared to protect and carry them.

Footwear

Shoes have seen many changes through the past century and have evolved to highly functional objects. Sport specific shoes are now developed in a science lab and are designed for optimum performance. Running shoes seem to have become a separate industry with highly evolved sensors implanted in the sneakers which tell you details of your workout like your time, distance, pace, and calories burned.

Fashion shoes are not bound by limitations of one designer or one trend. Seasonal changes and varied fashion trends offer lots of opportunity for creativity, which is widely accepted by a global demand. The only limitations for shoe designers right now are their own creativity. This boundless opportunity also applies to the other accessories we shall explore in the remainder of this book.

PROJECT

GOALS

To learn to conduct a conscious effort to find inspiration for accessory designs through research in history and to relate styles of the past to their cultural environment; to study the connections between past and present conditions and adapt design references of the past to current needs.

ASSIGNMENT

Pick a historic period described in this chapter and design a collection inspired by that period. You may select a full era, a century, or just a decade with a strong influence. Research not only what accessories were worn, but also the development of the arts, architecture, and the political and social environment. Design a collection of at least ten to fifteen pieces and merchandise it to have various shapes of bags, shoes, small leather goods, hats, gloves, scarves, and so on. Concentrate on functionality as well as design and feel free to include cases for modern technology gadgets like a laptop, iPad, iPod, cell phone, and cameras.

2

History of

CLASSIC ACCESSORY COMPANIES

CHAPTER TWO tells the stories of six classic accessory companies—Hermés, Louis Vuitton, Roger Vivier, Ferragamo, Coach, and Manolo Blahnik—and their contributions to the fashion accessories industry. After reading this chapter, you will be able to recognize the products that are central to each company's brand and how they have evolved over time.

THESE COMPANIES ARE THE LEADERS in accessory design, who have created lasting brand identity and are still setting the bar for beautiful products and quality workmanship. The stories of these design firms will help you understand how a brand's style evolves and how accessory designers fulfill their role in maintaining their brands' image in the minds of their target customers, contributing to their success as businesses.

Hermès

Hermès is known as one of the most elegant French accessory design businesses. The company has a reputation as one of the world's finest makers of luxury leather goods, luggage, accessories, home decor, jewelry, fragrances, and ready-to-wear (Figure 2.1). The Hermès trademark calèche, or horse-drawn carriage, is based on a drawing by Alfred de Dreux, and is reminiscent of its origins as a wholesale saddlery business. The meticulous craftsmanship started in saddle-making is the same throughout the company for every product that bears the Hermès label.

Thierry Hermès was born in 1801 in Kréfeld, in Rhénanie-Westphalie, which, following Napoleon's victories, was a French territory at the time. Thierry Hermès was the son of an innkeeper and the godson of a master suede worker. In his young years he traveled often, worked as a saddler, and eventually settled in Paris. He founded the Hermès company in 1837 as a saddlery business and produced bridles and harnesses, which he supplied to coachmakers and wholesalers. His company became famous for creating one-of-a-kind saddlery for European noblemen, including the Russian Czar. It was rumored that

coronations were sometimes postponed for years until Hermès could create original carriage designs. The company continued to custom-make saddles, investing 20 to 40 hours in each, throughout the nineteenth and twentieth centuries. The functional and decorative "saddle stitch" used by Hermès craftsmen to join pieces of leather together would come to represent the branded goods' quality and simple elegance. When executed by hand, as it always has been throughout Hermès's history, the technique involves punching holes through multiple layers of leather, then alternating needles at either end of a beeswaxed linen thread through the holes in a figure-eight pattern.

Thierry Hermès was a visionary and quickly adopted new ideas and inventions for his otherwise traditional products. While buying gear in Canada, he spotted the newly invented *fermeture éclair*, or zipper, and not only brought it back to France but purchased a two-year patent on this invention. The closure became so closely associated with Hermès products (handbags, jockey silks, and leather gloves) that Frenchmen came to call it a *fermeture Hermès*. One often-repeated "zipper story" is that the Prince of Wales, a well-known fashion icon, requested

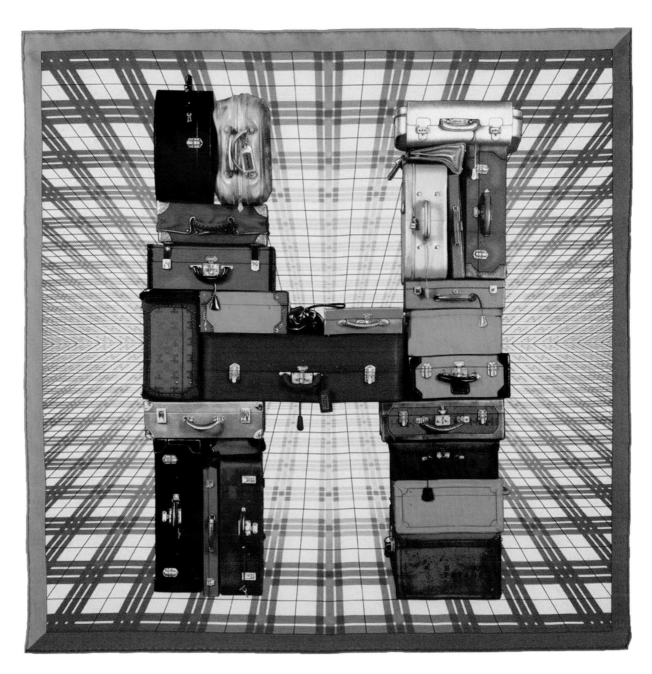

a zippered leather golfing jacket, thereby inaugurating the Hermès line of leather apparel.

When he realized that the days of the horse-carriage were numbered and Hermès's business might slow as a result, Thierry shifted the focus of the company away from the saddlery business and steered toward developing luggage and bags for plane, car, and train travel. Hermès manufactured trunks, bags, and overnight cases, using its signature saddle leather. Thierry

Hermès's grandson, Émile-Maurice Hermès, took control of the company throughout the 1920s and made a series of smart business decisions. He added new accessory collections and purchased the building at Rue Faubourg St.-Honoré 24 in Paris, which still houses the flagship store as well as the workshops. The legend has it that in 1922, the wife of Emile-Maurice Hermès complained that she could not find a handbag that she liked, and so he began making handbags, many with

FIGURE 2.1
The Hermès company has some of the most luxurious and elegant products, paired with truly whimsical presentations and advertising campaigns. Courtesy of WWD/Quentin Bertoux.

the revolutionary invention, the zipper. When Émile-Maurice Hermès died in 1951, two of his sons-in-law, Robert Dumas and Jean-Rene Guerrand, took over Hermès and added the name Hermès to their own surname. Robert Dumas-Hermès introduced the Hermès tie, the beach towel, and the perfume to the wide assortment of products.

The business has remained within the family for almost 200 years. When Robert Dumas-Hermès died in 1978, his son Jean-Louis Dumas-Hermès took over the company. He is the fifth generation of family involved in the business and is a chairman of Hermès. He travels extensively all over the world in search of new ideas and concepts, which go into development of Hermès products (Figure 2.2). Hermès still uses some of the best quality skins from all over the world. The Hermès leather storage facility in Paris contains hundreds of the finest animal skins: alligator from Florida; buffalo from Pakistan; crocodile from Australia; sharks from Thailand; lizards from Malaysia; and oxen, deer, calf, and goats from all over the world. They are dyed in every color, pattern, and texture imaginable and turned into elegant accessories.

The Hermès Scarf

Like the production of leather goods, the making of a scarf at Hermès is utterly dedicated to the pursuit of highest quality. Their first printed scarf was produced in 1937 and in the years since they have become the epitomy of sophistication and style. They are not just scarves; they are works of art, made from the finest materials with exquisite workmanship (Figure 2.3). Hermès oversees the entire process, from the purchase of the Brazilian cocoon silk, to its spinning into yarn and its weaving into a fabric, which is twice as strong and heavy as that found in most scarves. It takes 250 cocoons to make one scarf. The very first scarf was printed with

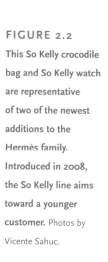

FIGURE 2.2
This So Kelly crocodile bag and So Kelly watch are representative of two of the newest additions to the Hermès family. Introduced in 2008, the So Kelly line aims toward a younger customer. Photos by Vicente Sahuc.

wooden blocks, and it wasn't until 1947 that Hermès started silkscreening the scarves. The scarf designs feature the artwork of artists from around the world. Some work for the company, some are comissioned, some are submitted by the artists themselves. It takes a minimum of two years from an initial design until a scarf comes to life. For the actual screening process, scarves are positioned on 100-yard long tables and individual screens for each color move onto every scarf to print each one. Colors are screened from lightest to darkest and from the smallest to the largest amount of surface. In the process, each color is allowed to dry completely before the next one is applied. Hermès artisans choose from a palette of over 200,000 colors; and the most complicated designs feature 40 colors. Hand-rolling and hemming the scarves completes the process and takes about a half-hour each. Despite this painstaking work, Hermès managed to put out two new scarf collections a year in the 1990s. Some were limited designs, part of annual themes, like "The Road" (1994) or "The Sun" (1995), while other perennial favorites remained in circulation for decades. Scarf motifs ranged from the French Revolution to French cuisine and flora and fauna of Texas. Hermès customers consider the scarves collectible works of art and are willing to pay any price to acquire them. In 2011, prices ranged from $385 to $580 for the 36" × 36" scarf and $760 for a dip-dyed giant 56" × 56" scarf (prices from www.Hermès.com).

FIGURE 2.3 The Hermès scarf is one of the most coveted accessories in the world. The official website, Hermes.com, offers downloadable booklets called "Playtime with Your Scarf," offering hundreds of fun and elegant ways to fold and wear it as headwear, neckwear, belt, and even a sleeveless top. Courtesy of WWD/Giovanni Giannoni (above); Courtesy of WWD/George Chinsee (below).

rêver (make us dream), Hermès designers and craftsmen fashioned unusual special orders. The custom items ranged from the functional, such as a calfskin fly-fishing tackle box, to the frivolous, including an ostrich-skin Walkman case. These limited-edition novelties did not come cheap either; indulgences such as $175 chewing-gum holders made of leather, $500 playing card holders, $1,000 silk kites, $20,000 alligator golf bags, and $12,500 mink jogging suits were out of reach for most of the world's consumers.

Hermès Handbags

Some of the most famous Hermès bags are:

- **The Kelly Bag** 1956 was named after the actress Grace Kelly, who became Princess Grace of Monaco; she was often photographed with it. The bag started out as a specialty nineteenth-century saddlebag and was reintroduced as a handbag in the 1930s. The attention to detail that had become a family hallmark was applied to the construction of each Kelly bag, requiring 18 hours of work by a single artisan.
- **Constance Bag** 1968 was named for the daughter of its designer, who was born the same day as the bag debuted. Jackie Kennedy Onassis wore this shoulder bag with the double strap and big H clasp, so regularly that people often ask for the "Jackie O bag."
- **Birkin Bag** 1984 named after Jane Birkin, the film star and model of the 1960s. She met Jean-Louis Hermès on a plane while struggling to get her handbag in an overhead compartment and dropped the bag, spilling everything that was in it. Hermès offered to design a bag especially for her. This handcrafted bag is so popular that even today it has the longest waiting list for any accessory (see Figure 2.4).

Here are some interesting facts about the Hermès scarves: A factory dedicated only to the production of scarves was established in Lyon in 1937. The first silk scarf in the Hermès collection was called "Jeax des Omnibus et Dames Blanches." The modern Hermès scarf measures a 36-inch square, weighs 65 grams and is woven from the silk of 250 mulberry moth cocoons. The per-pound cost of a scarf today is more than $3,500. The Brides De Gala scarf design, first introduced in the 1970s, has sold over 70,000 scarves.

Custom Articles

Over the decades, Hermès has earned a reputation for creating unique custom articles. Urging clients to *faites nous*

Louis Vuitton

Most of us know Louis Vuitton Moët Hennessy S.A. simply as Louis Vuitton, and everybody who knows fashion recognizes the LV logo from countless advertising campaigns featuring famous celebrities. This luxury French fashion and leather goods brand has its headquarters in Paris, France and is historically known as a supplier of luggage to the wealthy and powerful in their world travels. Even though in the most recent years, Marc Jacobs has been appointed the Creative Director, this brand has been a family affair for more than a century before that.

The Founder of Louis Vuitton

The company is named after its founder, who designed and manufactured luggage (Figure 2.5) as a *malletier*, or a trunk-maker, during the second half of the nineteenth century. Louis Vuitton was born in Anchay, the Jura region of France, a son of a carpenter. He left for Paris on foot in 1835 at age 14, and became an apprentice packer and trunk-maker, mastering the skill of woodworking and designing trunks. Within 10 years, he became an expert in packing wealthy women's clothes for their long voyages. Vuitton and his master, Monsieur Maréchal, were the exclusive packers to the Empress Eugénie and her ladies-in-waiting and regularly went to the Tuileries Palace to prepare their luggage. Because of his familiarity with wood, silk, and satin, he became well respected by the couturiers. They often hired him to pack their creations, and in 1854, Louis Vuitton opened his own business *Malletier à Paris* or "Trunk-Maker in Paris," situated very close to the couture houses around Place Vendôme.

He was the first to manufacture a flat-topped trunk, which was lightweight and airtight and allowed stacking on top of each other. Before that all trunks had rounded tops so water would run off when transported and exposed to rainy weather. This simple invention established his

reputation as a master luggage-maker. His business grew increasingly successful, and eventually the original store became too small, and he moved to a larger space where he focused on trunk-making rather than packing. Louis Vuitton became the supplier of luggage to many of the most famous people of the era, from King Alfonso XII of Spain to the future Czar Nicholas II of Russia.

The quality of the materials he used, the grey Trianon canvas, which was elegant and waterproof when varnished; the way the interiors were arranged; and the overall finish of the trunks made Vuitton's deluxe trunks far superior to anything previously produced. In 1867, Louis Vuitton entered the Universal Exhibition at the World's Fair in Paris and won the bronze medal, but that also created a slew of copycats, so in 1876, he started introducing new designs featuring stripes. By

FIGURE 2.5

Socialites like Gloria Vanderbilt (left) and her aunt, Gertrude Vanderbilt Whitney, not only used trunks for travel but proudly displayed their prized possessions.

© Associated Press.

1888, the LV red and beige and brown and beige striped canvases were imitated, and the LV designs were changed to a patented checkered material. The company started changing designs according to the latest fashion of travel. Vuitton designed classic wardrobe trunks for sleeping cars and lighter versions of the suitcase traditionally used by the English aristocracy. His first international branch was opened in London.

By 1880, his son Georges was given full control of the business and started playing a vital role in managing and keeping it fresh and current. In 1888, the Damier Canvas pattern was created by Louis Vuitton in collaboration with Georges, and bore a logo that read "marque L. Vuitton déposée," which translates "L. Vuitton trademark."

The Contributions of Georges and Gaston Vuitton

In 1890, Georges Vuitton invented the theft-proof five-tumbler lock, which provided each customer with a personal combination and made the luggage much more secure. Two years later, the company's first catalog presented a wide range of products, from very specialized trunks for transporting particular objects to simple bags with the typical traveler in mind.

Louis Vuitton passed away in 1892, and four years later, his son Georges Vuitton introduced a new canvas design in another attempt to deter counterfeiters. In memory of his father, Vuitton's new design featured Louis Vuitton's initials against a background of stars and flowers. This design was also trademarked and became an immediate and lasting success.

Being a smart businessman, Georges Vuitton became convinced of the importance of a sales network abroad, and by the end of the century, John Wanamaker began representing Louis Vuitton in New York and Philadelphia. By the early twentieth century, the company had expanded to Washington, Boston, Chicago,

San Francisco, Brussels, Buenos Aires, Bombay, Nice, Bangkok, and Montreal.

Georges Vuitton also foresaw the importance of the automobile as a form of transport and began designing automobile trunks, which imitated the lines of the car, to protect travelers' effects from rain and dust. He created iceboxes, canteens, and light and flexible steamer bags and adapted to the changes in the travel industry by manufacturing airplane and hot air balloon trunks and cases for spare tires.

During World War I, production was modified to the needs of the war effort, as simple and solid military trunks replaced delicate and luxurious models. But as the economy improved after the war, Louis Vuitton regained its stylish and affluent clientele, and special orders increased.

One of the most notable designs is the Milano case, presented at the exposition of 1925. It was lined with red Morocco leather and had crystal bottles with vermeil stoppers, ivory brushes, and toilet accessories, carved with fine geometric Art Deco details. Another one was the toiletry case, created especially for opera singer Marthe Chenal, which held bottles, brushes, mirrors, powder boxes, and other toiletries. The company also provided some packing services for foreigners who came to buy garments from the Paris couture collections and incorporated exotic skins, tortoise shell, lizard skin, crocodile skin, elephant hide, ebony, and unusual woods in its fabrications.

As economic conditions deteriorated worldwide in the 1930s, the Vuittons realized the necessity of increasing the company's profitability. Georges Vuitton's son Gaston Vuitton worked with his father to increase company efficiency. An advertising agency was set up, and a design office was created to make detailed sketches of products to show customers before fabrication. The designs expanded into such special items as the *Noé* bag. This bag was created in 1932 for champagne vintners to transport bottles.

By the time Georges Vuitton died in 1936, special orders had dramatically declined, and the company's sales depended more than ever upon its catalog offerings, which were expanded to include trunks for typewriters, radios, books, rifles, and wine bottles.

During World War II, delivery of Vuitton products was reduced, overseas contracts were terminated, and the Vuitton factory and stores had to close. The first important postwar order at the company was for the President of the French Republic, Vincent Auriol, who made an official visit to the United States. In 1954, the company's hundredth anniversary, Louis Vuitton moved from the Champs-Elysées to Avenue Marceau. As travel times were cut with the development of trains, cars, and airplanes, the company created and improved its soft-sided and carry-on luggage.

In 1959, Gaston Vuitton perfected a system of coating his motif canvases, making them more durable, waterproof, and suitable for shorter journeys. These lightweight, practical bags signified a new standard in luggage. Gaston had the visionary idea to invite well-known artists to take part in the design of accessories. From 1959 to 1965, an average of 25 new models of Vuitton luggage and handbags were created each year, and stars like Audrey Hepburn were used to help rebuild the image of the brand. With the company's success and reputation for luxury came a vast wave of counterfeit Louis Vuitton products. One year before his death in 1970, Gaston Vuitton decided to take action against the counterfeiters by opening a store in Tokyo and offering the real Vuitton product in the Asian market. With this, he hoped to better inform customers about the original products and their qualities and discourage the purchase and manufacture of imitations. The company also undertook a successful advertising campaign to battle the increase in counterfeiting.

Marc Jacobs at Louis Vuitton

In 1997, Marc Jacobs was hired as an artistic director, and as such he introduced the first prêt-à-porter fashion clothing line. Jacobs facilitated collaborations with other designers like Stephen Sprouse, Takashi Murakami, Richard Prince, and Comme des Garçons for the LV accessories. Those collaborations featured graffiti writing, "Cherry Blossom" patterns, and mismatched prints. In 2004, Louis Vuitton celebrated its 150th anniversary and inaugurated signature stores on the corner of Fifth Avenue and 57th Street in New York City, and in São Paulo, Brazil and Johannesburg, South Africa. It also opened its first global store in Shanghai. By 2005, Louis Vuitton reopened its Champs-Élysées store, known as the largest LV store in the world, and released the Speedy watch collection. In 2008, Louis Vuitton released the Damier Graphite canvas. The canvas features the classic Damier pattern but in black and grey, giving it a masculine look and urban feel.

Throughout its history, the Louis Vuitton Company has carefully positioned itself in the luxury market as one of the most coveted brands. Its products have a cult following among celebrities, actresses, and rich clients as well as fashionistas all over the world. A large part of that appeal has been cultivated through carefully crafted ad campaigns, using world famous models, actresses, and singers. Breaking from their usual traditions of employing supermodels and celebrities to advertise their products, in 2007 the company featured former USSR leader Mikhail Gorbachev in an ad campaign. After relying only on selected press for its advertising, Antoine Arnault, director of the communication department, recently decided to enter the world of television and cinema. The first ever LV video commercial, exploring the theme "Where will life take you?" directed by renowned French director

his career. He started designing for couture houses in the United Kingdom, France, and the United States. Roger Vivier saw every detail, curve, and technical aspect as an opportunity for novelty and beauty. He was an innovator, utilizing fabrics like clear plastic, which would initially be rejected by some houses.

In 1930, Roger Vivier started working for Elsa Schiaparelli, and his ideas found a perfect ground to flourish. He went on to collaborate with many couturiers, but the most groundbreaking inventions came while he worked with Dior around 1947. He designed extravagant richly decorated shoes that he described as sculptures.

FIGURE 2.6
Louis Vuitton still creates highly specialized custom cases like this monogram 2010 Soccer World Cup trophy case. Courtesy of WWD/Dominique Maitre.

FIGURE 2.7
Designer Roger Vivier. Deborah Feingold/ Corbis.

Bruno Aveillan was created and translated into 13 languages. Today, the LV logo is one of the most recognizable logos in the world of fashion, and the brand products continue to feature traditional craftsmanship and quality as well as groundbreaking design ideas and special custom cases (Figure 2.6).

Roger Vivier

Roger Vivier (1907–1998) (Figure 2.7) is best known for creating groundbreaking heel designs for women's shoes. His shoes are like pieces of jewelry and have been called "the Fabergé of footwear." He used silk, pearls, beads, lace, appliqué and jewels to create unique decorations. Vivier dressed the feet of such celebrities as Elizabeth Taylor and Sophia Loren. Ava Gardner, Gloria Guinness, and the Beatles were all Vivier customers.

A native of Paris, he studied sculpture at the École des Beaux Arts there and completed an apprenticeship in a shoe factory. The knowledge of visual beauty and technical practicality that he acquired from these two very different realms prepared him for

Vivier's Inventive Designs

When Dior's New Look brought emphasis to the ankle and foot, Vivier created a number of innovative heel shapes for Dior, including the stiletto and the comma heel. The thin high heels were around in the 1800s, as seen

in fetish drawings, but Vivier is credited with the reviving and developing this style in 1954 by using a thin rod of steel. The origin of the stiletto name goes back to the notorious and dangerous daggers with a long slender blade, primarily used as a stabbing weapon, favored by criminals to leave a deep wound upon its intended victim. Vivier wanted a new design to add height but maintain the femininity of his shoes. His answer was the heel from a long thin piece of metal, which kept it strong, thin, and powerful.

He experimented with many shapes for heels; one of the most famous is the comma heel. It is shaped like an inverted curve and might have not been the most balanced heel, but it was an exciting innovation that brought a lot of attention to the designer. His most iconic design, the Pilgrim pumps with an oversized square silver buckle (worn by Catherine Deneuve in the film *Belle de Jour*), became all the rage of their time and are still one of the most imitated designs (Figure 2.8).

An example of Vivier's ever innovative brand, the original coronation shoe for Queen Elizabeth II was responsible for the birth of the platform; a step was inlayed in the queen's shoe to give her support and stability so she would feel steady during the most monumental moment of her life. She was warned by her grandmother that she would be on her feet for at least three hours, and that at no time during the ceremony should she falter in her stance. Thanks to her Vivier shoes, the queen was able to stand gracefully through the entire ceremony.

The 1960s brought an epic social, political and cultural revolution, and Roger Vivier's thigh-high boot were no exception. With them he dared to delve into a sexual territory that had long been forbidden in female fashion. He appliquéd and bejeweled them and lined them with satin, creating powerful and beautiful statements.

FIGURE 2.8 The Pilgrim Pump as designed by Vivier for Catherine Deneuve in the film *Belle de Jour* (above) and a modern version of the shoe (below). The style has been copied countless times and is still in demand. Courtesy of WWD; Courtesy of WWD.

FIGURE 2.9

Modern Vivier shoe

designs. Courtesy of

WWD.

Vivier's Legacy

Roger Vivier passed away in 1998, at age 90, but his designs live on as inspirations to designers all over the world (Figure 2.9). A testament to his creations as works of art, Roger Vivier's designs can be seen at several museums including the Musée du Costume et de la Mode of the Louvre in Paris and the Victoria and Albert Museum in London as well as The Costume Institute of the Metropolitan Museum of Art in New York.

His design spirit lives on in a brand that is now stronger than ever, thanks to creative director Bruno Frisoni. In 2001, Frisoni was asked to join the rich heritage of the brand as Creative Director. Frisoni is himself obsessed with feminine allure and his ambition is "to create a brand, not to set up another shoe shop." For Frisoni, who cites Cate Blanchett and Isabelle Huppert among his muses, "The shoe is an accessory of seduction. Seduction is the watchword of my designs at Roger Vivier."

Salvatore Ferragamo

Salvatore Ferragamo was born in 1898, the eleventh of 14 children, in Bonito, a village about 62 miles from Naples, Italy. Early in his childhood, he revealed a great passion for shoes. At the age of 11, he was apprenticed to a shoemaker in Naples, and by the age of 13, he had already opened his own shoe shop in Bonito. At age 14, he went to America to join one of his

brothers, who was working in a large footwear company in Boston. Ferragamo was fascinated by the modern machinery but at the same time had a lot of appreciation for handmade, quality footwear. In the early 1920s, he moved to Santa Barbara, California, to join another brother, where he opened a shoe-repair shop. Being so close to the movie industry in Hollywood, Ferragamo started to design and make shoes for the cinema. In his constant search for "shoes which fit perfectly," he studied human anatomy, chemical engineering, and mathematics so he could create the ultimate shoes.

Ferragamo's Return to Italy

Salvatore Ferragamo opened his Hollywood Boot Shop in 1923, marking the start of his career as the "shoemaker to the stars" (Figure 2.10). The press and the stars loved him and his designs. His success was so great, he couldn't keep pace with the orders. Realizing the limitations of the American workforce, Ferragamo decided to return to Florence, Italy, which is traditionally rich in skilled craftsmanship. By 1927, the move was completed, and he manufactured handmade shoes as a constant stream of exports from his Florentine workshop to the United States.

Unfortunately, as a result of the great stock market crisis of 1929 and interrupted relationships with the American market, he had to close his shop. Ferragamo didn't lose hope and turned his energy into expanding to the national Italian market. By 1936, business was going so well he started expanding facilities and rented two more workshops and a shop in Palazzo Spini Feroni. Even though these years were marked by economic sanctions against Mussolini's Italy, Ferragamo used an array of innovative materials creatively to replace the leather and steel that were restricted at the time. During those years, Ferragamo developed some of his most popular and widely-imitated creations, such as the light cork wedges.

Ideas came from all around him, and as a true genius, he used common materials to solve high-end design puzzles.

> My first major problem was to find a substitute for the fine quality kidskins. I experimented with many materials, but none were satisfactory. Then, one Sunday morning, I found the solution. My mother was extremely fond of chocolates, and this day I brought a box back to the house. As I unwrapped a chocolate for her I was attracted by its transparent paper wrapping. I turned the paper over in my hands. Here might be the substitute I was seeking.

This marked the beginning of Ferragamo's production of shoes in cellophane to provide elegant summer wear. The cellophane was often worked in combination with cotton, rayon, and other threads by the same women who made his raffia bands and crocheted cotton uppers.

On the strength of his success, in 1938, Ferragamo managed to pay the first installment for the purchase of the entire Palazzo Spini Feroni, which remains the company headquarters. The shoes of Salvatore Ferragamo became a symbol of Italy's reconstruction all over the world in the post-war period. Those were years of memorable inventions: the metal-reinforced stiletto heels made famous by Marilyn Monroe, gold sandals, and the invisible sandals with uppers made from

FIGURE 2.10 Salvatore Ferragamo developed lasting relationships with Hollywood stars like dancer Katherine Dunham (above) and created shoes for some of the biggest names, like Sophia Loren, Marilyn Monroe, and Judy Garland (below).

nylon thread (which in 1947 won Ferragamo the prestigious Neiman Marcus Award, the Oscar of the fashion world, awarded for the first time to a footwear designer).

"Which of all materials is my favorite? None! Or rather, all. The material I work with today is my favorite today," Ferragamo wrote in his autobiography. "Nevertheless, if I like them all, I must still confess to a recurring and fond regard for the use of kidskin. It is a beautiful leather, smart and graceful and with a fine gentle feel to the fingers." Ferragamo often used kidskin, dyed in an extraordinary variety of colors, in combination with other skins, such as lizard and patent leather or with satin for his evening shoes. Bovine leather was used especially for casual and winter shoes and for soles.

Steel or brass heels have graced shoes by Ferragamo since the 1920s, but they were at the height of fashion above all in the fifties. In 1955, Salvatore Ferragamo filed a number of important patents. One was a metalized heel in various colors, lined with a lamina of aluminum; another was a "cage" heel, hollow and lightweight yet very strong and durable. The third and even more ingenious patent was for a multiple heel adorned with gem-spattered, gold- or silver-plated metal decorations, painstakingly handcrafted to look like lacework. But the most extraordinary invention has to be the metal sole that Ferragamo patented in 1956, when he created the most costly shoe he'd ever made, an 18-karat gold sandal.

The use of plant fibers and straw in the shoe construction was certainly not a novelty, but before Ferragamo revived them in the early thirties, they hadn't been popular or used for luxury shoes. When Ferragamo settled in Florence, straw manufacturing was one of the city's most thriving activities, and it inspired him to revive the use of this traditional material in shoes. The market sold straw, or bark treated with chrome, grass from Philippines, and Manila hemp made from banana leaves and skin. Ferragamo's favorite, however, was raffia,

a fiber derived from the young leave of an east African palm. Ferragamo's innovation was to adopt this weave for his uppers, especially for summer shoes, and in 1930, he called the new range "Pompeian by Ferragamo." The growth of this artisan industry lasted for a brief period of time, and by 1950, straw and raffia were in short supply. In the 1950s, synthetic raffia gradually replaced natural straw. Salvatore Ferragamo favored one of the synthetic raffia called "pontovo" or "pontova" produced mainly in Bonito, his home town in Campania.

Techniques Used in Ferragamo's Designs

From the very beginning of his career, Salvatore Ferragamo was strongly focused on handcraft techniques, especially the ones involved in the making of uppers. Here are some of his favorite techniques:

TAVARNELLE LACE

Before Salvatore Ferragamo, needlepoint lace was used only to decorate clothing, underwear, and household linen, but at the end of the twenties, Ferragamo created a new purpose for the lace by using it to form the uppers of his shoes and introduced an array of colors that had never been seen before. He adopted the Tavarnelle needlepoint lace in 1930s and 1950s, both periods of the revival of Romanticism in fashion. Tavarnelle, Mercatale, and Greve, all small towns in the area between Florence and Siena, were the centers of production, relying on pieceworkers.

PATCHWORK

The use of patchwork is one of the most recurrent themes in Salvatore Ferragamo's footwear since the very beginning, and it became one of his stylistic hallmarks. He had a talent for combining colors and materials and creating exciting combinations, even when using the most traditional leathers. He worked with Sonia Delaunay, wife of the painter Robert Delaunay and a key influencer in figurative

and applied arts, to develop new patterns. The inspiration behind patchwork wasn't only an expression of new artistic trends, it was also an interest in the tradition of handmade quilts in North America. The first patchwork uppers by Ferragamo appeared in the twenties and combined calfskin with crocodile and suede. These creations were cross stitched with silk or cotton thread and had variously colored suede in geometrical arrangements. They became a signature motif in subsequent collections, even after Ferragamo's death. These design motifs were adapted in the clothing as well as the footwear and in all the leather accessories.

EMBROIDERY

Salvatore Ferragamo's decision to settle in Florence in 1927 was influenced by the survival of local traditional artisans as well as by the beauty of the city and its works of art. He was confident that Florence would provide inspiration, materials, and expert hands for his new enterprise. Embroidery was one of the oldest of the city's handcrafts, with an impressive history of superb production. The embroiderers received the cloth or skin uppers

already cut, which then they worked in various ways, given a wide choice in the type of stitch and decoration. The result was an incredible variety of glorious designs.

TRAMEZZA STITCHED WELTING

At Ferragamo, workmanship is technical and precise. The complex construction process of tramezza stitched welting helps balance sturdiness and resistance with peerless flexibility and comfort. If the soles are periodically repaired and replaced, shoes with hand-stitched welting can be worn "forever," and their fit becomes shaped by the foot's imprint. The handcrafted welting process for just one pair of shoes takes several hours. The key operation in this type of construction involves the selection of the inner and outer materials. At Ferragamo, both are of the highest natural quality and are made to mold the shoe around the foot at first wearing.

When Salvatore Ferragamo died in 1960, he had realized the great dream of his life: to create and produce the most beautiful shoes in the world. Today his empire has expanded to include handbags, scarves, and men's shoes (Figure 2.11).

FIGURE 2.11

Various products from Salvatore Ferragamo, representing the large variety of luxury goods manufactured by this world-renowned label. The Ferragamo company currently creates a full line of handbags, small leather goods, belts, eyewear, and timepieces in addition to travel-related bags and shoes. Clockwise from top left: Courtesy of WWD/George Chinsee; © Condé Nast Digital Studio/Greg Vore; Courtesy of WWD; © Condé Nast Digital Studio/Ethan Palmer; Courtesy of WWD/ Thomas Iannaccone.

Coach

The Coach brand has defined classic, modern American style for more than 60 years with a broad range of classic lifestyle accessories. In a family-run workshop in a Manhattan loft founded in 1941, six artisans handcrafted a collection of wallets and billfolds, using skills handed down from generation to generation. In 1946, Miles Cahn, a lifelong New Yorker, came to work for the company. By 1950, he was running the factory for its owners. Cahn noticed the distinctive properties of the leather used to make baseball gloves and realized that with wear, the leather in a glove became soft and supple. He created a way of processing leather in order to make it strong, soft, flexible, and deep-toned in color and started making bags with it. Purses made of the sturdy cowhide were given the brand name Coach. These bags were revolutionary in the way they were made. The grain of the leather could still be seen, instead of the thin leather pasted over cardboard that was used for most women's handbags at the time. This innovation marked a new era for Coach and an entry into the field of classic luxury women's leather handbags that lasted a lifetime.

The Contribution of Bonnie Cashin

In the late 1960s, as fashion changed radically, Coach started introducing additional models that were designed to complement trendier styles in clothing and marketing seasonal items. They asked the visionary American designer Bonnie Cashin to become their designer. She was too busy with other projects and declined. They waited two years for her to clear her calendar, and in 1962, Cashin became the designer for their new label of leather accessories. Bonnie Cashin developed accessories according to her philosophy of contemporary dress and revolutionized the

handbag industry. She dyed leather to match her favorite candy colors of pink, orange, yellow and green, and lined bags with exquisite Belgian linens, Mexican cottons, or tweeds designed by her friend and mentor, textile designer Dorothy Liebes.

After years of rigid black and brown accessories, clients and the craftsmen in the Coach factory raved about the variety of shapes, colors, and textures available in the new "Cashin-Carry" designs, all with convenient wide openings or exterior coin purses and pockets. Cashin also designed matching wallets, makeup bags, key holders, and sunglass cases, which was rare for the handbag business. She pioneered the use of hardware on her clothes and accessories alike, particularly the brass toggle that became the Coach hallmark.

The Expansion in the 1970s and 1980s

In the late 1970s and early 1980s, Coach took two steps to diversify its channels of distribution. First the company began a mail-order business, and second it started opening its own specialty stores to sell Coach products outside a department store setting. Sales of Coach products grew steadily throughout this period, until demand began to outstrip supply. Department stores were selling all the Coach bags that the company could produce, and by the early 1980s, it had become necessary to ration the products to various vendors. Despite the potential for vast expansion of their market share, the Cahns continued to run their business in the same way that they always had. They kept the factory in urban Manhattan despite the high rents, taxes, and wages and preserved their methods of production with high quality of workmanship. They continued to run their business on a personal level, maintaining first-name relationships with many of their workers, and inviting department store buyers from New York to tour their factory to observe the craftsmanship that went into each Coach bag.

In 1983, the Cahns purchased a 300-acre dairy farm in Vermont as a weekend diversion from their business in New York, but it became more of a permanent home, and by 1985, they were commuting twice a week between Vermont and New York. After determining that none of their three children had any desire to take over the family leatherware business, the Cahns sold the company to Sara Lee Corporation for a sum reported to be around $30 million. The conglomerate took control of the company's factory, its six boutiques, and the flagship store on Madison Avenue in New York City and promised to operate Coach in the way it had always been run. Under its new owners and new president, the company started a rapid expansion, introducing a number of new products under the Coach name and opening new boutiques throughout the country. By November of 1986, the company was operating 12 stand-alone stores and 50 boutiques within larger department stores. The most significant product line introduction during that time was the Coach Lightweights collection. It featured lighter weight leather bags with new shapes for women who lived in the warmer climate of the South and West of the United States. The Lightweights line featured handbags in smaller sizes and lighter spring colors and quickly became successful, reaching 15 percent of the company's overall sales. The next product expansion for Coach was business items for men and women. Among the new products were briefcases, wallets, and diaries.

Coach's first nonleather product was introduced in 1988. Silk scarves, sold in four designs that related to leather goods, were planned to complement the rest of the Coach products. Each of the 36-inch silk squares was manufactured in Italy and priced at $60. However, the products were eventually discontinued after it was determined that their equestrian designs, featuring bridles and stirrups, made them look too much like products from a Coach competitor, Hermès.

Coach took its first steps overseas in 1988 when the company noted that many of the customers in its New York store were foreign tourists. The first boutiques were opened in England and Japan. These stores carried a full line of Coach products and mimicked the look of Coach stores in the United States, with mahogany and brass fixtures and marble floors. By 1989, the number of company stores had grown to 40.

Coach the Brand

Coach planned a dramatic shift in its identity in the 1990s. "We're going for positioning as Coach the brand, as opposed to Coach the leather company," the company's president told *Crain's New York Business*. "I can't see a limit to Coach's growth in the foreseeable future." To bolster that growth, Coach hired a designer to lead a 16-person product development department to create new objects that could be marketed under the Coach name. In its women's line, the company sought to introduce products in more fashionable colors, deviating from the timeless styling, but without watering down the Coach image and integrity. The company began to sell a line of accessory goods for men that included suspenders and socks. This fast-moving category allowed the opening of two Coach for Business stores, on Madison Avenue in Manhattan and in Boston. With these stores, the company hoped to shift its image, repositioning itself as a full-range accessory maker (Figure 2.12).

Coach started marketing its products to younger customers in 1991 and hired a new, young advertising agency, which designed a campaign featuring descendants of famous Americans using Coach products, with the theme, "An American Legacy." By early 1992, Coach had expanded its number of stores worldwide to 53 and added gift items, including picture frames and belts. As Coach broadened its product offerings, it also broadened the variety of its handbags and expanded its manufacturing facilities to Puerto Rico to keep up with the demand.

Reed Krakoff assumed the role of Senior Vice President and Executive Creative Director in December 1996 and soon after unveiling his first collection, he became an influenial creative leader (Figure 2.13).

In 1999, Coach launched its online store at www.coach.com and evolved it into an effective marketing and advertising vehicle for Coach both domestically and abroad. By mid-2000, there were 106 Coach retail outlets in the United States and 63 outlet stores.

Coach in the Twenty-First Century

In November 2001, Coach introduced its first jewelry collection in a joint effort with Carolee Designs, Inc. The silver jewelry line featured some items that combined silver and leather. It seemed clear that Coach was well positioned to leverage its strong reputation for prestige and quality and its tradition of producing classic, classy products into a successful era of independence.

FIGURE 2.12
Various Coach accessories featured in an ad campaign shot.
Courtesy of Coach.

The most vibrant and exciting collection yet was introduced in July of 2009. The Poppy collection mixed preppy with a youthful quirky appeal in bright colors and eclectic prints. "When designing Poppy I really wanted to explore who the Coach woman could be," said Reed Krakoff. "With its bright colors, prints, sequins, and new fabrics, Poppy is a natural extension of the brand while simultaneously proving to be an exciting draw for new customers and age groups. Poppy offers a different attitude that is younger in spirit," he said. "It's playful, with more prints, interesting fabrics and more experimentation. [These ideas] are always countered with a more classic shape or a more traditional construction." The line featured handbags, tiaras, footwear, watches, and select apparel and marked the beginning of a new era: a trendy, fun, and edgy Coach.

Now greatly expanded, Coach continues to maintain the highest standards for materials and workmanship. The values of the brand: classic American style, customer satisfaction, integrity, innovation, and collaboration are the reason people are still seeking the Coach craftsmanship in handbags, briefcases, luggage, and accessories. There are currently over 400 Coach stores in the United States and Canada, and while Coach continues to be one of the most recognized accessories brands in the United States, its corporate headquarters remain in midtown Manhattan on 34th Street, in the same location as its former factory lofts.

COACH
EST. 1941

Introducing the first
Fragrance from Coach

FIGURE 2.13 Reed Krakoff has been instrumental in developing the first fragrance, as well as overseeing design and all creative aspects of the Coach Company and even venturing into photographing advertising campaigns like this one. Courtesy of Coach.

JUDITH LEIBER

Handbag designer Judith Leiber.
© Condé Nast.

Judith Leiber is an American luxury brand synonymous with elegance and sophistication, and its handbags are considered art pieces sought after by collectors. Each Judith Leiber product is created with meticulous attention to detail and flawless handcraftsmanship. In addition to designing handbags and minaudières, the company also produces eyewear, fur, and cashmere accessories. Various handbags are included in the collections of the Metropolitan Museum of Art, The Smithsonian Institution, The Corcoran Gallery, and The Victoria and Albert Museum, among many others.

JUDITH LEIBER'S EARLY CAREER

Judith Leiber, the founder of the company, was born Judith Peto in 1921 and raised in Budapest, Hungary, where she studied the craft of handbag making during World War II. She became the first female apprentice and then master in the Hungarian handbag guild. When the war finally ended, Judith met an American GI, Gerson Leiber. They had a whirlwind courtship and were married within the year. An avid art lover, Gerson began his formal art training at the Royal Academy of Art in Budapest.

JUDITH LEIBER IN THE UNITED STATES

In 1947, the Leibers immigrated to the United States, filled with ambitious dreams. He wanted to succeed as an artist, and she wanted to design handbags. Gerson continued to study art at the Art Students League, while Judith took jobs with various fashion houses on Seventh Avenue in New York. Judith's reputation for creativity and uniquely beautiful designs was apparent, and her handbags were featured in *Vogue*, *Harper's Bazaar*, and other top fashion magazines. Beginning in 1953, many first ladies, from Mamie Eisenhower on, have carried a Judith Leiber handbag to their husbands' inaugurations. In the world of high-fashion handbags, Leiber was known as a designer creating magnificent finished product, each one a unique work of art.

THE JUDITH LEIBER COMPANY

Finally, in 1963, Judith and Gerson decided it was time for her to start her own handbag company. Department stores were happy to display her collections, and customers loved her unique designs. First ladies, celebrities, and socially prominent arbiters of fashion quickly became devoted collectors of her artistic accessories. Opera diva Beverly Sills owned nearly 200 Judith Leiber bags. In addition, many prestigious museums began collecting Judith Leiber handbags and exhibiting the bags as part of their permanent collections.

In 1993, the Leibers received an offer they couldn't refuse. A British company bought the company with all its inventory, asking Judith Leiber to remain as a consultant. A name once on a Nazi list of Jews to be exterminated had become a world famous brand, now worth millions of dollars. Her remarkable story of survival, determination, and visionary creativity now inspires countless new dreams.

Hundreds of her artful handbags can be seen in a magnificent Palladian-style museum in East Hampton, built by the Leibers. Judith Leiber is truly an iconic American brand and her collections are available at Judith Leiber boutiques in New York and Los Angeles, The Forum Shops in Las Vegas, South Coast Plaza in Costa Mesa, California, and the department stores Neiman Marcus, Saks Fifth Avenue, and Bergdorf Goodman.

The whimsical Judith Leiber bags often feature multicolored rhinestones and pearls like this Fabergé egg–inspired bag. Photo by Gary Mamay, Courtesy: The Leiber Museum, East Hampton, NY © Judith Leiber.

Manolo Blahnik

Manolo Blahnik's career spans over 40 years, and he has dominated shoe design since setting up business in London in the early 1970s (Figure 2.14). What is even more remarkable is that he is solely responsible for the design and prototype of every one of the thousands of shoes that bear his name and has no formal training in shoemaking. "I didn't need it," Blahnik told a friend, Michael Roberts, only half-jokingly in the late 1970s, "because I've got the best taste in the world."

Born in 1942 in Santa Cruz de la Palma in the Canary Islands to a Spanish mother and a Czech father, he and his younger sister Evangelina were homeschooled, but the family often traveled to Paris and Madrid, where his parents ordered clothes from his mother's favorite couturiers. His first encounter with shoe making was when his mother persuaded the local Canary Islands cobbler to teach her how to make Catalan espadrilles from ribbons and laces. Blahnik loved to watch her making them. "I'm sure I acquired my interest in shoes genetically or at least through my fingers, when I was allowed to touch them as they were made," he later claimed.

Blahnik's Early Career

Hoping that Blahnik would become a diplomat, his parents enrolled him at the university in Geneva to study politics and law, but soon he switched to literature and architecture. In 1965, he left Geneva for Paris to study art and made ends meet by working at GO, a vintage clothes store. After a few years in Paris, his father suggested that he move to London and enrolled him at a language school to perfect his English, but Manolo spent most of his afternoons watching film after film. Barely earning a living in boutiques and from occasional design jobs, Blahnik decided to become a stage set designer and took a portfolio of drawings to New York in 1971 hoping to find work there. His friend from Paris, Paloma Picasso, arranged a meeting with Diana Vreeland, the editor of *Vogue*, and

FIGURE 2.14
Manolo Blahnik.
Courtesy of WWD.

his career was launched. When she looked at his drawings, Vreeland exclaimed, "How amusing! You can do accessories very well. Why don't you do that? Go make shoes. Your shoes in these drawings are so amusing."

Blahnik at Zapata

Upon his return to London, he began designing vividly colored men's shoes for Zapata, a boutique in Chelsea, but he found proper English brogues limiting. Blahnik started visiting the factories during production to learn about the process and got his break in 1972, when the most famous London fashion designer at the time, Ossie Clark, asked him to design the shoes for his next collection. The shoes looked extraordinary but were structurally unfinished. "I forgot to put in pins that would support the shoe; when it got hot the heels started to wobble. It was like walking on quicksand," he remembered years later. British *Vogue* warned its readers: "If you're buying [his] shoes, employ a sense of humour." But by then, his shoes at Zapata were sought after by

Vogue editors, and famous actresses popped in. Blahnik searched for a reliable manufacturer to correct his technical shortcomings and found one in Walthamstow, northeast London. He spent time learning the craft of shoemaking, and as much as fashion editors loved Blahnik's shoes, he was usually portrayed as a handsome, cultured man-about-town rather than as a designer. His celebrity status symbol solidified in 1974, when he became the first man to appear on the cover of British *Vogue*, photographed by David Bailey in a passionate embrace with Angelica Huston.

In 1973, Blahnik borrowed £2,000 to buy out Zapata's owner so he could run it with his sister Evangelina. It became a meeting place for celebrity clients and fashion designer collaborators including Jean Muir, Fiorucci, and Ossie Clark. In 1978, he broke into the U.S. market by creating a collection for Bloomingdale's and opening his first U.S. store on New York's Madison Avenue. By that time, Blahnik had found a successful formula for his collection: a combination of "occasional avant garde looks for the affluent few" and "good solid looks that will wear forever." They were both inspired by his eclectic passions, ranging from favorite Visconti and Cocteau films, and grandes dames like Elizabeth of Austria and Pauline Borghese to the paintings of Velázquez, El Greco, and Zurburán, and the work of couturiers he admired: Cristobál Balenciaga, Coco Chanel, and Yves Saint Laurent. He had become a craftsman, perfecting the exquisite shapes of lasts and heels with his own hands in a distinctive signature style. Always stylistically innovative, he revived the sleek stiletto heel in the 1970s, when mainstream shoes were dominated by chunky platforms. He refined the rustic Mediterranean mules that he remembered from his childhood into an elegant shoe that is now a staple.

The Master Shoemaker

Throughout the 1970s and 1980s, Blahnik concentrated on mastering the techniques of shoemaking by finding the best possible factories to work with and studying them carefully. He has made the most of his collaborations with fashion designers (Figure 2.15) like Perry Ellis, Isaac Mizrahi, and John Galliano. His partnership with Calvin Klein taught him a great deal about designing for a broader market. The United States has recognized Manolo Blahnik's design brilliance over the years with numerous awards in 1987, 1990, and 1998. The British Design Coucil presented him with awards in 1990, 1999, and 2003 and his native Spain has presented him with La Agija de Oro in 2001 and La Medalla de Oro en Merito en las Bellas Artes, awarded by His Majesty Don Juan Carlos I, King of Spain.

Even now the process of creating a Manolo Blahnik shoe begins with Blahnik himself sketching it with a Tombo Japanese brush pen. He then takes up to a day to carve the last from beechwood, and then sculpts the heel by hand. When Blahnik is satisfied, an aluminium mold is made of the last and then the plastic last from which the shoe will be made.

"I have the advantage of study," he told Colin McDowell. "I've been studying the art of the shoe . . . for over 20 years. I know every process. I know how to cut and cut away here [the side of the shoe] and still make it so that it stays on the foot. And the secret of toe cleavage, a very important part of the sexuality of the shoe. You must only show the first two cracks. And the heel. Even if it's 12 centimetres high, it still has to feel secure, and that's a question of balance. That's why I carve each heel personally myself on the machine and then by hand with a chisel and file, until it's exactly right."

FIGURE 2.15 Manolo Blahnik's continued success lies in creating classic elegant shoes as well as collaborating with young designers on modern edgy styles. Left, a Manolo Blahnik shoe designed specifically for Zac Posen, and, right, a sandal designed for Calvin Klein. Courtesy of WWD; © Condé Nast Digital Studio.

PROJECT

Classic Product Redesign

GOALS

To do what is expected of an accessory designer in the professional environment: create a fresh design for an established brand name company, using the branding already in place.

ASSIGNMENT

You have been hired to work for an established classic accessory company such as Louis Vuitton, Ferragamo, Hermès, or Coach. Choose the company you will be working for, and a season to design for. Your task as a head designer is to develop a collection that reflects the identity of the company and serves the established customer, but the collection needs to be fresh and modern. The collection needs to consist of handbags, clutches, luggage, and wallets. It can also include shoes, hats, belts, and scarves. The collection must include the existing logo as-is, a new print, and newly developed hardware. Keep in mind the particular functions of the accessories for the season you design for. Prepare sketches for presentation of your collection.

3

CONTEMPORARY
ACCESSORY DESIGNER
PROFILES

CHAPTER THREE profiles seven of today's leading accessory designers and design firms—Miuccia Prada, Carlos Falchi, Nike, Christian Louboutin, Kate Spade, Jimmy Choo, and olsenHaus. After reading this chapter, you will understand how building and maintaining a strong brand image leads to success in this competitive design business.

THE CONTEMPORARY DESIGNERS featured in this chapter are key influencers in the accessory industry. Year after year they develop collections that define the latest trends while staying true to their own philosophy.

Miuccia Prada

FIGURE 3.1
Miuccia Prada is the controversial designer behind Prada and the younger hipper label Miu Miu. Courtesy of WWD/Davide Maestri.

Prada as we know it today signifies style and luxury in designer handbags, fabulous shoes, and forward thinking clothing, a brand image due in large part to the role of Miuccia Prada in creating that trendsetting look (Figure 3.1). Her personal imprint on the family company started with rugged nylon bags, but over the years she developed a signature utilitarian look with odd, muted colors, unusual prints, and forward design shapes. She took her father's traditional handbag company and with her husband Patrizio Bertelli created an accessory empire churning out groundbreaking design ideas.

The Beginnings of Prada

The Prada empire started from the leather goods store Mario Prada opened in Milan in 1913. In addition to his own creations, he also sold steamer trunks and handbags imported from England to a customer base that included Italian nobles. When the signature Prada suitcase, made from heavy, cumbersome walrus skin, proved to be ill suited for air travel, Prada concentrated on designing exquisite leather accessories and waterproof handbags.

Miuccia Prada, the founder's granddaughter, was born in 1949. In spite of, or perhaps because of, her affluent upbringing, she flaunted leftist tendencies, handing out Communist leaflets on street corners. She received a doctoral degree in political science in 1973 and studied mime for several years. Miuccia Prada joined the firm in 1970 and inherited it eight years later. The label was still mainly a leather goods manufacturer and struggled financially for several years, affected greatly by competition from other fashion houses like Gucci and Versace.

The Personal Stamp of Miuccia Prada

In 1977, Miuccia Prada met Patrizio Bertelli, who had started his own leather goods manufacturing firm when he was 17 and had strong commerce skills. Prada readily followed the charismatic Bertelli's business advice, which included dropping the firm's English suppliers and revamping old-fashioned luggage styles with new, trendy ideas. After their marriage, Patrizio Bertelli took on the role of business manager, allowing Miuccia to focus on designing and perfecting the new Prada look. As a Prada CEO, Bertelli has earned a reputation as a brilliant and temperamental but very effective micromanager. His design mantra, as quoted in *Fortune* magazine is: "It is not fashion that changes lifestyles. It is lifestyles that change fashion."

In 1979, following the utilitarian concept, Miuccia Prada designed what became her first commercial hit: backpacks and totes made of a tough, military spec black nylon that her grandfather had used as a protective covering for steamer trunks. Success was not instant, but in the next few years, Prada and Bertelli sought wholesale accounts for the bags at exclusive department stores and boutiques around the world. They were a hard sell because of their high price tag and complete lack of company advertising. It wasn't until 1985 that a black nylon version of the famous Chanel tote was introduced by Prada, as the classic Prada handbag. Simultaneously simple and sleek, functional and sturdy, practical and fashionable, the bag became an overnight sensation. The high price tag that accompanied the handbags caused an onslaught of designer knock-offs, which only helped to make the genuine Prada articles more in demand. A shoe line was released in 1984, and with its trend-forward ideas, it also contributed to the success of the company.

While other labels were creating designs that played on sexuality, with frilly, lacy details, Prada often favored offbeat retro elements and unusual color schemes. Venturing on groundbreaking ideas, Prada's popularity skyrocketed. By the 1990s, Prada was a leading force in fashion, with reported $31.7 million in sales. The garments and accessories were smart, sophisticated, and extremely high quality. Accessories included skinny leather belts, elegant high-heeled shoes, and classic handbags. In 1992, Miuccia Prada presented the more affordable Miu Miu line, which targeted a younger consumer. "It's about bad taste, which is part of life today," she said in *Time*. Much of the Miu Miu line was constructed out of tacky synthetic fabrics but had the high-quality workmanship of the Prada line.

The Prada look has become more famous over the years, and Miuccia Prada is credited with many innovations in fabric and design. She has added everything from mirror fragments to beaded latex to her garments and experimented with new and unique fabrics and concepts. One thing that is consistent throughout all collections is the immaculate quality of workmanship.

Prada has commissioned various artists and architects for numerous collaborations. Rem Koolhaas and Herzog & de Meuron have both designed flagship stores in various locations. One of the most interesting commissioned projects is the unusual multipurpose building called the Prada Transformer in Seoul (Figure 3.2). Funded

FIGURE 3.2

This unique Prada store, called Transformer, was designed by Rem Koolhaas. It transforms into one of four different shapes, depending on the needed function. Courtesy of WWD.

by Prada and designed by Rem Koolhaas, the building has the shape of a tetrahedron, or somewhat of a pyramid, composed of four triangular faces, three of which meet at each vertex. It transforms into one of four different shapes, depending on the function for which the building is needed at any given moment. Cranes rotate the building so that different surfaces of the tetrahedron face downward, thus changing the building's form and function. The base is a hexagon when used for a fashion exhibition, a rectangle when used as a movie theatre, a cross when used for an art exhibition, and a circle when used for special events.

In 2007, Prada joined forces with cell phone maker LG Electronics to produce the LG Prada KE850 phone with a retail price of $800. In 2009, a second generation of the phone was launched in Europe. The KF900 had a 3G capability and featured a new sliding QWERTY keyboard. The phone also works with the new Prada Link watch, with which users can view text messages via a Bluetooth connection to their phone (Figure 3.3).

American financial newspaper, the *Wall Street Journal*, has named Miuccia Prada one of the 30 most powerful women in Europe. From fabulous runway shows to gracing the bodies of actresses like Uma Thurman and Cameron Diaz, Miuccia Prada and Patrizio Bertelli have taken her grandfather's struggling leather goods business and created a luxury empire (Figure 3.4).

FIGURE 3.4 Prada accessories often lead the newest trends in fashion accessory (above) design. Spring 2008 Art Nouveau shoes (below) featured sculpted heels inspired by a psychedelic garden.
(From top to bottom) Catwalking/copyright © 2007 Christopher Moore Limited; Courtesy of WWD.

Carlos Falchi

Carlos Falchi was born on September 26, 1944, in Brazil and has become famous for his handbags, featuring unusual collages of exotic skin patchwork designs (Figure 3.5). From his early career, dressing rockers in the West Village of New York City to selling luxury exotic handbags at Bergdorf Goodman, creating a handbag line for Target, and selling products on the Home Shopping Network, Carlos Falchi has been enjoying a longevity few designers can brag about in their lifetime. In all that time, his office and his luxury handbag production have remained on three floors of a building on West 39th Street in New York City.

"I feel that I should have been a fortune teller," says Carlos Falchi. "My job is to predict the future. So, my focus first is colors and materials, mixing style and shapes. With that in mind, I embark on a great adventure in design. Trips to the museums and to Central Park are required to soak up all those beautiful colors, textures, and nature; then I come home, get the watercolors and the trip begins."

Falchi first started designing clothing and handbags for himself and his musician friends in the seventies and counted Miles Davis, Herbie Hancock, Elvis Presley, and Mick Jagger as fans and Jimi Hendrix as a neighbor. After he studied traditional arts in Japan in the late 1970s, he reinvented his approach to design and in 1979 created his first unconstructed and unlined buffalo satchel. It was made from a single skin with only two seams. Until then, handbag production was based on traditional rigid construction, and this new approach initiated a revolution in handbag making. His style was improvised and somewhat rebellious. His handbags were made by hand, imperfect, and always unique and could be distinguished by unusual collages of exotic skins.

Retailer Geraldine Stutz of Henri Bendel was one of the first to give Falchi's designs floor space and contributed to his rise to success. Neiman Marcus and Bergdorf

Goodman also gave him an early break and remain among his biggest retail partners.

Even though the late 1980s collapse of the Japanese economy seriously affected his sales, he became a part of the "It Bag" trend of the 1990s–2000s. His business has seen a series of ups and downs, and at one point he even lost his own name brand to another company, but he managed to relaunch his collection in 1999 and has enjoyed a resurrection and increased interest from a large following of loyal customers. His designs have been featured in television shows and movies like *Sex and the City*, and his customers range from fashion icons to young starlets and fashionistas.

Falchi often uses python, alligator, and ostrich skins and has worked for decades to develop

FIGURE 3.5

Using exotic skins is part of Carlos Falchi's signature style.

Courtesy of WWD/ Robert Mitra.

FIGURE 3.6

Falchi's bags have an unmistakable organic quality to them. He uses every piece of the leather to create original designs, which are often unique even within the same basic style. (From left to right) Courtesy of Carlos Falchi; Courtesy of WWD/Robert Mitra.

and increase farm-bred, exotic skins. The farms he works with protect the species, provide environmental controls, and bolster employment in underdeveloped areas of the world. The success of these programs, coupled with Falchi's dedication to being green has increased the availability of quality exotic skins. His collections have always showcased inventive finishes and new tanning techniques, and he works with tanneries to develop new techniques that are more protective of the world's ecosystems.

His Buffalo Satchel was declared by *Women's Wear Daily* "the most copied bag in the industry," in 1980, and today his designs grace the runways of Donna Karan, Catherine Malandrino, Vera Wang, Ralph Rucci, and Bill Blass; and his collection prices range from $1,500 to $5,000. In 2009, American retailer Target, famous for contracting young hip designers for collaborations, chose Carlos Falchi to produce a line of ten lower-priced bags, using synthetic materials. In the same year, his lower priced line, Chi, launched on the Home Shopping Network.

He has remained relevant and competitive for more than 37 years and the industry has recognized his talent with numerous nominations and awards. The acknowledgments of his talent spans from a 1983 Coty Award to two CFDA award nominations and Lifetime Achievement Awards from the Accessories Council of America in 2004, and from the Independent Handbag Designers of America in 2007. Several of Falchi's designs have been placed in the permanent collection of The Costume Institute of the Metropolitan Museum of Art. On April 23, 2009, Carlos Falchi celebrated 30 years at Bergdorf Goodman with a retrospective exhibition and designed ten one-of-a-kind bags for the occasion (Figure 3.6).

Nike

The origin of the name Nike lies in Greek mythology. Nike, pronounced *[NI-key]*, means "Victory," and throughout the ancient Greek culture Nike was known as the Winged Goddess of Victory. She was close to Zeus, king of the gods in Greek mythology, and presided over the battlefields.

From Blue Ribbon Sports to Nike

The company Nike, as we know it today, was originally called Blue Ribbon Sports. Founded by University of Oregon track athlete Philip Knight and his coach Bill Bowerman in January 1964, it initially was just a distributor for the Japanese shoe maker Onitsuka Tiger. They operated from Knight's automobile and made most sales literally on the track. Bowerman's

desire to create a lighter, more durable shoe and Knight's love for the sport and a sense for business created a perfect combination for a winning strategy. Philip Knight earned his MBA at Stanford in the early 1960s and proposed the idea of a quality running shoe as a semester-long project, including a marketing and a business plan. Even though that was just a student project, he had found his niche with the idea of producing high quality/low cost shoes in Japan and importing them to the U.S. market.

The project came to realization after Philip Knight graduated and took a trip which included Japan. He scheduled an interview with a Japanese running shoe manufacturer called Tiger and presented himself as a representative of an American distributor interested in their product. He quickly thought of the name Blue Ribbon Sports and struck a deal with the Japanese company.

The Tiger shoes sold quickly, and the company's profits grew accordingly. Bill Bowerman and Philip Knight opened their first retail store in 1966, located on Pico Boulevard in Santa Monica, California. By 1971, the relationship between Blue Ribbon Sport and Onitsuka Tiger came to an end and the two business partners prepared to launch their own line of footwear. They wanted to have a distinctive symbol for their shoes that suggested movement

and Knight asked Portland State University graphic design student Caroline Davidson to design one. She came up with various designs, and the swoosh logo was the one that got Knight's approval. Pressed for time, he made a decision, telling Davidson: "I don't love it, but it will grow on me." The logo was registered with the U.S. Patent and Trademark Office on January 22, 1974 (Figure 3.7). The first shoe using the swoosh was a soccer shoe, which came out in June of 1971. In February 1972, BRS introduced its first line of Nike shoes, with the name Nike, and in 1978, BRS, Inc. officially renamed itself to Nike, Inc. Sponsorship of athletes became a key marketing tool for the rapidly growing company, with professional tennis player Ilie Năstase the first athlete to be signed.

Nike Designs

Nike's first self-designed product was based on Bowerman's "waffle" design. He started experimenting with various potential outsoles that would grip the newest urethane tracks more effectively. Bowerman decided to pour liquid urethane into his wife's waffle iron and his efforts were rewarded with the idea for a new sole design. He developed and refined the idea in 1974 but kept the name "waffle" sole which evolved into the now-iconic Waffle Trainer. This design focus on function

FIGURE 3.7
The Nike swoosh has become an iconic symbol of the company and is recognized worldwide.
Courtesy of WWD.

FIGURE 3.8 **Nike's ultralight LunarGlide shoe.** Courtesy of WWD.

FIGURE 3.9 **Nike Trash Talk Shoe, created entirely out of scrap material and worn by Steve Nash at an All-Star basketball game.** Courtesy of WWD.

is critical to Nike's success as a producer of athletic shoes.

With design innovation like this one and implementation of new technologies Nike reached a 50 percent market share in the United States athletic shoe market by 1980, and the company went public in December of that year. During the 1970s, Nike relied on "word-of-foot" advertising (a quote from an ad from the late 1970s), and didn't run any national television commercials until October 1982 during the broadcast of the New York City Marathon. The ads were created by a brand new Portland-based advertising agency called Wieden+Kennedy, which worked closely with Nike to create all of its print and television ads and continues to do so today. Dan Wieden, co-founder of Wieden+Kennedy is the one who came up with the now-famous slogan "Just Do It" for a 1988

Nike ad campaign. The "Just Do It" trademark was filed by Nike, Inc. on October 3, 1989 with the description attributed to sports clothing, on which the mark was to be affixed.

Throughout the 1980s, Nike expanded its product line from running shoes to a wide range of sports and recreation use and started a revolution by developing specific technologies to be used in its shoes. Beginning in 1985, Nike designed shoes for basketball great Michael Jordan, and since then, vintage Air Jordans have become collectors' items. One of the most significant partnerships to introduce technological innovations is the one with Apple Inc., which produced the Nike+ products. They track the pace, distance, time, and calories burned of a runner and send the data to an Apple device like iPod or iPhone or a SportBand. The data can be sent to the Nike website where any runner can review them, set challenges, and connect with other people in the online Nike+ community.

Some of Nike's newest shoes contain *Flywire* (a superlight but very strong thread) and *Lunarlite Foam* (Figure 3.8), which reduces the overall weight of the shoe and gives it more support. It is inventions and partnerships like these that propelled Nike to the top of the athletic footwear business and helped it get ahead of giants like Puma and Adidas.

Unfortunately, with its sheer size of manufacturing business, Nike impacts the environment negatively, but the company makes an effort to counteract its influence with other projects and currently ranks in the top three climate-friendly companies. One of those projects is the Reuse-A-Shoe program, which was started in 1993 and benefits the community and the environment by collecting used athletic shoes and recycling them to create padding for basketball courts or surface for running tracks, tennis courts, baseball fields, and playgrounds. Nike's Trash Talk is another project where athletic shoes are made entirely of scrap from Nike shoe plants in Asia (Figure 3.9).

Today Nike produces not only shoes, but also a wide variety of accessories and athletic clothing for sports and outdoor activities. A large portion of its business includes licensing deals for bags, hats, and socks, which bear the Nike logo but are created by other companies. These items contribute to the fashion component of Nike's image. Another fashion feature of Nike's athletic footwear is NikeiD, an online service that enables customers to custom design their own shoes, selecting colors and materials for the parts of the shoe; adding a personal identification; and fitting the shoes with the correct size, even if that is very small or very large or differs between the left and right feet. Nike's efforts to create competitive products, using the latest technology has paid off for the owners. The company revenue for 2009 was estimated at $19.2 billion.

Christian Louboutin

Christian Louboutin launched his high-end line of women's shoes in France in 1991, and the red-lacquered soles have become his signature since 1992. Christian Louboutin has topped the Luxury Institute's annual Luxury Brand Status Index (LBSI) for three years; the brand's offerings were declared the Most Prestigious Women's Shoes in 2007, 2008, and 2009 (Figure 3.10). (In 2007, he was followed by Manolo Blahnik and Jimmy Choo, rated second and third, respectively.)

Louboutin was born in 1964 in Paris, France and as a child, regularly sneaked out of school to watch the showgirls at some Parisian nightclubs. He was fascinated by their costumes and cites this as his main inspiration for becoming a shoe designer: "[The showgirls] influenced me a lot. If you like high heels, it's really the ultimate high heel—it's all about the legs, how they carry themselves, the embellishment of the body. They are the ultimate icons." He was 11 years old when he was struck by a strange drawing on the wall of the Musée des Arts Africains et Oceaniens. It was a woman's shoe with a sharp

heel, crossed out with a red line in a sign, stating that women could not enter while wearing sharp stilettos, for fear of damage to the wood floor. This image stayed in his mind and catapulted his creativity. Later he used this idea in his designs. "I wanted to defy that," said Louboutin. "I wanted to create something that broke rules and made women feel confident and empowered."

He knew he wanted to design shoes and became obsessed with sketching and designing them. He decided to pursue his dream although his family opposed his decision to leave school. He claims that his resolve was strengthened after watching an interview on TV with Sophia Loren in which she introduced her sister, saying she had to leave school when she was only 12 but when she turned 50 she got her degree. "Everybody applauded! And I thought, 'Well, at least if I regret it, I'm going to be like the sister of Sophia Loren!'"

FIGURE 3.10

Designer
Christian Louboutin.

Courtesy of WWD.

FIGURE 3.11

Christian Louboutin's creations combine elegance and whimsy and can always be recognized by their signature red outsole.

Courtesy of WWD/ Thomas Iannaccone.

eveningwear designs incorporating bejeweled straps, bows, feathers, patent leather, and other frills.

In 2002, Louboutin created the shoes for Yves Saint Laurent's farewell haute couture show. Referred to as "Christian Louboutin for Yves Saint Laurent Haute Couture 1962–2002," it was the only time that Saint Laurent associated his name with that of another designer.

In 2007, he collaborated with David Lynch on the exhibition "Fetish" and created sexy one-of-a-kind shoes; fetish objects of desire, photographed by Lynch. In 2008, the Fashion Institute of Technology paid a tribute to Christian Louboutin by creating a retrospective of his work.

The red soles of his shoes have become a signature (Figure 3.11), and on March 27, 2007, Christian Louboutin filed an application for U.S. trademark protection of this design element. In his U.S. trademark application, Louboutin explains the inception of the red soles: "In 1992 I incorporated the red sole into the design of my shoes. This happened by accident as I felt that the shoes lacked energy so I applied red nail polish to the sole of a shoe. This was such a success that it became a permanent fixture." As he explains, "[He] did not really choose the red sole. It's more like the red sole came to [him] and had to stay with [him]."

Christian Louboutin's designs have gained popularity among socialites and celebrities. A pair of size five black Christian Louboutin shoes once owned by Elizabeth Taylor sold for £10,000 at a charity auction in 2005. His shoes regularly show up on the red carpet at the Oscars and other glamorous events. When asked if there was a famous star on which Louboutin was glad to see his shoes he responded, "I admire Angelina Jolie. I think she is gorgeous, generous, talented, and [a] free-minded person. I am lucky that she is already wearing my shoes."

Christian Louboutin currently has six boutiques in the United States, two in London, England, one in each of Hong Kong, Indonesia, and Singapore and several in Australia. The first in South America is in Shopping Iguatemi, São Paulo, Brazil. In addition to being sold at 46 signature boutiques internationally, the shoes can be found at Saks Fifth Avenue, Barneys, Bergdorf Goodman, and Jeffrey and through online stores and boutiques. His shoes demand prices as high as $1,400, and he continues

The Launch of Louboutin's Career

Louboutin got his first apprenticeship at the Folies Bergères and followed it with freelance work for Chanel, Yves Saint Laurent, Maud Frizon, and Roger Vivier. After a three-year stint in garden design, he opened his own boutique in 1992. By 1995, he was designing for Jean-Paul Gaultier, Chloe, Azzaro, Diane Von Furstenberg, Victor and Rolf, and Lanvin with ready-to-wear and couture creations and helped bring stilettos back into fashion. His designs often featured heel heights of 120mm (4.72 inches) and higher.

Louboutin's Signature Style

Christian Louboutin's professed goal is to "make a woman look sexy, beautiful, to make her legs look as long as [he] can." And while he does offer some lower-heeled styles, Louboutin is most famous for his dressier to create shoes for young and talented designers like Roland Mouret and Rodarte as well as his signature. He is famous for his quirky and down-to-earth personality and rides a humble Vespa to work and professes not to own a television. During his prolific career Christian Louboutin has received two FannyAwards from the International Fashion Group in 1996 and 2008.

Kate Spade and Jack Spade

Katherine Noel Brosnahan, now Kate Spade, was born on December 24, 1962, and grew up in Kansas City, Missouri. She graduated from the University of Kansas and always had an air of charming originality about her, a sense of preppy and quirky style, and a keen wit.

The Launch of Kate Spade's Career

Kate started her professional career in the accessories business in 1986, taking a job in the accessory department of *Mademoiselle* magazine, but while working there, she started designing her own stylish, practical handbags. She left *Mademoiselle* in 1991 with the title of senior fashion editor/head of accessories and promptly started creating her own line. She delved into sketching designs, browsing local flea markets, investigating manufacturers, and researching costs. She created a collection of classically shaped bags in interesting colors and fabrics. With her fingers crossed, Kate and her partner and husband, Andy Spade, launched kate spade handbags in January of 1993 (Figure 3.12).

In 1996, kate spade opened its first shop in New York City's trendy SoHo neighborhood, and in 1998, kate spade opened its doors in Boston. By 2000, stores were springing up in Chicago; San Francisco; Greenwich, Connecticut; and Manhasset, Long Island. Further expansion through numerous store openings continued through 2004, when the first international store opened doors in Japan. Nowadays there are around 46 boutiques in the United States and about 44 internationally (Figure 3.13). The kate spade brand was sold

FIGURE 3.12

The creative duo Andy and Kate Spade.

Courtesy of WWD.

FIGURE 3.13

The kate spade stores have a preppy and fun atmosphere with brightly colored furniture and decorations and are recognizable by their bright green awnings.

(top) Courtesy of WWD;

(bottom) Courtesy of WWD/Tyler Boye.

FIGURE 3.14

Tamara Mellon, the creative force behind Jimmy Choo. Jordan Strauss/WireImage.

to Liz Claiborne for $124 million in 2007 and has grown to sell a variety of items including stationery, personal organizers, address books, shoes, beauty products, perfume, raincoats, pajamas, and eyewear and in recent years has been featuring designs and special editions by guest designers and is no longer the sole artistic vision of the husband-and-wife team.

Related Brands

Jack Spade is a fictional name and is the men's complement to the kate spade brand. Its founder and principal designer is Andy Spade. The line features men's utility and messenger bags, briefcases, luggage and travel bags, small leather goods, apparel, and books.

In 2004, the design duo launched "kate spade at home." The home collection includes bedding, bath items, china, various items for the home, and wallpaper.

Recognition and Accolades

Kate Spade has won numerous awards throughout her career. In 1996 the Council of the Fashion Designers of America named her "America's New Fashion Talent in Accessories" for her classic designs, and in 1998, CFDA bestowed upon her the "Best Accessory Designer

of the Year" award. In 1999, Kate Spade was honored when her handbags were exhibited at the Cooper-Hewitt National Design Museum for the first national design triennial, celebrating American design excellence. Kate Spade's home collection won her three design awards in 2004, including *House Beautiful*'s "Giants of Design Award for Tastemaker," *Bon Appetit*'s "American Food and Entertaining Award for Designer of the Year," and *Elle Decor*'s "Elle Decor International Design Award for Bedding."

Jimmy Choo

Tamara Mellon is the founder and president of Jimmy Choo, the luxury lifestyle accessory brand that took over the hearts and wallets of countless shoe lovers around the globe (Figure 3.14). She oversees the creative vision, encompassing women's shoes, handbags, small leather goods, sunglasses, and eyewear, around the world by building a full luxury house with shoes at the core.

Mellon was born in London and was raised and educated in England, Beverly Hills, and Switzerland. She started her career as an accessories editor at British *Vogue* in 1996, where she realized the potential demand for stylish but wearable shoes. She approached Jimmy Choo, a couture shoemaker based in the East End of London and partnered with him to start the ready-to-wear shoe company. Together they sourced factories and production in Italy and opened the first stand-alone boutique on Motcomb Street. The wholesale part of the business also grew strong, and in 1998, Jimmy Choo opened its first boutique in New York, followed by one in Los Angeles in 1999. Mellon pioneered the act of offering the award nominees and presenters customized shoes for their red carpet appearances. Hollywood starlets fell in love with the Jimmy Choo shoes for their edgy and glamorous style and often wear them on the red carpet. They have been called a lucky charm for Oscar winners Cate Blanchett, Halle Berry, and Hilary Swank.

In 2001, Jimmy Choo introduced handbags and expanded throughout the world. In October 2009, Jimmy Choo announced a new license agreement with Inter Parfums SA for the creation, development, and distribution of fragrances under the Jimmy Choo brand.

Today, Jimmy Choo's glamorous accessories are available in over 100 store locations in 32 countries (Figure 3.15). Jimmy Choo has been awarded the 2008 ACE Designer Brand of the Year award, 2008 British Designer Brand of the Year Award from the British Fashion Council, the 2008 *Footwear News* Brand of the Year Award, and the 2009 Nordstrom Partners In Excellence award.

olsenHaus

The philosophy of olsenHaus and Elizabeth Olsen, its founder, is anchored in respect for all beings, commitment to producing 100 percent animal-free and cruelty-free products, and a high standard of ethical social responsibility in animal and human rights and the protection of the environment (Figure 3.16). The company's functional and fashionable vegan shoes are all made of sustainable materials. Olsen herself never wears fur or leather and has been outspoken against the use of animals for food, clothing, experimentation, and entertainment, as well as advocating for environmental causes and social justice. Her activism dates back to her childhood. When she was 15 years old and read about what happens to animals during factory farming, she knew she wanted to get involved in protecting them, and to spread the word, she co-founded an animal rights club in her high school. She became a vegetarian and more recently, a vegan. As an adult, Olsen carried her philosophy into her shoe designs. Based on the conviction that a vegan diet is optimal not only for the body, but also for the planet, she creates shoes that use only environmentally friendly, nonanimal materials.

Elizabeth Olsen attended the University of Florida studying art and art history, and then

FIGURE 3.15 Jimmy Choo is synonymous with elegance, femininity, and a luxurious lifestyle. Courtesy of WWD.

FIGURE 3.16

This olsenHaus vegan shoe from the Fall 2010 collection is created from 100% recycled industrial waste from television screens, that have been made into an ultrasuede material. olsenHaus-Pure Vegan LLC Photo.

FIGURE 3.17 OlsenHaus shoes are not only created entirely of nonanimal products but feature stylish and elegant design. olsenHaus-Pure Vegan LLC Photo.

FIT in New York City for Accessory Design. Her work experience came from designing for Calvin Klein, Bulga, Nine West, and Jodi Arnold MINT, and being a creative director at Tommy Hilfiger. Her own company creative concept is based on a passionate pursuit of consciousness, purpose of life, ethics, and, of course, function. In short: olsenHaus is the fruit of Olsen's journey so far. The company name pays homage to her heritage by combining her last name with "haus," the German word for house. The concept of olsenHaus is to showcase alternative materials that are sophisticated, fun, and on trend, while promoting her philosophy. Olsen works to change the face of what a vegan product looks like. She creates stylish women's shoes along with a consciousness of a new kind of luxury, while seeking innovative methods that lessen the impact of her products on the environment (Figure 3.17).

Materials

OlsenHaus uses sustainable, renewable, plant-based, and manmade materials such as ultrasuede, organic cotton, canvas, nylon, velvet, linen, cork, and a synthetic eco-lining. These materials account for far less pollution than leather and use only a fraction of the energy in processing. "Most synthetics available today are flexible, breathable, and biodegradable and have a much smaller negative impact on the planet," Olsen says. No leather, fur, wool, or silk is ever used. Soles are a composite of rubber; glues are rubber-based; paint is nontoxic. Nothing is ever tested on animals. Many designer brands create additional

collections that are marketed toward the eco-conscious customers to capitalize on the current trend, while still maintaining a leather line, but olsenHaus has been totally vegan from the start.

Manufacturing

The company produces as locally as possible in Central America and works only with people and factories with high standards of quality and accountability. OlsenHaus continually searches for innovative techniques and encourages its factories and suppliers to use safer processes and recycled materials. The factories are personally checked for fair trade practices, fair wages, clean and comfortable working conditions, and safe machinery. Olsen makes sure that employees are respected for their skills and there are no child-labor practices or outsourcing to other factories or countries. She believes that everything is interconnected, including all life forms, and the manufacturing processes can evolve toward a respect for animals, ecosystems, and people.

olsenHaus's Focus

Currently olsenHaus concentrates on women's shoes with clean lines and unexpected material mixes but includes children's and men's lines of footwear. It creates comfortable shoes through slightly lower heels, padding, or the addition of platforms. Olsen's shoes can be worn for many seasons because of their modern and classic look.

Elizabeth Olsen actively aims to educate through her products. She embraces accountability, welcomes feedback, and believes that it is very important to give back and support organizations doing educational work towards increasing public awareness in animals' rights and the environment. Some of the organizations olsenHaus works with, donates to, or is a member of are Farm Sanctuary, PETA, Humane Society, and Greenpeace. Future plans for her company include an expansion into further study of metaphysics, theosophy, and yoga and building a completely environmentally friendly home and family.

Market Research Project

GOALS

To enhance your skills of observation and recognizing sources of inspiration based upon what is happening in the real world of accessory brands. To see how different brands develop in store presentations for their product groups.

ASSIGNMENT

Go to at least *two* established accessory brand signature stores such as kate spade, Jimmy Choo, Sigerson Morrison, Christian Louboutin, or Coach. If signature stores are not within your reach you can look for a designer/brand boutique within a department store like Bloomingdale's, Nordstrom, or Neiman Marcus. As a last option you may use the brand's website, but keep in mind that nothing replaces the look and feel of actual products on display within a store designed specifically to entice the customer.

When you visit the store, walk around the whole area and different floors if any. Get a sense of the label's branding and specific technique of displaying the accessories. Notice the unique accessory market for this particular brand/retailer. Understand who the customers are by observing them. Look at prices and compare different product groups. Look at displays and how products are positioned and merchandised together. Takes notes as soon as you leave the store.

Write your final report, on *one* store/label, based on your observations and taking into consideration the questions below. Be sure to take pictures of the products displayed in the windows (from outside) of the store you choose to profile.

QUESTIONS

1. What is the brand you chose and why?

2. What is the interior design feel or look, and how does it relate to the brand?

3. What are the specific displays?

4. Do the displays play a role in the desirability of the product? How and why?

5. How many groups of products are in the store?

6. What are the groups based on? (Design details, pattern, concepts, functionality, or customer age or sex.) What are the price ranges within the different groups? Is there a price-range difference, and why may that be important?

7. What is the range of products within each group?

8. What design elements keep the different accessories consistent with the brand identity you know and recognize?

Feel free to add other observations and thoughts that relate to the report.

4

Basics of

ACCESSORY DESIGN

CHAPTER FOUR describes the basic design process for all accessories and traces the steps of product development from first prototype to full-scale manufacturing. After reading this chapter, you will understand how accessory designers develop a concept into a seasonal line that takes target market, functionality, and price point into consideration.

THE DESIGN PROCESS for all accessories is similar in its basic steps. It goes through recognizable stages that are a natural evolution of the collection development from research and inspiration through sketching and design to actual product development. For each of these steps, the process might vary, depending on the type of accessory you design and the company you work for, but overall, you can recognize a basic pattern that repeats every single cycle. A large corporation typically has a design process that is strictly repeated, and designers have clear responsibilities within the structure of the company. A smaller design studio with fewer people involved in the process is more likely to have designers involved in a variety of aspects of the design process, from research to collection development. While in a large company, the fabric, leather or print development could be handled by a separate department; in a small design studio a single designer might be responsible for sourcing and designing the full collection and its material and hardware components. The basic steps of the design process can be identified as follows:

- Research and inspiration
- Concept and mood board preparation
- Collection creation
- Sample development
- Manufacturing

For each of these steps, the process can stretch from a day or two to weeks of scheduled work. Here is a more in-depth examination of the process.

Research and Inspiration

The very essence of a designer is to feel inspired and to constantly search for new ideas. The American Heritage Dictionary defines *inspiration* as "stimulation of the mind or emotions to a high level of feeling or activity."

For designers it is extremely important to be inspired while designing a new collection. They need to create countless groups of product one after another and need inspiration for every single one. Even though there are many resources for inspiration, being in this fickle state can be evasive and it takes some effort to maintain. The reality is that it takes a disciplined approach, a methodical search, and persistence in order to be constantly inspired. The true process of stimulation for a designer is an investigation process with a final goal of creating a beautiful and functional piece. The designer is always looking for the next idea to spark that initial instinct of designing a new collection.

Being inspired is a personal experience, which could start with the smallest piece of trim, music, or an amazing find from a flea market. Any of those items could put you in a creative state of mind. The overwhelming desire to create can be spontaneous, or it can be provoked with preplanned visits to leather and component shows or a trip to a museum or a vintage fair. What separates a professional designer from a hobby crafter is the capability to evoke those feelings when they are needed to design a collection, the ability to seek out and recognize sources of inspiration. Every season, a designer creates more than one collection, and each accessory collection needs to be grounded with solid design ideas gathered into a concept. The process of researching for inspirational materials is about investigation and gathering information that will keep you in that state of mind and will show everybody else, from fellow designers to customers, the collection concept. The collected research materials will keep you inspired throughout the whole design process. In order to start with the research you need to be clear about what your guidelines are. The main constraints you need to think about are as follows:

- Brand identity
- Target consumer characteristics, including age range and gender
- Season
- Functionality and lifestyle
- Price range

Each of these elements is important to consider and keep in mind, even before you start the design process. Once you establish these parameters, you can start searching for design ideas and concepts keeping the parameters in mind. Very often, if you work in a large corporate design company, there will be concepts that are valid for all design teams and are in line with the overall philosophy and direction of the company. As a designer, you will be given guidance about where and how you should direct your research. In a smaller design studio, you might have a bit more freedom in picking and introducing new design ideas. Either way, the directions should just channel your research into a focused process.

Brand Identity

The most important element of a company is its image, from the logo to the signature shapes, materials, and even the spokesperson or models who represent the company. Each component must be very well-thought-out. The research for a new collection includes knowing the history and the future plans of a company and must reflect both. It is extremely important to have each finished accessory embody the "look" of the company. A consistent message through design and advertising keeps bringing back the customers for more, as the brand becomes a part of their life. Almost anybody anywhere in the world, who shops for accessories, would recognize the LV logo of Louis Vuitton or the intertwined GG for Gucci. These iconic logos were built over many years with consistent exposure establishing the brand identity.

Age Range and Gender

The gender and age range of the customers is usually specified by the brand you work for. Each designer satisfies a very specific consumer, who needs to be targeted with each collection. All products within each group every season need to satisfy the needs of that girl, boy, woman, or man. It is possible that the company develops different collections to reach out to different groups, and you, as a designer, need to be aware of the differences among them all. It is imperative to create product that relates to the intended customer and reflects the brand identity. When the brand image is closely identified with the customer, it is dangerous to deviate from the existing representation. That would be a sure way to alienate existing customers who come to find a specific product.

Functionality and Lifestyle

Every collection reflects the lifestyle of the customer. Each group has different requirements and designers need to satisfy those specifics. A socialite who needs dressy designer high heels and a unique "it bag" would not be satisfied by a cheap imitation or a casual backpack, just as an active athlete does not need a Swarovski-covered clutch when headed to a training session. In addition, the same person performs

FIGURE 4.1
This assortment of
spring accessories
features lightweight
leather and fabrics
and is a great example
of typical colors and
materials that are
used for that season.
Courtesy of WWD/
George Chinsee.

different roles throughout his or her life. A busy
professional woman has a heavy work schedule
with social obligations in addition to family and
personal ones. Each of those functions needs
appropriate shoes, bags, and other accessories.
A successful designer understands the lifestyle-
related requirements and approaches them with
the style and finesse that the brand requires.
Researching the appropriate functions and
developing the right products defines the core
responsibility of a designer.

Season

Each season has specific requirements for look
and functionality as well as materials that are
usually used. Some activities, like going to the
beach, usually happen during the summer, and
bags that cater to that function are usually
created for the summer collections. Seasonal
materials also change. Raffia, straw, shells,
flowers, and canvas are popular during hot
months or for resort locations, while fur and
heavy leather are much more desirable for fall
and winter. Color and pattern are also affected
through the changes of Mother Nature.

Bright floral patterns and colors like white,
yellow, orange, or natural shades are much
more popular during the warmers months of
the year while darker colors or furry animal
prints might become more relevant for the
colder months. See Figure 4.1 for an example
of spring accessories and Figure 4.2 for fall/
winter accessories. Naturally, there are always
exceptions to the rules, and trends change every
year, but the main brand identity would lead
the designer through the seasonal changes.

Price Range

Each company has a specific price range that
corresponds to its customers' capabilities.
Consumers on the other hand, also have an
expectation for a certain price range when they
go into a store. A lower-price company would
not be able to sell an expensive product, simply
because its customer cannot afford it, no matter
how luxurious the product might be. At the same
time, luxury companies must continuously offer
a range very high-end bags and shoes, created
from rare, exotic materials and unique designs
in order to keep their image. It is expected that

high-end designers might create some outrageous designs that are used mostly for the runway, photo shoots, and magazine editorials. That's exactly what their customers would expect, and nothing less should be offered. Either way, the finished product must fall within the price range for each particular company.

Resources

You should start the research process with familiar resources. The local library and an appropriate museum are a great beginning, and as you discover new information, you can expand onto new sources. While you are visiting flea markets and vintage stores, talk to the shopkeepers and learn about other happenings that might carry similar objects. Seasonal fairs or pop-up flea markets might have a fresh, new variety of inspirational pieces. Talking to other customers while shopping could also give you new ideas. When visiting leather and component shows, let the vendors introduce you to their new products. Those might spark new thoughts for your collection and could lead you into a direction you never saw before.

Naturally, your research can expand into online sources. The Internet offers endless possibilities of information resources. It is important to remember to look for original sources of information. While looking for images on a particular subject, note where the image comes from, and if it is found in a gallery, museum, or an artist-dedicated website, then search deeper within that source to discover other similar works. The Internet is one of the best tools to discover dates of trade shows and fabric, leather, and component shows. Visit their websites if it is impossible to go to the actual event. Paid trend services can also provide all of the above information and actually give suggestions for concepts and materials to be used as well as finished mood boards with all necessary information.

Shopping the competition is a tried-and-true way of figuring out what other brands create to cater to the same customer as you do. Knowing who your customers are and what they need is a great start, but knowing what your competition sells to them could help you distinguish your designs even better.

FIGURE 4.2

This accessory assortment shows some choices for fall materials and colors.

Courtesy of WWD/David Sawyer.

It is no secret that people shop around for the coolest item, or the biggest sale, or the most interesting design. Nowadays with so many designers churning out product, it is hard to keep customers coming back to your shop if your designs are not innovative or functional and at the right price for the right customer. Keep your eyes open for amazing solutions or even mistakes of other companies in order to stay current with your own product.

Regardless of the sources, the inspiration you gather must be useful for the design process. It should contain shapes and structure, textures, design detail references, color, prints (if applicable for the selected concept), and hardware and visual references for components. Once the initial research is complete, you need to identify the concept of the collection.

Research Stages and Goals

The initial goal of the research is to find the concept or idea for the current collection. Once the concept is established and finalized, the next stage of research is to gather enough information and examples of design elements, with the goal to inspire the design process. In the final stage it is important to source materials and hardware that are not only appropriate for the collection but are also at the right price.

Different collections require different price points, and even though most companies develop their own hardware with a branded logo, it is extremely important to work within the development deadlines. Developing specific patterns to be printed or embossed in addition to ordering leather and fabrics can take its share of research and investigating in order to determine what is possible, at what costs, and how long it takes until it is produced. Using exotic materials as a handle or a heel might seem like the perfect idea for the chosen concept, but if the desired material is not available in the right color, pattern, weight, and price when needed, then the collection cannot be produced.

Developing new hardware requires new molds for each new piece, and knowing how long it takes to develop each one allows for proper planning of the sample-making and manufacturing process. Scheduling well in advance allows a designer to react when materials need to be replaced or any other changes need to be made.

For a design student who is still in school, it might seem a bit far in advance to think of all these production deadlines, but learning to do a thorough research of available materials and hardware is an essential step of the process at any stage of your career. Looking for the right hardware for an accessory you are developing in a school project can become even more challenging because your imagination is probably much wilder than what is available in the local store or even on the Internet. Spending the time to look for the right leather or hardware might be crucial to executing your project.

Concepts

Within the conceptual stage, you, as a designer, need to consider all the components of a collection and satisfy the needs for each one of them. While searching for the right concept you should be gathering information and examples for each one of the following integral parts of a collection: color story, materials, hardware, and prints.

Identifying a Concept

Choosing a theme or a concept for your collection is the most important step of the initial process. The concept will guide the research and the rest of the design process and needs to be clear and easy to understand. It is the essence of the collection and what makes it unique and appealing to the customers. A concept can be very abstract or it can be directly connected to a historical period or an architectural theme with exact references to existing design elements that are widely accepted as typical for that era. The theme can revolve around a particular artist and reflect his or her work characteristics or simply the artist's style and influence. A famous brand can have a guest artist create a particular print like Stephen Sprouse for LV or an updated interpretation of the legendary LV print from Takashi Murakami (Figure 4.3) and thus the whole collection is based on that idea. A collection concept can be destination driven and capture the beauty of a special place, and reflect the function of the accessories used in that destination. That could be a resort town in an exotic location or a safari. An accessory collection can be based on a specific culture with all its unique costume and historic beauty or a sociological or political event. Themes like recycle and sustainability can easily drive not just one season, but also the direction of a whole brand. In short, a concept can relate to a narrow group of people or to a very wide audience. It's in the hands of the designer to choose the most appropriate concept for each particular brand.

Picking a Color Story

Developing a **color story** is usually driven by the concept, the season, and the overall trend direction. It is a palette of colors for the materials, prints, and hardware that will be used in the accessory collection. Some companies match their colors to an established system like Pantone. It is a world-renowned and recognized way to identify, match, and communicate color choices. Other companies, like Ralph Lauren for example, have a color lab where they develop their own color tones and colored fabric swatches every season and give them names that are recognized solely throughout the company itself. A designer might use a color service to see what the general direction of colors is for each season or might come up with an independent color story that works for the specific brand.

After all colors are selected, designers give them names according to the concepts they belong to. A variety of names can be used to identify the same color. A brown shade can be called "chocolate" by one company and "rust" by another. The practice of romanticizing color names is widely used by design houses and is a way to create excitement with a new collection

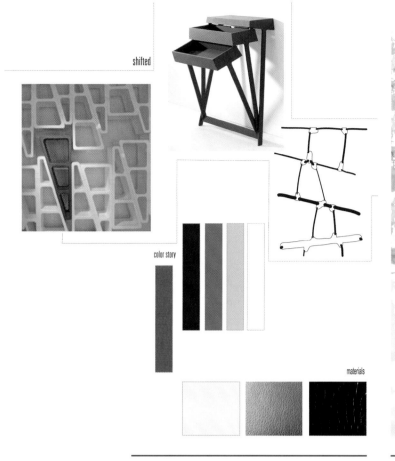

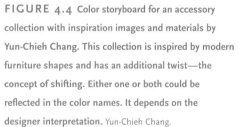

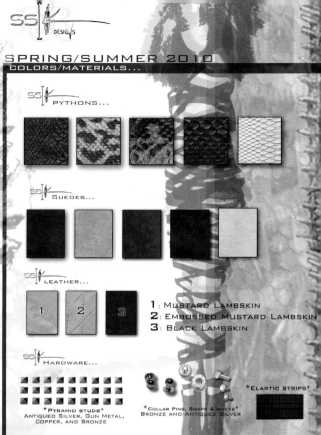

FIGURE 4.4 Color storyboard for an accessory collection with inspiration images and materials by Yun-Chieh Chang. This collection is inspired by modern furniture shapes and has an additional twist—the concept of shifting. Either one or both could be reflected in the color names. It depends on the designer interpretation. Yun-Chieh Chang.

FIGURE 4.5 The hardware and materials board can be presented as part of the mood board or separately and should include all materials used in the accessory collection. It should be well organized and clearly labeled. This materials and hardware presentation board is created by Fashion Institute of Technology accessory design graduate Kristina Gress. Created by Kristina Gress.

every season. See Figure 4.4 for an example of a color story with some of the inspiration images. In this case, color names could refer to geometric shapes or to the idea of the concept "shifted."

Picking Materials and Hardware

Picking the right materials and developing hardware are extremely important in the accessory business. The hardware is the most recognizable part of a handbag, and a logo or a signature shape can attract enormous attention. Because they are three-dimensional pieces that do not have to conform to the human body shape, they offer an endless opportunity to play with hardware and

shapes. Using a metal plaque with a logo might be a simple execution, but when that plate is oversized and placed on the outside, then it becomes a signature design element. Combining an exotic skin with precious metals can also be a way of bringing attention to a handbag. In Figure 4.5, you can see a great example of an organized presentation board with all materials and hardware to be used in an accessory collection.

Developing signature prints is another way of creating interest that brings attention to the brand identity and identifies with a specific customer base. Most large accessory companies have a group of signature print accessories every season. The print is specifically developed to reflect on the current trend and color story and might relate to another concept in the collection or might be a separate story. Merchandisers and designers usually get together to identify prints that have sold well in previous seasons and might decide to do variations on them. This is also the place to invite a guest artist to develop a variation of the existing signature print. Some companies, like LeSportsac, base their collections solely on prints and develop multiple groups per season. They invite guest artists like Simone Legno from Tokidoki (Figure 4.6) or designers like Stella McCartney (Figure 4.7) to develop new ideas, artwork, and prints and then apply them to a whole array of familiar bag shapes to create a collection.

Mood Boards

A mood board reflects the finalized concept and represents the compiled research for each collection to be designed. It contains visual references to the overall mood and specific design elements to be used in the collection. It defines the colors and represents materials, hardware and any other possible ideas. The collage of images can be constructed in any way you like as long as it shows the concept clearly. You can crop images to perfect shapes and create a linear presentation as in Figure 4.8 or you can create a collage in which images blend into each other and flow into one idea to present the concept, as in Figure 4.9.

A **mood board** is the refined presentation of the finished research. A good mood board contains images, and references to fabrics, prints, and trims, as well as hardware and logos to be used in the final collection. It can contain rough sketches of shapes to be used as design details as well as some potential body shapes that correspond well to the concept.

A great mood board presentation shows the complete concept, with enough visuals that a designer can create the full collection without

FIGURE 4.6 Italian artist Simone Legno, the artist behind the Tokidoki brand, has created numerous prints for collaborations with clothing and accessory companies. The LeSportsac collection included multiple color ways of different prints, and custom-designed hardware and trims. ©TOKIDOKI, LLC. Designed by Simone Legno.

FIGURE 4.7
A collaboration with a designer like Stella McCartney brings the designer philosophy to an established brand like LeSportsac and creates an interesting take on familiar shapes with new colors and prints. Including signature items like this bunny backpack creates a cult following, always looking for the next new item. Stella McCartney for LeSportsac, courtesy of WWD/John Aquino.

FIGURE 4.8

Hyeyoung Kim's mood board uses cropping of images in motion to create an interesting juxtaposition.

Hyeyoung Kim.

Precision

Suspension

Chromed

Circular Form

Balance

Scale

FIGURE 4.9 In this mood board for Devi Kroell shoe designs, the images are placed in a more organic way, combined with swatches, hand sketches, and words to enhance the design ideas and represent the overall mood of the collection. Devi Kroell.

looking for any other images. After looking at the presentation, observers should have no questions as to what the group is about. The season, the customer, and the customer's lifestyle, as well as the colors, materials, hardware finishes, and design details for this concept should all be clear. In order to represent the colors, you can pick actual swatches or images that are in the right colors for your concept, or you can tweak them to look "correct." Either way, at the final stage of the finished mood board, those colors should be obvious. Take a look at the mood board by Fay Leshner, Figure 4.10. This particular board has plastic clown figurines, which represent the colors of the collection and are a part of the collage. They are not presented on a separate color board but are three-dimensional shapes that are attached and stand out from the flat surface. This technique creates an easy distinction from the rest of the presentation and makes an interesting and engaging presentation.

Be creative and employ all inspirational resources when making the boards. You could use Pantone color square chips or you could cut out the color swatches from the fabrics or leather you will be using. The shapes should match and fit in with the overall theme and concept, and should be neatly cut and presented.

FIGURE 4.10 This whimsical mood board by Fay Leshner targets a younger consumer who responds to bright colors, busy prints, and bold slogans. The three-dimensional clown shapes help the color stand out from an already overwhelming presentation. Fay Leshner.

FIGURE 4.11 In this mood board, the luxury handbag designer Gabriella Zanzani created a collage of inspiration images and leather swatches, which represent the general direction and feeling for the collection and provide color and design references for shape, materials, and techniques to be used in the design process. Gabriella Zanzani.

A mood board can be a collage presented on one page or it can take a whole wall covered in pictures and actual objects. Some companies make concepts a large portion of the design process and a presentation can be so elaborate as to take a whole room, complete with repainted floors in the right shade and furniture and related objects that belong in the lifestyle of the customer. Creating this kind of a presentation requires a lot of research and helps the designers completely immerse themselves in the theme and understand the customer they are designing for.

Here are some questions to consider while building a mood board (Figure 4.11):

- Is my idea or concept clear and focused or has it become too broad?
- Do I have enough shapes to draw inspiration from?
- Are there any details that I can use?
- Are there patterns that I can use?
- Are the colors I want to use represented?
- Do I have too many pictures?

Collection Development

By the time you start designing the collection, you have the following information:

- Consumer gender, age, and occupation
- Functionality of the accessories
- Season for this collection
- Materials, leather, fabrics, trims, special techniques
- Colors, swatches, and prints
- A clear concept and complete research in the form of a mood board or a collage of photographs and real samples of techniques, swatches, and hardware

Design

To review the steps up to the point where the concept is clarified by the mood board, you need first to identify the customers who will be buying the product. Knowing who you are targeting with your product defines the variety of styles you will be designing. A young teenage girl will be buying a very different product from a professional middle-aged man.

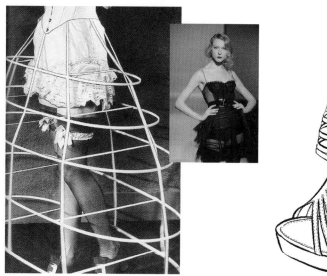

The function of accessories and where they might be used are defined by the customer. An evening clutch would be very different in shape, size, and materials from a day tote that needs to fit a laptop and paperwork. Knowing the season is the next and most important defining element in the design process. And finally, picking the right fabrics, leathers, trims, and hardware will solidify the idea and bind the collection with a cohesive look and feel. All you have to do now is think of the different ideas and sketch them out.

Sketching

Sketching the initial collection ideas can be done in any shape or form that suits your personality as a designer or the company you work for. Most designers keep a sketchbook in which they draw random ideas and hardware ideas and make collages of photos and tear sheets that evoke design ideas. You might want to sketch as you go anything that pops into your head, but once the concept for a particular collection is clear, it is time to create some focused ideas derived from the actual research. Start developing ideas by dissecting all design elements from the mood board and sketch every possible variation that could be created with those details. You can add photos from the research next to sketches to show where design details come from and how they were interpreted. In Figure 4.12, a shoe development sketch from Ann-Marie Mountford-Chu, you can clearly see how

inspiration, drawn from a crinoline hoop skirt is translated into a crinoline-like cage design, adorning an elegant high heel shoe.

During this process it is important to show close-ups of key design elements and to show different views of the accessory and the continuation of design details from all angles. As shown in Figure 4.13, front and back views of the hobo bag show how the strap connects to the main body of the bag. It is important to show how a detail like that works, even though it looks exactly the same on each side. In addition, the designer must show a close-up of the strap detail. In this case, Melinda chose to sketch this detail in a flat view. Notice that all hardware is shown attached to the strap as it would be in the finished product. The circular rivets show you how it would be attached to the bag.

Some companies have a general template of how accessories should be sketched and on what kind of paper and use that template over and over again in order to achieve a consistent look of the sketches. Designers at these firms often trace a basic shape and then add trims and details or change the shape from the initial one. As vast as the different sketching techniques can be for different companies, it is most important to express the design ideas and all detail clearly for everybody to understand. Some designers, like Rafe Totengco, like to sketch multiple smaller drawings with a variety of ideas and have them in one sketchbook (Figure 4.14).

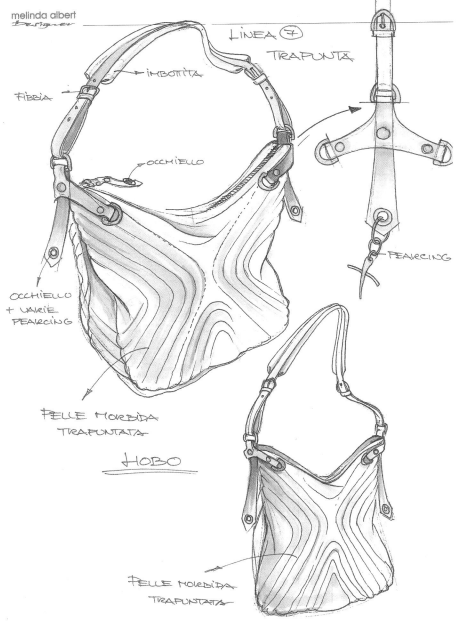

melinda albert
Designer

FIBBIA

IMBOTTITA

LINEA ⑦
TRAPUNTA

OCCHIELLO

PEARCING

OCCHIELLO
+ VARIE
PEARCING

PELLE MORBIDA
TRAPUNTATA

HOBO

PELLE MORBIDA
TRAPUNTATA

FIGURE 4.13
Handbag sketch
by Melinda Albert,
showing front and
back view and enlarged
side detail of the strap.
Melinda works in Italy
for various design
labels, and her notes
are geared toward
Italian manufacturers.
Melinda Albert.

FIGURE 4.14
A designer can
sketch multiple
ideas in a sketchbook
until all designs are
ready to be edited.
In this photo, designer
Rafe Totengco uses
a spiral-bound
sketchbook for this
purpose. © 2009
Rafe Totengco.

FIGURE 4.15

Han Josef is an
experienced footwear
designer with a lot of
technical knowledge,
which comes across
in his realistic shoe
sketches for Cole Haan.

Han Josef for Cole Haan.

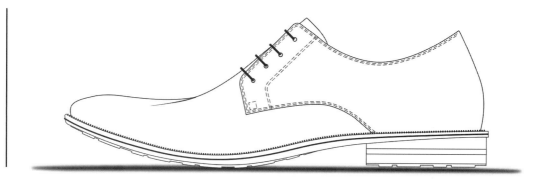

Others, like Han Josef, draw one style per sheet of letter-size paper. It looks realistic and is almost in actual size (Figure 4.15). He can easily present all single sketches arranged by concept on a board and look at them with his design team to decide what stays in the collection. There is no wrong or right way of doing this part of the process. This is more of a personal choice or an overall company directive.

Merchandising

Make sure that the collection of accessories is well merchandised. That means that there is a good variety of different shapes and functional items that satisfy the diverse needs of a variety of customers. If you are designing shoes, you should offer different heel heights from stilettos to flat, keeping in mind the current trends and your specific customers. If you are designing handbags, then you need to offer a good variety of shapes from hobo to clutch and wallets that can be bought for different reasons. A belt collection would offer different widths and various buckles and a hat collection would certainly present different crown and brim shapes, which are in vogue for the season. A complete collection satisfies all the needs of the existing customers and strives to attract new ones. Most companies have a merchandising team that tracks which styles are best sellers and asks designers to create similar models or run the same exact model from the previous season in updated

colors or new prints. The relationship between designers and merchandisers is a key one in creating a sellable line that translates well to the consumers.

Line Sheets

A **line sheet** has a grid chart that contains all the pieces from the accessory collection with their names, colors, logos, fabric, leather, trim, and hardware information. Usually it contains a thumbnail sketch of each style with a designated style number in the group and has information on fabric costs and wholesale and suggested retail prices. Some companies also include the factories where each style is produced and information on trim, logos, hardware, and print development. The line sheets are created by the designers after the whole accessory collection is sketched and are used by merchandisers and planners for the business strategy of the company. They give a concise and organized view of the whole collection and are a very important tool in judging the overall count and variety of styles. Depending on the number of styles per group the whole collection might fit on one or several pages.

Tech Packs

The next step after designing the collection is providing all measurements and specifications for samples and manufacturing and creating **tech packs**. A tech pack contains a black-and-white flat sketch of the design and all technical

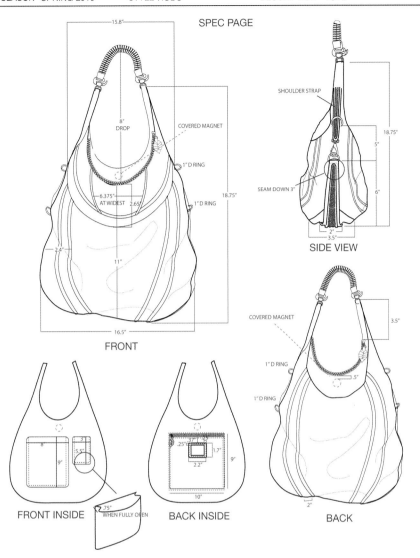

SPEC PAGE

FRONT

SIDE VIEW

FRONT INSIDE   BACK INSIDE

BACK

FIGURE 4.16
This spec page is not created on a particular template. For handbags, it is a common practice to draw detailed black-and-white sketches, with all measurements and views showing the front, back, side, and inside with pocket placement, on company letter-head and use those sketches as a tech pack. Khirma Eliazov New York.

information needed to make the accessory. That includes detailed measurements, multiple sketches of different views of the accessory, color combinations, trims, and techniques for executing every single detail. If all information fits on one page, then designers refer to it as a **spec page**. A tech pack can have multiple pages containing all needed information, and later on fitting notes, and can be created in designated software or written by hand. Some companies employ technical designers, who fill in the information in the tech packs, relay them to overseas factories online, and follow up with the manufacturers, but it is still the responsibility of the designers to provide all measurements. Assigning the correct measurements, designating the proper materials, and providing detailed sketches of every element is imperative to getting a sample that looks like the initial design idea. Nothing confuses a manufacturer more than missing or vague information. If you open the door to interpretation, you never know what you will receive back as a sample. A small clutch might turn into a large bag without the proper measurements. The more detailed notes and measurements you provide, the smoother the process will be. Figure 4.16 shows an example of a Khirma Eliazov handbag spec page from a tech pack, created in Illustrator.

REED KRAKOFF

Originally from Weston, Connecticut, Reed Krakoff received a degree in Fashion Design from Parsons School for Design and entered the fashion world at the bottom of the design ladder. His first job was at Anne Klein, and he perfected his craft at various prominent design houses, including Ralph Lauren, where he worked for five years.

Krakoff's pioneering talents landed him in the design offices of the renowned classic American accessories company Coach. He assumed the role of senior vice president and executive creative director in December 1996, and soon after he unveiled his first collection, it became clear that with his creative force he would lead the company in an influential role. His creative ideas led to an inspired renaissance by injecting trendy ideas at a traditional accessory company and managed to strengthen the brand image while bringing new customers throughout the world. As the architect of the brand, he led design, store concept, marketing, and worldwide positioning. Two and a half years after becoming senior vice president, Krakoff was appointed president, executive creative director, where he continues today.

Krakoff has been triumphant in revamping the brand for over 14 years and has shepherded two fragrances, the Legacy concept boutique, a jewelry line, and notable design collaborations with fashion designers Phillip Lim and Eugenia Kim and artist Kiki Smith, among others. Krakoff has garnered the respect of his industry and peers and has received countless awards. In 2007, Krakoff was elected vice president of the Council of Fashion Designers of America (CFDA), an institution that has been extremely supportive of his work. In 2001 and 2004, the CFDA named Krakoff Accessories Designer of the Year.

Recently, Krakoff has added "photographer" to his responsibilities

Reed Krakoff. Courtesy of Coach.

at Coach. Following in the footsteps of Mario Testino, Mikael Jansson, and Peter Lindbergh, who all shot Coach's advertising campaigns, Krakoff himself styles and photographs the campaigns and has worked with well-known celebrity faces Kate Bosworth and Mandy Moore and style icon Iris Apfel. His work has been shown in exhibits in New York City and Tokyo and featured in magazines such as *Elle Décor*, *Town & Country*, and *Interview*.

In 2010, he introduced his own Reed Krakoff Collection, a line of luxury goods including women's ready-to-wear, shoes, handbags, and jewelry.

Krakoff is a patron and supporter of the arts and is closely involved with the Cooper-Hewitt National Design Museum and the Whitney Museum. In addition to serving on the board at Parsons School for Design, he is a mentor for the CFDA Vogue Fashion Fund. He has also published several books of his photography, including *Claude & Francois-Xavier Lalanne*, *Fighter: The Fighters of the UFC*, and *Mattia Bonetti*.

Concept sketches for ad campaigns from Reed Krakoff and the photographic executions. Courtesy of Coach.

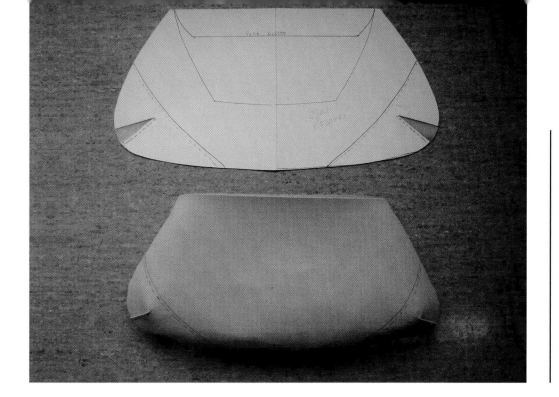

FIGURE 4.17

A paper pattern piece for a clutch and a first proto made out of salpa. The first proto gives a good idea for the overall shape of the accessory and allows designers to make key decisions before proceeding to the final piece.

Courtesy of Aneta Genova.

Proto Development

The next logical step in the design process is to create the patterns and develop the first prototype, or **proto**, of each accessory in the collection. This step can vary significantly from designer to designer and is strictly regimented in a large corporation. A mock-up can be created from an existing bag, wallet, belt, or shoe to better illustrate the design sketch. This is usually done when an existing body from a previous season is reused, but some small changes are made to it. For example, different pockets or a new strap or closure can be added. Some elements can be drawn on, others attached with clips or tape to resemble the designed final product. The mock-up is sent to the sample maker to help show the sketched idea in real size and three dimensions.

If a sample maker is located in the same city as the design offices, you should be visiting the sample room and making yourself readily available to answer any additional questions or check on the development during the process of creating the prototype. Most mistakes can be avoided by providing plenty of notes, detailed sketches, precise measurements on the tech packs, and clear communication. That is especially important when communicating with factories abroad. Do not leave anything open for interpretation.

Language barrier and culture differences might create unexpected changes to your original idea.

Once the factory or sample room receives the tech pack and possibly an accompanying mock-up, it creates the first prototype from the chosen leather or a material that resembles the final choice. Some sample makers create a simplified example without any pockets just to see the overall shape of a bag; others make the prototype with all finalized materials and trim. Most of the time, it is early in the process, and leather or hardware might not yet be available. In that case, the manufacturer or a sample maker usually makes a simplified sample out of salpa, to show the overall look of the accessory. Pockets and straps can be drawn on top of the salpa to show placement and details. **Salpa** is a material that gives handbags structure and comes in different thicknesses. It resembles thin cardboard or thick tan paper but is a blend of various materials that makes it flexible and stiff at the same time. It is often used for creating a prototype, and some designers and manufacturers might call the actual first prototype a salpa too. A salpa is the muslin of the accessory industry, the basic and cheap material used for experimenting. See Figure 4.17

for an example of a pattern and the corresponding bag made from salpa.

A shoe designer usually asks for one shoe as a sample of each designed style to see whether the heel and the overall proportions look satisfactory. It can be made of substitute leather, but the actual material always gives a better idea of any potential problems and best shows the qualities of the finalized design.

The factory usually returns the first proto within two to three weeks for review.

Sample Corrections

When the first prototypes come back to the designers, they are reviewed by the whole design team and design directors. This is judgment time. This is the first opportunity to see a real example of the design sketch according to the specifications in the tech pack. Designers analyze the overall look and fit and provide feedback on any corrections. A shoe should be placed on a foot in order to see any problems with the upper and heel. All details, closures, and trims should be carefully inspected before approval. A handbag should be carried and worn around as well as opened and closed multiple times to see whether everything looks and functions as expected. The same is valid for small leather goods. Always make sure that bills and credit cards fit in a wallet or a card case. Belts should be tried on and their hardware inspected closely. Any corrections

should be clearly marked on the proto and also written in an e-mail or a designated space in the tech pack. Comments and notes include measurement, revisions, and photographs of the drawn correction, as well as instructions how to correct the proto. A clear communication will ensure that the desired corrections will be made by the factory and a perfect accessory can be produced.

A second prototype is usually made in the correct leather, fabrication, trim, and hardware. All measurements are revised at that point, and a perfect or near-perfect proto is created. Once this prototype is approved, sales samples are made for the showroom. The number of sales samples depends on the number of showrooms that sell the accessory collection. The cost of developing samples could be quite high, and a designer might choose to develop only one set of samples or create only one color of each style. Some companies choose to create samples in multiple colors or prints to show the full strength of the collection. Buyers are notorious for buying what they see made. It is much harder to buy from photographs and a sample made in a different material. Visualizing the actual product can prove to be elusive for some people, so designers usually like to make a great variety of samples and accompany them with colored sketches and actual swatches of all available options.

Manufacturing

The next and final step of the process is producing the accessories that have received orders. Most manufacturers have a minimum number of each style that they are willing to produce, or they are not willing to manufacture the style. In this case, it helps to have the same accessory made in different colors or materials. To prepare for the manufacturing process, designers need to make sure all sample corrections have been made and tech packs have been updated with the latest fit and correction notes. As long as all materials, components, and hardware are available and shipped to the appropriate factories, the production process should be smooth. It is important to communicate with the factories and make sure all questions are answered as soon as they are raised.

The development process of an accessory from a wonderful idea to a finished product takes a few months and many steps in between and involves various other professionals. A brand usually develops multiple collections with different concepts each season. In order to maintain a bit of sanity, a designer needs to be organized and disciplined every workday. All design companies have a calendar of milestone dates that need to be achieved every week so the collection gets developed. Having a great idea for an accessory is a great start, but following through with the rest of the process is the key to success.

PROJECT

Identifying Trends

GOALS

To practice observation and compiling information from various sources and organize it in a trend report.

ASSIGNMENT

For this project, you will need to arm yourself with a simple camera (any camera will do) and go on a hunt for emerging trends. Visit a popular neighborhood where trendy people go out to socialize or stroll around. Pick a location where there is a lot of foot traffic on a busy early evening or during the weekend and spend at least half an hour observing fashionable passersby. Look for repeating trends, unusual accessories, and creative ways of reinterpreting familiar design ideas. Feel free to stop people, ask what they are wearing and how they construct their look, and take photos of them. Compile numerous photographs that you can review later.

For the final presentation look through all your photographs and find three different trends that can be identified in various users. Write a short report accompanied by supporting photo collages for each trend.

DESIGNING HANDBAGS

and Small Leather Goods

Part Two

5

Introduction to

HANDBAGS AND SMALL LEATHER GOODS

CHAPTER FIVE provides an overview of the handbag industry and the responsibilities of a handbag designer. After reading this chapter, you will be able to recognize and describe styles and components of handbags, travel-related bags, and small leather goods.

HANDBAGS HAVE BECOME an extremely important accessory. They are considered to be a status symbol that reveals much about their owners. From a simple hold-all tote to a luxury crocodile bag, women need a carrier to hold their precious possessions while away from home. Having the "It Bag" of the season can provoke jealousy, get one noticed, and propel the owner to instant fashionista status, while the wrong purse could potentially ruin the reputation of an otherwise highly regarded style-seeker. Furthermore, having the right matching or unique wallet or small purse adds to the challenge and the opportunity to complete the outfit.

Today, with advancements in technology and our busy work lives, we tend to carry more than one bag containing hundreds of items in a variety of pockets, compartments, pouches, and wallets. Each one of these bags has been researched, thought about, designed and manufactured by a specific brand that caters to the wishes and demands of its loyal customers. More and more large companies and independent designers get into the handbag industry because it is a lucrative business, and women tend to buy multiple handbags every season. Today there is a handbag, travel-related bag, or small leather item to equip us for every role or function we perform. From work to gym to a weekend getaway you can find the perfect carryall complete with specially designated compartments for every single thing you might carry.

Handbags

The word *handbag* is often shortened to just *bag*, and because it can describe so many different variations, it might just be easier to use it instead of the specific name.

Some Common Characteristics of Handbags

The actual terminology has changed over the centuries as our needs developed, but nowadays a variety of handbag styles can be described as having some of the following features (Figure 5.1):

- **Cross-body bag** A handbag of any size, but usually small, with a long strap, designed to be carried over one shoulder across the chest.
- **Drawstring bag** Any bag that can be closed or cinched with a drawstring on top can be called a drawstring bag. One of the most popular and recognizable drawstring styles is the Louis Vuitton Noe bag.
- **Purse** The term purse started out as a small container holding coins and now may contain a wallet, keys, cell phones, make-up, and anything else one might be able to squeeze into it. The term is used much more as a general synonym for a woman's handbag.
- **Shoulder bag** Any handbag with a long shoulder strap.
- **North-south bag** A designer term for any bag that is taller rather than wider. Compare to portrait orientation.
- **East-west bag** A designer term for any bag that is wider rather than taller. Compare to landscape orientation.

CROSS-BODY
BAG

SHOULDER
BAG

PURSE

DRAWSTRING
BAG

NORTH-SOUTH
BAG

EAST-WEST
BAG

FIGURE 5.2

Styles of handbags.

Courtesy of Aneta

Genova.

BRIEFCASE

CLUTCH

DOCTOR'S
BAG

Styles of Handbags

The following common styles of handbags are shown in Figure 5.2:

- **Briefcase** Usually flat, rectangular case, designed to carry documents, books, files, and personal items like a wallet and electronics. It is most often made from leather and has a single carrying handle.
- **Clutch** A woman's small purse that can be carried in the hand and usually has no handle or strap.
- **Doctor's bag** Large handbag shaped like the traditional doctor's bags, usually made from leather, with two handles.
- **Fold-over bag** A zippered-top bag, usually flat, that may be folded over (doubled up) and carried under the arm or in a hand.
- **Hobo** Single strap women's bag, with a curved crescent shape and slouchy look, usually with a zipper closure on top.
- **Pouch** A relatively small bag of soft fabric or leather (alternatively suede) gathered with a drawstring as means of closure, which usually extend as handles.
- **Satchel** A rigid-bottom bag of varying sizes with one or two handles. It is usually carried on the arm rather than the shoulder. Originally used to carry books, this bag has become a popular women's everyday bag.
- **Tote bag** A large handheld bag with two handles, open top, and simple structure. Often made from canvas, it is usually used to carry groceries, beachwear, or books.

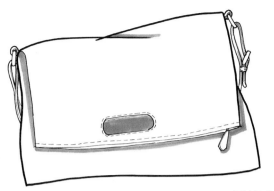

FOLD-OVER
BAG

HOBO

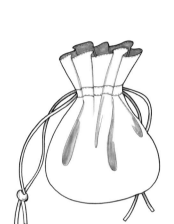

POUCH

TOTE BAG

SATCHEL

FIGURE 5.3

Examples of travel-related bags. Courtesy of Aneta Genova.

TRAVEL BAG

DUFFEL BAG

Travel-Related Bags

Travel-related bags range in size from luggage large enough to hold a wardrobe and other necessities for a long trip to smaller bags for transporting items on the daily route to and from home to work or school. Figure 5.3 shows a sampling of travel-related bags.

- **Backpack** A bag of varying shapes and sizes carried on one's back and secured with two straps that go over the shoulders.
- **Duffel bag** A large, cylindrical bag with a zipper opening on top, usually made out of canvas or leather for carrying personal belongings. It was originally used by

military personnel; nowadays it is used to carry belongings while on short trips.
- **Fanny pack** A small zippered pouch suspended from a belt around the waist.
- **Messenger bag** A rectangular bag with a single flap closure and an adjustable long shoulder strap.
- **Suitcase** A rectangular large bag with solid structure and reinforced corners, used to carry luggage on trips.
- **Travel bag** Generally a rectangular bag with multiple compartments and pockets, used as carry-on luggage on airplanes or short trips. Usually designed to fit in the overhead compartment of an airplane.

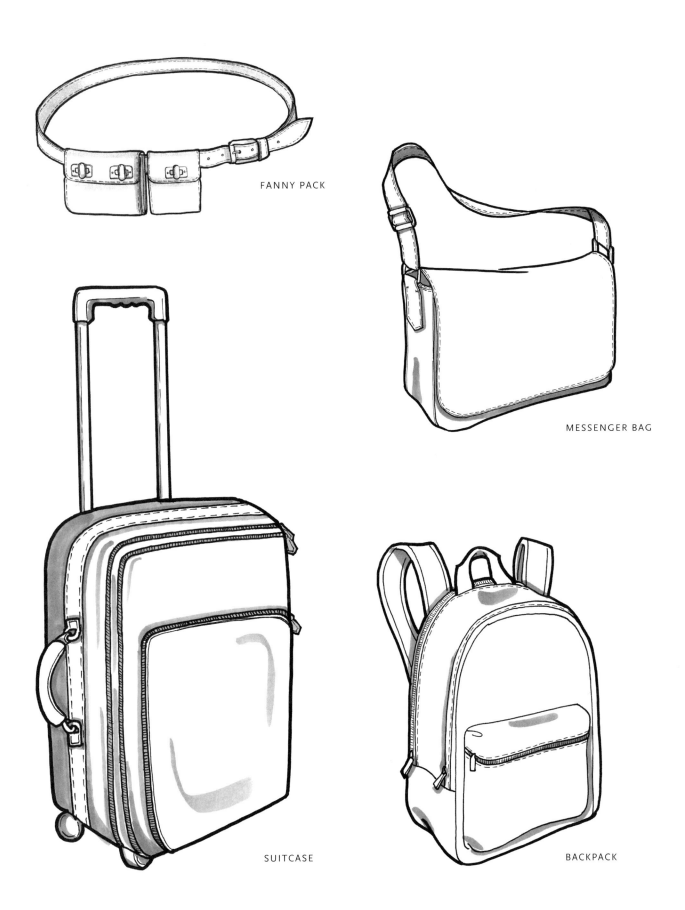

FANNY PACK

MESSENGER BAG

SUITCASE

BACKPACK

FIGURE 5.4

Examples of small

leather goods.

Courtesy of Aneta Genova.

COIN
PURSE

KEY
HOLDER

Small Leather Goods

The term **small leather goods** (SLGs for short) encompasses a variety of containers that women typically carry in their handbags and men may carry in a pocket or briefcase to hold small items. Despite the term for this category of accessories, not all small leather goods are made of leather or even synthetic materials simulating leather. Textiles and other materials are also used. Figure 5.4 shows a variety of small leather goods.

- **Checkbook case** A single-purpose case to hold and protect a checkbook. It has the signature rectangular shape and might have a few more slots or pockets for credit cards, ID, or a pen attachment, as well as an external pocket for change and bills. It could also be a part of a wallet.
- **Coin purse** A small, one compartment purse used to carry coins, bills, and cards.
- **Cosmetic bag** A small bag with zipper closure usually lined in plastic, which holds cosmetics.
- **Credit card holder** A flat smaller version of a wallet, designed to carry only a small number of credit cards and an ID card. It has no space or designated pocket for loose change or large bills.
- **Eyeglass case** An eyeglass case holds sunglasses and reading glasses and protects them while carrying them in a bag or pocket. Shapes and construction vary widely but it always resembles and closely fits the eyewear.
- **Key holder** There are quite a few variations on this small item. It can look like a wallet that opens up to expose a metal frame with hanging rings where one can attach keys, or it can look like a coin purse with a single chain and ring for keys. The term key fob is also widely used to describe a single ring that holds numerous keys and has a metal or leather attachment with a company logo or an image.
- **PDA** or **cell phone case** With the advancements in technology and the fact that almost everyone carries a cell phone or some kind of personal digital assistant (PDA), there are a variety of leather cases that suit them. They vary in shape, size, and closure, but their purpose is to carry and protect these mobile devices.
- **Wallet** Small flat case, usually with multiple compartments and a zipped coin section, used to carry money, credit cards, coins, and other personal items like ID and checks.
- **Wristlet** A small, usually flat bag with a very short strap that only fits around the wrist. The most common shape is a rectangle with a zipper closure.

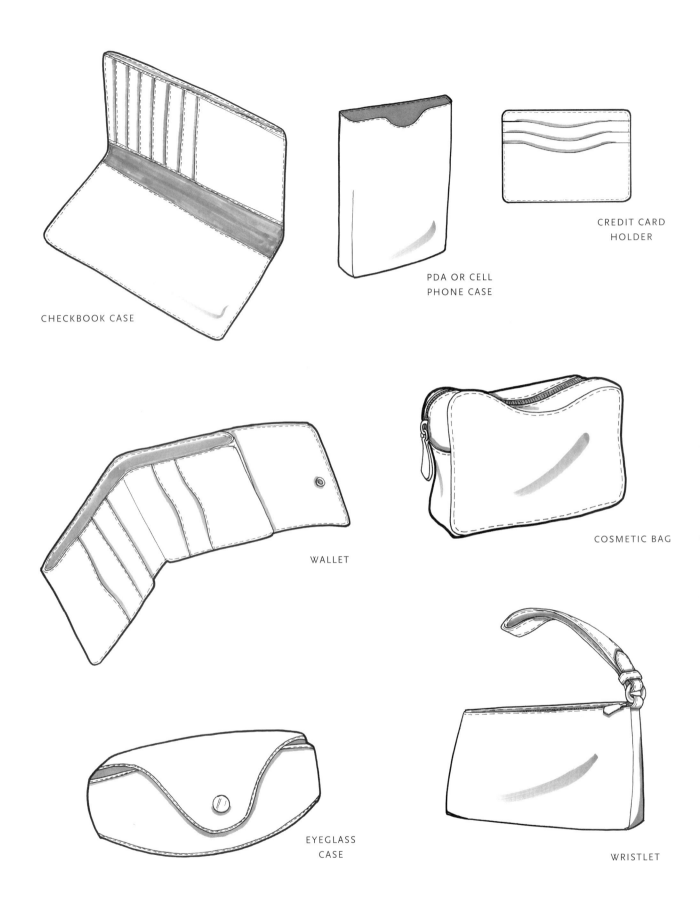

CHECKBOOK CASE

PDA OR CELL
PHONE CASE

CREDIT CARD
HOLDER

WALLET

COSMETIC BAG

EYEGLASS
CASE

WRISTLET

FIGURE 5.5

The main components of a handbag. Courtesy of Aneta Genova.

STRAP CLOSURE

FLAP

BODY

GUSSET

POCKET

FOOT

HANDLE

HARDWARE

Components of Handbags, Travel-Related Bags, and SLGs

A handbag can be as simple as a tote bag or as complicated as any designer wishes. There is no limit to materials and components to be used. Although bags vary in shapes and sizes, we can distinguish some characteristics and components of most if not all handbags (Figure 5.5). Most of these features are also found on travel-related bags, and some apply to small leather goods.

It's not to say that these are all the elements of a handbag, or that all bags have all of the described components; surely some bags are very simple and others have multiple characteristics that make them hard to place in a single category. The same is true of travel-related bags and small leather goods. This is where a talented designer like you comes into play. There will be time to design simple and possibly boring styles, and then there will be opportunities to design your dream bags. Having the knowledge of the construction and components is what will make you a better designer.

Body

The overall handbag can be constructed from one or more materials; usually it is made from leather, textile, hard material like plastic, polycarbonate, or wood, or a mixture of different materials. The general shape determines the function and use of each particular accessory.

Handles

A bag usually has one or two handles or a shoulder strap, by which it is carried. Some bags have both. Handles fit in the hand or around the shoulder. They can be made out of the same material as the bag or a specifically constructed durable material that holds weight very well like webbing. They are usually reinforced or have padding for comfort, especially for shoulder straps. It is possible that a bag has no handles. An evening clutch or an envelope bag for example can be carried by hand without any handles or straps.

Flap

Some bags, like the messenger bag, for example, have a flap attached to or extending from the back wall and falling over the front. How the flap is attached or how it closes on the front is a significant design detail in the overall construction and purpose of each handbag. A signature closure on the flap or a logo print is as important to the brand identity as not having any details on it. Either choice defines the style of the bag and the characteristics of the design company.

Pockets and Compartments

Inner or outer pockets are extremely important in modern bags. Our busy lives demand a variety of items to be carried at all times, and organization is imperative for any individual. Pockets can be decorative and functional at the same time and are an easy way to define a particular bag style. Two front pockets with large metal closures, for example, have become quite a signature look for Marc Jacobs handbags.

Gussets

Rectangular or triangular panels, or gores, usually positioned on the side of a bag, designed to expand the handbag.

Lining

Most bags have a lining made of a light fabric. The purpose of the lining is to protect the shape of the bag from stretching, to add more compartments and pockets, and to add a design element to the overall concept. The choice of lining is just as important as the outside body. A colorful print adds a whimsical feeling to a bag, while a luxurious leather or silk lining will add even more value to a bag. No lining can signify lower quality bag or a simple rustic look. Either way, the lining speaks a thousand words about the purpose and the designer of the bag.

Hardware

Hardware includes all metal components of a bag like metal closures, rings, D-rings, buckles, lock and key, feet studs, studs, snaps, zippers, and the logo plate.

Feet and Wheels

Feet seem to be appropriate for certain bag shapes and not others. The feet studs on a Birkin bag are a signature design element, while a hobo or a coin purse might never need them. For today's travel, flexible maneuverable wheels are a must on suitcases. Gone is the time of steam trunks that had to be lifted by more than one man. Some of the high-tech luggage even has a four-wheel system with swivel wheels for easy maneuvering and a foot brake. Whatever the case may be, consider that feet can play an important role in building the brand image with their shape, position, and logo placement.

Closures

All bags have an opening but not all bags have a closure, yet the closure plays a significant part as a design detail. The concept usually dictates elements that can easily be implemented in the

RAFE TOTENGCO

By 1989, Ramon Felix Totengco, more popularly known as Rafe Totengco, already had a successful clothing business in Manila, Philippines, but he was dreaming of a bigger career in New York City. He showed interest in fashion design early in his childhood and used to modify his school uniforms and get specially tailored clothes for himself and his friends. By the age of 18, with no formal training in design, he had his own clothing and accessory business called Schizo, sold throughout the Philippines. Looking to pursue his dreams in a bigger arena, Totengco left for America and enrolled in the fashion program at FIT (Fashion Institute of Technology). He supported himself as a design assistant while he studied, and in 1994, he produced his first collection of accessories: skinny mod belts and watchbands for a SoHo boutique. The accessories sold well, and he was asked to design handbags to go with the items. Totengco enthusiastically said "yes" even though he didn't have a single bag designed or made yet.

A year later, the first collection of Rafé New York handbags debuted at the luxury store Bergdorf Goodman. By 1995, Totengco was designing and working out of his apartment with one assistant and making bags and belts in local Manhattan factories. In order to grow his business, Totengco personally made cold calls and brought his own collection to new stores. With the help of his friends and family, he raised the money he needed to expand, and by 1999, his products were sold in more than 60 department and specialty stores worldwide. He started Rafe Studio Ltd. in 2000, and his products are now distributed at department

stores and boutiques worldwide, and sold through his own website, www.rafe.com. In 2006, Totengco received the honor of being tapped by Target as the first accessories designer to create a capsule collection for the mass retailer.

Since his humble beginnings, Totengco has become one of the most acclaimed young New York designers. His brand has grown to include women's handbags, shoes, and small leather goods, as well as men's bags and accessories. The Rafé accessories are known for their balance of fashion and function, blending uptown sophistication with downtown edge. He cares passionately about quality, style, and comfort and strives to bring satisfaction to each customer. Each item is crafted using top grade leathers, original fabrics, and a fierce attention to detail. The industry has acknowledged his accomplishments and has recognized him with numerous awards, including the following:

- 1996: Fresh Faces in Fashion—Gen Art
- 1997: The "Ten Best" Award—ENK International
- 1997: Membership Council of Fashion Designers of America (CFDA)
- 1999: Finalist: Perry Ellis Accessory Design Award—(CFDA)
- 2000: Rising Star Award—Fashion Group International (FGI)
- 2001: Best Accessories Designer (ACE Award)—Accessories Council
- 2005: Entrepreneurship Award—*Filipinas* magazine
- 2007: Asian Entrepreneur of the Year—*Asian Enterprise* magazine

Portrait of Rafe Totengco in his work area. © 2009 Rafe Totengco

Rafe's ad campaigns exude the energy and excitement of his accessory line. His handbags are as elegant and functional as they are edgy. © 2009 Rafe Totengco.

closure design. A heavy zipper with a signature zipper pull, a branded metal closure, or an arrangement of precious designed details make all the difference in the overall look of the bag. Closures offer protection from pickpockets and prevent the contents of the bag from falling out. Closures range from a magnet or a simple zipper to complicated and fun metal frames. Each one of them should be designed with thought and consideration of the designer label.

It's not to say that these are all the elements of a handbag, or that all bags have all of the described components; surely some bags are very simple and others have multiple characteristics that make them hard to place in a single category. And this is where a talented designer like you comes into play. There will be time to design simple and possibly boring styles, and then there will be opportunities to design your dream bags. Having the knowledge of the construction and components is what will make you a better designer.

Designer's Responsibilities

For accessory designers it is much more important to understand how bags and small leather goods are made and what the customer needs and wants than to blindly follow the latest trends. To be a good designer you need to have design ideas, but to be a great designer you need to know how to present your ideas in clear sketches and how those ideas can be made into actual final products. Construction is essential if not crucial to the final appearance of a handbag. In the following chapters, you will go through the natural process of creating a handbag and small leather goods line from concept and inspiration to a final product, but first you need to learn the responsibilities of a designer.

A handbag designer is usually a graduate of a fashion design school and has specific interest in the accessory industry. Various titles from assistant to associate to designer, senior designer, and design director can indicate more or less responsibility and creative power to a designer within the company.

Research and Forecasting

The designer is responsible for researching the current trends, selecting materials and hardware, conceptualizing ideas, and designing the full collections of handbags and small leather goods. Very often accessory designers travel to textile, leather, color, and trend shows to follow the latest development and see the latest innovations in each area. This helps bring new ideas to life and gives a good overview of the industry as a whole.

Sketching

It is important for an accessory designer to sketch very well, as that is the only way to present the concept and the original ideas to the rest of the design and merchandising team, the sample-makers, and the manufacturers. Most designers sketch their ideas on paper, but some technically savvy designers can draw directly in Photoshop or Illustrator, bypassing the pen on paper stage. A precise technical sketch is needed for the tech packs used for sample making and production. The designer is responsible for creating the black-and-white sketch with all measurements and in most cases also fills in all the information on the technical package.

Developing Hardware

Handbag and SLG (small leather goods) designers usually develop all the hardware that goes into each concept. That might include buckles, closures, zipper pulls, feet, logo plates, rings, chains, and any other trims. For each idea, the designer needs to research metals and metal finishes or any other material to be used and produce a black-and-white sketch with precise measurements of all possible views. The designer is responsible for following up with the factory making the hardware and approving the final look and feel of it. In some large corporate companies, this responsibility is assigned to a trim development team. In that case, the designer meets with the trim specialist to discuss ideas and hand in any concept sketches. The ideas still need to be presented with actual measurements noted on the sketches, but the designer is not required to follow up on the making of the hardware. That becomes the responsibility of the trim developer.

Approving Prototypes

Another designer responsibility is to approve the first prototypes and participate in corrections to the shape and hardware. The designer corrects any mistakes and hands off all paperwork that is needed in order to proceed with the manufacturing. Some designers are in constant communication with the factories, following production and answering questions; others can leave that to the production team if there is one.

Designers usually travel on a development trips and ensure samples are done correctly until all issues are cleared and the actual orders for production are written. Until then, designers comment on fabric lab dips, wash finishes, and stitch and leather quality, among other issues. And even after bulk production is manufactured, designers still examine at least one sample to make sure it looks good.

Merchandising

In some companies, a designer also needs to work closely with the merchandising teams in order to have knowledge of which styles and colors sell well and which ones do not. This helps the designer understand the customers of the brand and create accessories that will keep selling. A designer usually also presents the latest collection to the merchandisers and hears the feedback firsthand. The next step in the process is following up with the visual teams and knowing where and how the handbags are displayed in the stores. That helps a designer understand why and if certain styles sell better than others. In some cases, a designer might be involved in the PR or advertising photo shoots and give direction as to the concepts and themes of the collection.

Growing on the Job

Naturally, each accessory company is different, and responsibilities might vary from team to team, but the main ones outlined here are valid for any company. You should have a positive attitude and be flexible and ready to learn new skills and take on new challenges. Be prepared to work hard and consistently produce relevant ideas, and every company you work for will enrich your knowledge and prepare you for the next level in your career as a designer.

Define the Customer Profile and Parameters for the Accessory Group

GOALS

To give you practical experience in defining parameters, like customer profile, season, and functionality, before designing a unique group of handbags and small leather goods.

ASSIGNMENT

You are preparing to design an accessory collection. For this project, you need to define the customer who will be buying the products, start looking for sources of inspiration, and researching a possible theme or a concept. You will identify the customer characteristics through visual means and build a collage to showcase them. Consider the following questions while searching for materials and building the customer profile.

What is the age group and gender of your consumer?

What does this customer do, and where will he or she use the accessories you will be designing?

Where does the customer live?

What does the customer do for a living?

What clothing labels is the customer wearing?

What other interests of your consumer might influence the choice of accessories he or she uses?

How will this customer use your accessories?

Compile photographs, drawings, cutouts, fabrics, trims, and so on that answer these questions and visually represent your customer, and present them as a finished collage mounted on a board. The same can be achieved in Photoshop by layering digital photos or scanned materials in a cohesive presentation and printing it.

6

INSPIRATION AND
RESEARCH

for Handbags

CHAPTER SIX explains how handbag designers conduct research and find inspiration. After reading this chapter, you will be able to identify research stages and goals, locate sources of inspiration, and choose design concepts, materials, and hardware. You will also learn how to build a mood board to present your completed research.

RESEARCH IS THE SEARCH PROCESS that feeds the imagination and keeps a designer inspired. It consists of investigating and collecting any objects that stimulate the mind and spark ideas (Figure 6.1). Those items could be pictures, drawings, materials, objects, and actual samples of fabrics, leather, hardware, and finished products. The research helps you learn the subject and delivers design ideas in front of your eyes. We all know that trends are changing all the time and designers are always expected to come up with the newest, hippest "It Bag" every season. There is pressure to be innovative and at the same time to keep the integrity of the brand you represent and create for. Different companies have different customer requirements and expectations, and you need to conduct extensive research to design a successful collection satisfying every need of that particular market.

FIGURE 6.1

Collecting photographs and tears of favorite images on a corkboard or a wall in the workspace keeps a designer focused on the muse, the customer, and the particular concept. Even partial pieces of any object can bring ideas and spark a collection. Images from the inspiration wall of luxury handbag designer Gabriella Zanzani. Gabriella Zanzani.

Research can also be used to bring knowledge of all aspects of the customer and the brand you design for. It is essential to understand the history of the brand you work for in order to keep its integrity, and this is where research comes into place. It's through research that designers look into new technologies and advancements so that they can propel the new designs into the future.

Handbag designers need to be collectors of objects that inspire new structures and shapes, as well as mechanisms for closures. As technology is evolving, there are new possibilities of implementing it into accessories. The essence of research is searching through the past and looking into the future of all aspects of design and storing and absorbing the new information. Historical influences can be interpreted through new materials in order to look trendy and fresh. It is the exploration and the journey of research that bring the inspiration into mood boards and the finished product.

Research Stages and Goals

Research is an integral part of the design process and can have a few different goals. The initial goal is to find the concept or idea for the collection. Once the concept is established, the next stage of research is to gather enough information and examples of design elements, to inspire the design process for the collection. In the final stage, it is important to source materials and hardware that are not only appropriate for the handbag collection but also available and at the right price.

Different collections require different price points, and even though most companies develop their own hardware with a branded logo, it is extremely important to work within the development deadlines. Developing specific patterns to be printed or embossed in addition to ordering leather and fabrics can take its share of research and investigating in order to determine what is possible, at what costs, and how long it will take to produce. Using a horn as a handle might seem like the perfect idea for the chosen concept, but if horn in the right

FIGURE 6.2
Developing every single hardware piece requires multiple steps, which are costly and time consuming but imperative for brand recognition. A wax model is carved by hand (left), and then a mold is made from it before the final metal piece (right) can be created. Courtesy of Aneta Genova.

FIGURE 6.3

Even a simple frame
might take weeks
to develop, so it
fits in the designer
specifications.

Courtesy of Coach.

than what is available in the local store or even on the Internet. Spending the time to look for the right leather or hardware might be crucial to executing any project. Even the simplest frame or closure takes time to find or develop from scratch (Figure 6.3).

Sources of Research and Inspiration

Where to begin the research depends on the stage you are at. If you are looking for a concept, the research can be very broad, and the whole wide world is your source. An art gallery, a poem, or a vintage flea-market find can be equally inspiring for the searching eye. At this stage it is important to be aware of the following influences:

- Current trends in fashion and design
- History
- Cultures
- Technology advancements
- Socio-economic events or the political environment
- Sampling and manufacturing capabilities
- Budget

color, pattern, weight, and price is not available then the collection cannot be produced. On the other hand, if there is enough time you can come up with a new design solution.

Developing new hardware requires new molds for each new piece and knowing how long it takes to develop each one allows for proper planning of the sample-making and manufacturing process (Figure 6.2). Researching all design elements and making sure they will be available within the time constrains ensures a timely production and delivery at the end of the process. For a design student who is still in school, it might seem a bit far in advance to think of all these production deadlines and costs, but learning to do a thorough research of available materials and hardware is an essential step of the process at any stage of the career of a designer. Looking for the right hardware for an accessory you are developing in a school project can become even more challenging because your imagination is much less limited

Once the concept is chosen, the research is narrowed by the chosen theme. At this stage, you can conduct the research in any way that works for you as long as it delivers the information and materials to inspire your collection. Each designer has specific needs and a different style of searching. For a seasoned designer who knows all the sources that work for his or her style, this might be a quick process, while a young designer might explore a variety of sources until satisfactory results are achieved.

Some sources that are available to all include the Internet, magazines, museums, art and art galleries, libraries, architecture, product designs, flea markets, travel, flora and fauna, movie stars, professional services, new technologies, the market, and the competition.

The Internet

The Internet seems to offer endless possibilities of information, but if you are looking for specific inspiration for a handle or a trim you need to refine your search and dig deeper than just typing a word in a search engine. You need to look for sources that will give you the desired image results and information. Use the Internet to find more information on the subject you are researching. Look for original sources and websites dedicated to the subject. For example, if you want to create a Bakelite handle, you should research the 1920s and 1930s when it was extremely popular. Explore the Internet for sources that offer its history or find places where you can go see actual pieces in person. Those could include museum exhibits, events, art fairs, and vintage shows, for example. Fashion and style websites have regular accessory reports and feature the latest trends. Look through music videos online to stimulate your visual senses and inspire a particular state of mind through the music. The Internet is such an accessible and easy source that most students tend to do all their research there. In reality it should give you information and be just the starting point of an extensive research.

Magazines

Monthly fashion and accessories magazines are a great source of current trends and information. They deliver knowledge and insight of lifestyle and culture of the country where they are issued. This can be very useful when researching the needs of your customers. Looking through industry magazines like *Accessories*, *WWD Accessories*, or *ELLE Accessories* will build your awareness of other designers and trends in the industry and should be done regularly. While looking for inspiration, though, keep in mind that what's published in the magazines is already created and already in the stores, and in a way, it is already old news. Do not use current magazines to design a new line. However, looking through vintage magazines will prove to be an endless source of information and inspiration for handbag shapes, color, and design details, especially if you are focused on a particular decade.

Library

Search for books that feature the history and development of handbags. Looking through vintage or haute couture styles will give you ideas for shapes, structure, hardware, and color combinations. Once you have an established theme you can visit the local branch of the library to browse through its archive. Very often libraries have a collection of vintage magazines, as well as an image archive on various subjects.

Museums

Museums are an amazing source of inspiration. They allow us to see a variety of styles and media within one place and can immediately take your artistic mind to a higher level of creative enthusiasm. Most costume museums feature clothing, but every so often there are exhibitions that highlight accessories, accessory designers or an iconic accessory company. "London Fashion" exhibit at FIT, New York featured Vivienne Westwood handbag creations. The Costume Institute at the Metropolitan Museum regularly features accessories in its exhibitions.

Art and Art Galleries

Art galleries are not only a source of inspiration because of the actual works of art, color, print, and concepts but also because of the people who walk through them. Art galleries attract creative people and art lovers and are one of the greatest

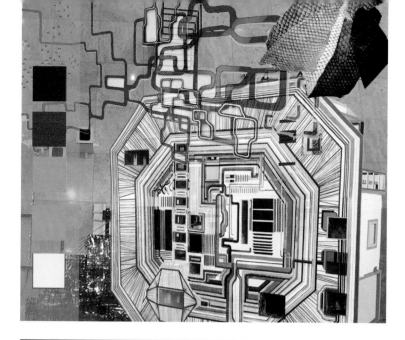

places to see the latest "It Bag" or a fresh new idea for a new shape or a closure. Use a single piece of art or multiple paintings or sculptures to develop a concept and a mood board (Figure 6.4).

Architecture

Architecture provides references for different styles and historical events. You can use design elements from building facades and interior decor or the overall structure of a building, for example, and recreate the feeling or surface texture or mimic the shape (Figure 6.5). Architecture from a particular period like Art Nouveau can provide the whole concept of a group, complete with shapes, colors, and materials.

FIGURE 6.4 A mood board with color chips and exotic skin textures, based on one single piece of art, which provides clear direction for colors, as well as vivid lines and possibilities for 3-D design. Nayany Katayama.

FIGURE 6.5 Clockwise from upper left: The wrought iron door of a building in Buenos Aires can provide inspiration for beautiful floral and ornamental shapes to be used in a print, embossing, or hardware; the overall shape, pattern, and color combination of this kiosk can be used for inspiration; the unique color of this building in Buenos Aires and its contrasting doors can be a great addition to a concept pursuing those qualities; and geometric shapes and figures or the ceiling in an Art Nouveau hotel lobby in Prague can provide inspiration for a great pattern. Courtesy of Aneta Genova.

Product Design

Accessory designers often look for inspiration into various objects from interior and industrial design and sculpture (Figure 6.6). Overall shape and construction or single elements can carry a lot of information applicable to accessories. Very often product designers themselves design accessories along with their other work.

Flea Markets

Flea markets are probably the best source for vintage bags and unique finds that can serve as inspiration. You might be surprised with the variety of materials used and the workmanship that you will find in some antique bags. The well-preserved pieces could be expensive, but having a good sample in perfect shape can be priceless. Building a library of samples can prove very useful in the long run. Sometimes unusual combinations just thrown together on a table can spark an idea for color combinations or materials. Make it a habit to go out to flea markets and buy or photograph interesting ideas and look at all kinds of objects not just handbags. Great shapes and patterns come in all objects around us (Figures 6.7 and 6.8), and furniture pieces are very often designed with a concept that can just as well be used for a handbag or other leather goods.

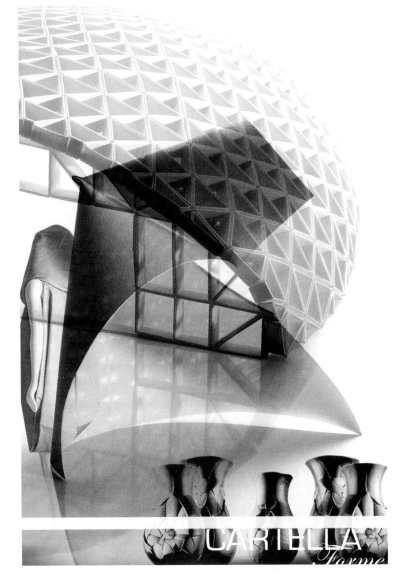

FIGURE 6.6 Inspiration images from various design fields by Sabato Riccio. Sabato Riccio.

FIGURE 6.7 The ornaments on the cash register and the overall copper and brass color combination can also be inspiring in an appropriate concept. Courtesy of Aneta Genova.

FIGURE 6.8 Photographs of antique pieces, like these gramophones, can play an important role in a concept related to a tango or other dance concept. They can also be used for color and shape inspiration and reference. Courtesy of Aneta Genova.

FIGURE 6.9 Designer Alexander McQueen went as far as using taxidermied fauna on the runway to complement his nature-inspired designs. Courtesy of WWD.

FIGURE 6.10 Handbag designer Gabriella Zanzani uses a poppy flower in her mood board for color and pattern reference. This close-up of the blossom reveals color nuances and textures that create powerful inspiration. Gabriella Zanzani.

Travel

Experiencing a variety of cultures will enrich your mind and will help you understand how different cultures use bags. This knowledge will serve as immediate inspiration, and later on it also might come in handy if you are designing for international markets. Observing patterns and shapes and storing them in your mind will also spark ideas when you need concepts driven by a destination.

Flora and Fauna

Rare birds, fish, and animals provide skins and feathers for use in the construction of a handbag. Flowers and leaves have naturally exquisite lines, and people easily associate them with beauty (Figure 6.9). They can also inspire shapes and patterns as well as general silhouettes (Figure 6.10).

Movie Stars

Use movie stars and other celebrities for historical reference and understanding of how and when certain styles of bags were used. Use them for pure inspiration if they bring an artistic element. Starlets of the past and present have the power to catapult a bag into immediate status of "must-have" accessories. Many bags have been named after a glamorous star who inspired the initial design. Some of the most famous examples are the Birkin bag, which was named after actress Jane Birkin and the Kelly bag named after Grace Kelly, who was seen carrying it throughout her life.

New Technologies

Since the technology breakthrough finds of synthetic fibers and digital printing, designers have the opportunity to use new materials or print on almost any surface. If you can imagine it, it can probably be done. With the invention of Gore-Tex® and HyVent™ fabrics, The North Face technical backpacks use a PU coated 210D nylon ripstop fabric with dual-sided PU coating to create a water resistant body, necessary for climbers who spend days exposed to high-altitude elements. Researching new technologies is imperative if you work for a brand that creates modern shapes or travel luggage. Utilizing them will give you an edge up on the competition.

Professional Services

There are vintage shops and antique dealers who work specifically with design houses and professional clients. These services are usually found in the fashion capitals like New York, Paris, and London and are listed in fashion resource books and websites. You can call them in advance and let them know what concept you are researching and what decade you might like to reference. With that information, they can pull a selection of styles from their archive and will either invite you to their studio or they will come to your office and deliver a variety of objects as requested by you. Such services are usually expensive, but the advantage is in knowing you will see quality finds and will not be wasting time traveling and looking through countless sales or shops. You can establish a relationship with a vintage dealer and have its staff look on your behalf for original pieces that fit your style.

Shopping the Market and the Competition

As part of ongoing research, a designer needs to know what the company's competitors are creating and selling. Your direct rivals are selling handbags and small leather goods to the same people you are, and it is important to know whether they have gained a design advantage in some way. It is also imperative to keep your brand identity (Figure 6. 11) and to be different enough from other companies to attract attention but at the same time serve the needs of the same customers.

Choosing Concepts

Having a concept or a theme keeps the group of different styles together and gives the designer focus. Depending on the company you work for, concepts for handbags and small leather goods can be driven by the main clothing line or they can be developed for each original new group. If you work for a designer label for which the main business is the clothing, the

FIGURE 6.11

The Louis Vuitton windows on the Fifth Avenue store in NYC feature unique ideas in both accessory design and window creations. Courtesy of Aneta Genova.

LULU GUINNESS

Lulu Guinness's motto is, "Dress to suit your mood! Don't keep all your most glamorous things for special occasions."

Lulu Guinness, famous for exquisite, witty handbags and accessories, was born in 1960 as Lucinda Jane Rivett-Carnac. She launched her company in 1989, but success didn't happen overnight for her. She always wanted to be in the fashion industry but she went through a trial-and-error period. She was working in video production when she had the idea to create a feminine briefcase inspired by a Filofax. She made it out of patent leather with lots of clear pockets and bright suede lining and started making phone calls herself to buyers at Liberty's and Joseph in London. Her creation was a bit expensive and didn't leave much margin for profit, but her eclectic dress style caught everyone's attention, and she was asked to design more like the way she dressed. She went back home and set up a shop in her basement. "I was born with endless creative ideas," says Guinness. "I was born not to want to be like everyone else. For me it is not a Eureka moment."

Appealing to women who want nontraditional, colorful bags, Lulu Guinness started creating an endless array of whimsical shapes and grew a business that became a "must" in every handbag aficionado's closet. She drew from her strong personal style to create partly retro, partly chic, glamorous handbags. In 1995, she opened a collaborative store on Elizabeth Street in London which, attracted customers like Madonna and Jerry Hall. The first of her world famous collectable handbags was designed in 1996 and was called the "Original House." It had hand embroidery on black satin with a red suede roof. Receiving praise in the fashion media paved the way for the world of Lulu Guinness creations. Her first international order came from Lane Crawford in Hong Kong, followed by

Lulu Guinness. Tim Whitby/Getty Images.

a store opening in New York in 2000. The year 2001 marked the launch of a Lulu Guinness shoe collection to complement the handbag's range. It was produced in collaboration with the British shoe company Lambert Howarth and embodies her stylish and feminine design touch with an element of humor. For Guinness, this development was a long-time ambition coming to fruition. "I have always wanted to design shoes. For years people have been asking me when they could have a pair of Lulu Guinness shoes."

By 2002, she had branched out to other accessories, like umbrellas, parasols, and wallets, followed by a fragrance in 2003, stationeries in 2004, and sunglasses in the following year. In 2006 Guinness launched a luxury Italian handbag collection, called "Couture," containing exquisitely detailed, modern-day, classic handbags made in leather.

The classically Guinness phrase, "Put on Your Pearls, Girls!" was also the title of Guinness's first book, a "pop-up book for adults," published in March 2005. It includes her famous sayings

and her philosophy of living well and has a foreword written by Helena Bonham Carter.

Nowadays her unique creations are sold in department and specialty stores worldwide including Harrods and Selfridges in the UK, Bergdorf Goodman in New York, Collette in Paris, and Harvey Nichols in Dubai and Istanbul. There are six Lulu Guinness retail boutiques around the globe, including, London, New York, Tokyo, Osaka, and Fukuoka. Guinness's collectable bags have been subjects of two exhibitions in Sotheby's London and New York. The Florist Basket and the Violet Hanging Basket are just two of the designs that have been included in the permanent fashion collection at the Victoria and Albert Museum, London. Her bags are seen on the arms of an ever-expanding list of celebrities; among them are Dita von Teese, Helena Bonham Carter, Jemima Khan, Sophie Dahl, Rachel Weisz, Keira Knightley, Claudia Schiffer, and Debra Messing.

Guinness also has designed other unique items including a Sky+ box, (a personal video recorder which works with the British Sky Broadcasting service and is very popular in England and Ireland); a stylish luxury travel bag for the Ford Focus car; and a bespoke bag for the Sony Playstation.

In October 2006, Guinness was awarded an OBE (an Order of the British Empire) from Her Majesty the Queen in recognition for her contribution to British fashion.

Signature Lulu Guinness lipstick bags like these have been collected by handbag aficionados all over the world. Courtesy of Aneta Genova.

accessory designers follow the concepts and colors of the collection and keep the handbags within the same theme. The materials usually change a bit from the ones used in the clothing line. Leather and exotic skins as well as sturdier textiles might be introduced in order to create sturdier, more structured shapes. Hardware needs to stay within the theme and reflect the chosen concept and colors, but the designers might add new metals for logo plates, rivets, feet, and other trims.

If you create handbags for an accessory-driven company, concepts can focus on a single technique, texture, or a pattern. Original patchwork, an animal print, or a rare and expensive skin can be the base for a full line of accessories. Carlos Falchi has made a long career creating handbags on the concept of unusual collages of exotic skins. See Figure 6.12 for an example. Some companies like Louis Vuitton keep doing variations on the same, already famous monogram print and keep it fresh by having different artists as contributors, who tweak it according to their style. In that case, the concept is driven by the artist.

Concepts are always given a name that represents them, and it is displayed on mood boards, line-sheets, tags, ad campaigns, store display windows, and wherever else the concept is promoted. Destinations, city names, trendy neighborhoods, female names, and word play on holidays are often used, as well as the actual leather quality name or the logo print if it's already recognizable. Here are some examples of concept names:

- Bleecker
- Tribeca
- Poppy
- Cambridge
- Damier Canvas
- Monogram Multicolore
- Pop Novelty
- Graffica
- Copacabana
- Atlantis

Picking Colors, Materials, and Hardware

Once the concepts have been solidified, it is time to focus on colors, materials, and hardware. Some of these will be already identified while researching the theme; others will need to be added.

Colors

It is important to narrow color choices to the essential few that truly represent the concept. Choose too few and there won't be enough of a range to merchandise the collection well. Choose too many, and the group can look watered down and unfocused. You should look carefully into the research pictures and study the essence of the main idea. This is the perfect time to examine the images and make sure you are extracting the colors that make them fit perfectly into the concept. Do not choose too many similar shades of the same color, and do not be afraid to narrow your choices. This is also the time to find out whether the skins and textiles you would like to use are available in all colors you need. Careful planning will pay off later in the manufacturing process.

FIGURE 6.12
Carlos Falchi is known for creating handbags that follow the natural lines and qualities of different leathers. In this bag, he combines short-hair leather and an exotic skin.
Courtesy of WWD/ George Chinsee/ Thomas Iannaccone.

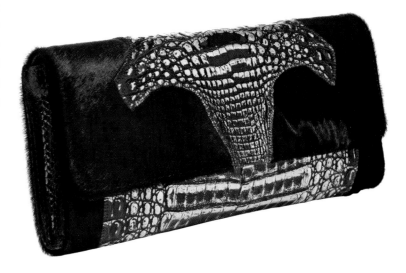

FIGURE 6.14 A single photograph like this lineup of soda bottles at Plaza Dorrego flea market in Buenos Aires can represent all colors to be used in a collection. Courtesy of Aneta Genova.

Once you've selected all colors, organize them and represent them on the mood board. They can be organized as a simple raw of square shapes, or you can create theme-specific shapes (Figure 6.13) to fit the overall concept and arrange them in an attractive formation. You can use one of the inspiration photographs to represent the colors (Figure 6.14) and just name them in a list. The selected image can already be in the right colors for your concept, or you can tweak it to look "correct." As long as it is obvious what the colors are, you can present them any way you think is best for the collection (Figures 6.15 and Figure 6.16).

Materials

Materials for each design group need to be chosen for their look and feel as well as their performance qualities. Naturally, you need to choose leather, fabrics, and hardware depending on what makes sense for each group. At this stage it is fundamentally important to understand the qualities of each material and

how it holds shape. Depending on the concept of the collection, you might want to use softer lambskin leather for an overall slouchy look or a fabric body with sturdy backing and vachetta leather for trims. Your knowledge of leathers, textiles, and hardware is extremely important at this stage. Knowing which leather will wear well and which one will look trendy and cool are two completely different criteria; both are viable as long as they are conscious choices aimed at the right consumer (Figure 6.17). It is also important to make sure that all leather and fabrics are available and can be delivered on time to ensure meeting your development deadlines.

Hardware

Hardware needs to be selected with a clear idea of the concept for the collection (Figure 6.18). You might use antique brass hardware for a vintage feel group and a high-polished gold for an evening one. It is also important to consider the look and the actual mechanism of the closure for each concept. A modern

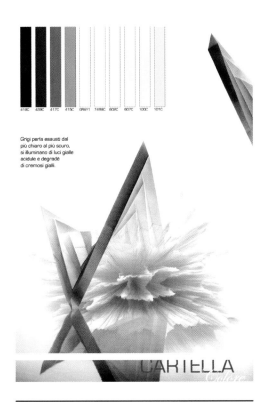

Grigi perla esausti dal
più chiaro al più scuro,
si illuminano di luci gialle
acidule e degradé
di cremosi gialli.

FIGURE 6.15 Color board by accessory designer Sabato Riccio. As of 2009, Sabato designs accessories for Dolce and Gabbana and his past experience includes Hugo Boss Black label and Moncler. Sabato Riccio.

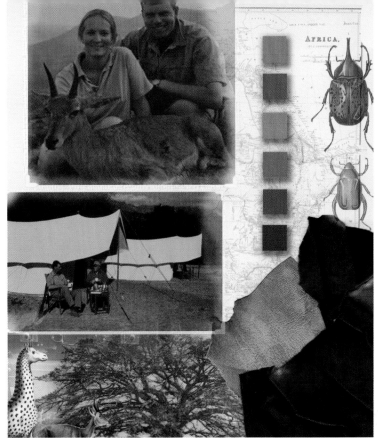

FIGURE 6.16 This concept and color mood board by Brianna Allen features all colors in a uniform lineup and actual swatches of leather for her African Safari luggage collection. Brianna Allen.

FIGURE 6.17 LV handbags are as recognizable by design as they are by their durable materials.

Photo by: Antoine Rozes.

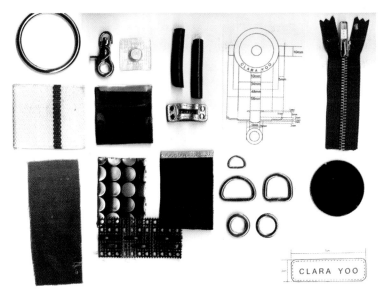

FIGURE 6.18 Materials and hardware page from Clara Yoo's portfolio. Clara won the CFDA fashion student completion in 2007 with her accessory collection and currently works for Cole Haan. Clara Yoo.

FIGURE 6.19 Simple hardware complements the geometric shapes and clean lines of this handbag. Courtesy of Aneta Genova.

FIGURE 6.20 A careful look into the inspiration photos might spark ideas for hardware development in addition to everything else. Architectural elements and door handles, as in this photo, provide perfect inspiration for a bag handle. Courtesy of Aneta Genova.

futuristic group might be complemented by an innovative metallic closure (Figure 6.19) or a hidden magnet, while a vintage group can benefit from ornate buckles inspired by a vintage door handle (Figure 6.20). Well-designed hardware that works with the concept will upgrade a beautiful bag and make it even more desirable (Figure 6.21). Expensive bags are usually associated with heavy hardware while inexpensive ones utilize hollowed out, cheaper metals.

Another factor for consideration is the time it takes to develop hardware. A mold must be opened for each new piece, and that can take a significant amount of time and investment. Each piece of hardware on a single bag needs to be well thought out and coordinated with all others (Figure 6.22). Zippers, buckles, grommets, and rivets can all match, or they can be designed to have different finishes in order to achieve a particular look.

FIGURE 6.21 The oval shape in this bag is carried through all the hardware and complements the overall handbag design and all trims. © 2009 Rafe Totengco.

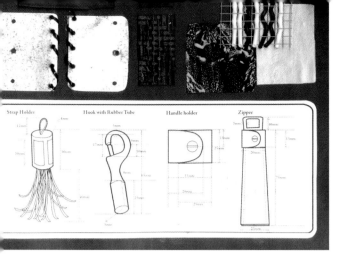

FIGURE 6.23
This mood board by designer Brianna Allen complements the one in Figure 6.16 and brings additional inspiration for shapes, pattern, and texture from animals and insects found in their natural environment and vintage luggage used in an African safari. Brianna Allen.

FIGURE 6.22 Materials and hardware page from Clara Yoo's accessory project for a CFDA fashion design competition. This accessory collection won the 2007 competition. Note the detailed measurements of every single hardware piece to be developed for her collection. Clara Yoo.

Building a Mood Board

A mood or a concept board is the refined presentation of the finished research. A good mood board contains images, fabrics, leather swatches, and trims as well as hardware and logos to be used in the final collection. It can contain rough sketches of shapes to be used as design details as well as some potential body shapes that correspond well to the concept.

A great mood board presentation shows the concept in its completion, and after looking at it, there should be no questions as to what the collection is about. The season, the customer and her lifestyle, the colors, materials, hardware finishes, and design details for this concept should all be clear. Figures 6.23 through 6.27 show how different designers' mood boards meet these criteria in representing different concepts.

Be creative and employ all inspirational resources when making the boards. You could cut out the color chips from the actual fabrics or leather you will be using, or you could use Pantone colors for example. Whatever shape you decide to cut the colors in, make sure it fits in the theme and is neat.

A mood board can be a collage presented on one page or it can take up a whole wall covered

FIGURE 6.24 Mood board by Jovana Mirabile. She developed a concept based on the Tibetan culture and it's colorful rich patterns. Notice how her materials are woven within the presentation instead of organized in one section. Jovana Mirabile.

FIGURE 6.25
A mood board by Nayany Katayama featuring artwork by Peter Reginatos. Notice how she has organized the chosen colors and hardware finishes on the left side and presented them in shapes mimicking the artwork. Nayany Katayama.

FIGURE 6.27 Mood board by Frank Nathan, based on mantis creatures and butterflies, uses symmetry as a tool to show the concept. Notice how colors are represented in uniform butterfly shapes. Frank Nathan.

FIGURE 6.26

Mood board with actual fabric swatches and peacock feathers from Fay Leshner.

Fay Leshner.

in pictures and actual objects. Some companies make concepts a large portion of the design process, and a presentation can be so elaborate as to take a whole room, complete with re-painted floors in the right shade and furniture and objects that belong in the lifestyle of the target customer. Doing this kind of a presentation requires a lot of research and helps the designers completely immerse themselves in the theme and understand the customer they are designing for.

Here are some questions to consider while building a mood board:

- Is the idea or concept clear and focused, or has it become too broad?
- Are there enough shapes from which to draw inspiration?
- Are there enough details that can be used in the design process?
- Are there sufficient patterns?
- Are the colors well represented?
- Are there too many or too few pictures?

Building a Concept Rig

Some large companies create **concept rigs** that represent not just the theme of the collection but also the complete lifestyle of the potential customer (Figure 6.28). They can take up a whole wall and sometimes a whole showroom with multiple concepts together. They consist of samples of all kinds of accessories and clothing

that would be worn within the concept. Past season and current or vintage clothing is added to create the true feeling of a complete outfit. In most cases, there would be large printouts of photographs representing the destination or the inspiration, and specific titles, tags, and signs would be created with appropriate colors and fonts that represent the theme. Some companies have specific concept designers who work only on the concept rigs and scout through countless archives, vintage shows, and new sources to find concept-specific items to represent the ideas. The point of a concept rig is to show a complete picture of the customers and their lifestyle and how they would wear the accessories. It is a great inspiration tool, and when executed right, it feels as if you are walking into the world of the named concept.

Concept rigs are certainly the most elaborate and time consuming type of presentations but are an important reminder of the concept so that each design in the collection will reflect every aspect of the theme. A designer working with a small budget can opt out for a simpler presentation that doesn't involve displaying actual samples or furniture but can still make an impression with ample sketches, hand-painted illustrations, swatches, and trims. The most important thing is to have a well-defined concept in a focused presentation, which will help the design process along.

FIGURE 6.28
Nine West concepts
called "After Nature,"
"Suited Symphony,"
and "Great Crusade."
Courtesy of Nine West.

PROJECT

Building a Mood Board

GOALS
To give you practical experience in researching inspiration materials and building an actual mood board.

ASSIGNMENT
Find sources of inspiration and compile research materials. Identify a concept for a handbag collection, research through all possible sources, and find images that represent it best. Compile those images in a collage that gives enough information (design details, shapes, and overall direction) for designing a collection. Choose your colors and find appropriate swatches that represent them. Select materials and hardware to be used in your design collection.

Create a presentation with a complete mood board, color story, and materials page.

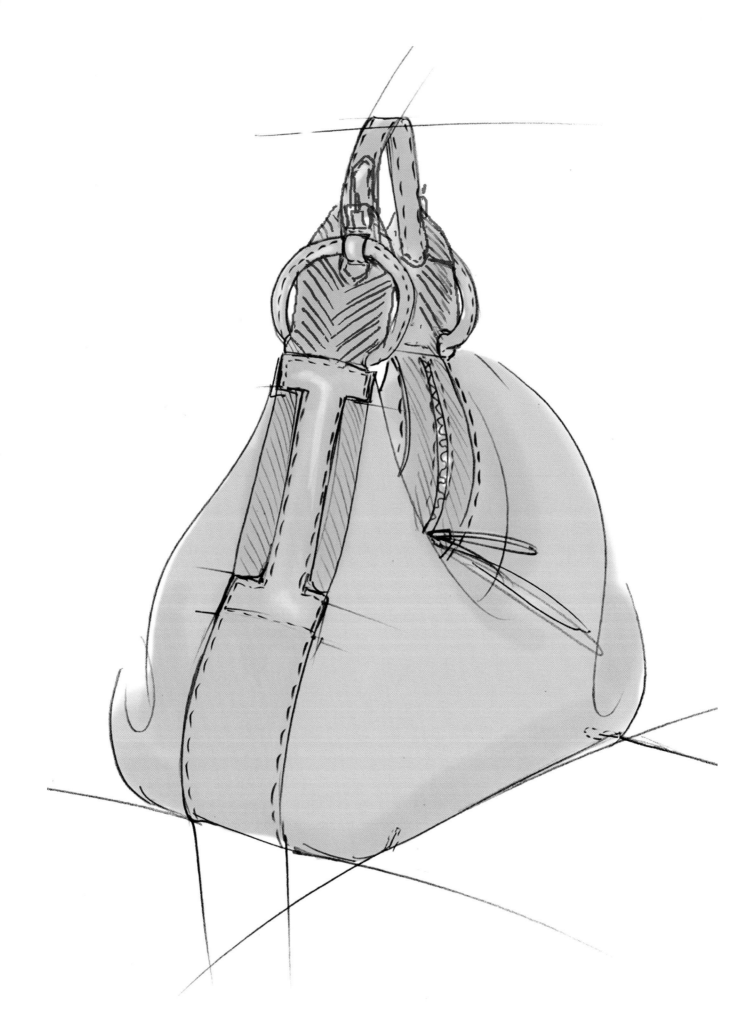

7

DESIGNING, SKETCHING, AND PRESENTING

Handbags and Small Leather Goods

CHAPTER SEVEN applies the design process to the creation of a handbag or small leather goods collection. After reading this chapter, you will be able to develop and edit designs according to a specific target market and brand identity. You will also appreciate the variety of techniques for preparing flat sketches and be able to present final ideas with both hand-drawn and computer-aided illustrations.

THE PROCESSES OF INSPIRATION, research, and design for handbags and small leather goods are similar to the processes for any other fashion item, but the designer has more freedom in creating three-dimensional objects and using a wide variety of materials. The difference between designing clothing or even shoes and designing handbags is that for handbags and small leather goods one can create new shapes that do not have to fit the human body and can stand on their own as masterpieces. That gives you, the designer, freedom to explore endless sources of inspiration: sculptures, art, architecture, vintage finds, and new techniques or materials.

Overview of the Design Process

The design process for handbags and SLGs, just like that for other accessories, is guided by a set of required elements for which you gather information. It is about incorporating familiar design details in new ways to create original ideas as a result of the gathered research and the defined concepts.

Identifying the Concept

In the design process, concept is the first and foremost component to consider. Depending on the company you work for, concept ideas can be a part of the overall direction of the company or can be chosen for each individual group. Inspiration can vary from a destination to a purpose to a single print, hardware, and shape. After the theme is chosen, it will guide your research process and define the places you will look for inspiration. Going to flea markets and vintage stores might not be an appropriate choice if you are researching a futuristic idea. Having a clear idea about the main concept, the season, and the customer is imperative to creating a successful collection. For more detailed explanation of research, concept and mood-board development, see Chapter 6.

Determining Materials and Sketching Ideas

After the concept and season are identified, and research is underway, the next step is to discover the materials you will be using for the body, handles, trims, lining, and hardware and look at the inspiration for shapes. With these elements in mind, you can start sketching design ideas. In this stage, you should use whatever technique works best for you. You can use pencils, pens, or markers, create collages to develop different proportions or just doodle away until you feel that you have developed enough valid ideas. There is no right or wrong way of approaching this step of the process. Just start sketching silhouettes that fit the concept and work in the media that is most comfortable for you. Keeping in mind the design development elements, you should sketch various shapes and details until you develop multiple ideas for the same group.

Editing the Ideas

The next step is to edit all the ideas and create a well-merchandised collection. That means defining a good array of sizes and shapes that satisfy various customers. A great collection is

composed of various functional pieces and is held together by the concept; the inspiration; the materials; the colors; and the hardware; and possibly a unique print, texture, or technique. Designing one cohesive collection means that you develop hardware, stitching details, and embellishments specifically for this concept and you use them throughout the designs for every single accessory in the group.

If you develop a braided pattern for the handles, then you use that pattern throughout the whole collection. Every group should have concept-specific trims and hardware finishes, and they should be used consistently for each style; otherwise there is no clear concept that can be followed in the next stages from merchandising to store display, photo-shoots, and ad campaigns.

While you are designing the collection you should always keep in mind the following guidelines: brand identity, customer, and seasonal requirements.

Designing with Brand Identity in Mind

Keeping the main characteristics of the brand in mind while designing is one of the most important responsibilities of an accessory designer. Learning the history of the company and looking at past collections give you the necessary information to identify the existing customers. For any future collections, the role of the designer is to understand the current trends and translate them into ideas

that work for these customers. An established company does not want to alienate its current customers while trying to attract new ones, and every accessory designer needs to be able to work within these parameters.

Whatever the target group of customers is, they all need to wear an assortment of handbags according to their daily activities and occupation, and a customer who loves a specific brand will buy various products from the same label. It is important to understand that when you are hired to design for a specific company, you need to immerse yourself completely in the identity of the brand. Learn its history and origins. Look at the various collections from the very beginning of the brand. See what other designers before you created to keep the image and identity of the company, and then think how you can update that image and offer a fresh new take on it.

Adapting Current Trends to the Brand's Identity

Looking at current trends is necessary and provides a starting point for any collection, but regardless of what type of company you work for, trends can be translated to fit the core image of the brand. The signature shapes that have been used for decades can be updated with new hardware and exotic leathers or new materials to follow the latest trends (Figure 7.1). If you work for a company that

FIGURE 7.1

The Hermès Birkin bag does not change its signature shape but gets updated with new materials, trim, and hardware finishes. A tan version (left) of the classic red bag (right). Simon Cowling/Alamy; Courtesy of WWD.

is driven by a clothing line and creates accessories to complement the clothes, then you need to work with the concepts of the main collection. In this case, you need to make sure you recognize and feature elements that are part of the clothing and create accessories that flow well with them. If you design for an accessory company, you still need to conform to the brand identity, but you have more freedom to create a signature look. No matter what company you work for, it is important to keep its integrity and design within the existing brand identity.

Designing for the Right Customer

The purpose of the bag you are designing and the target customer are just as important as the brand name and concept for each group. Designing within the brand identity guidelines and knowing your customer are the two most important rules every designer faces. The lifestyle of your customer is a leading factor in the decision you will be making. That particular style might not be your personal philosophy, but your job at your company is to design for this consumer. If you are not the target client or you do not actively pursue the activity you design bags for, then you must learn as much as possible about their needs or that activity. A handbag and small leather goods line geared toward a teenager is very different from a group designed for a professional mature adult. A travel suitcase differs greatly in shape and materials from a yoga bag. Your role as a designer is to study the needs of your customers and to understand their lifestyle and create objects that are desirable and functional. This will ensure a successful line of accessories. Always keep in mind that men and women have different needs and buy bags for different purposes. Women buy on impulse and collect multiple handbags to complement different outfits, while men buy lasting quality and don't change accessories as often.

The women's market is the most directional and conceptual and is driven strongly by the latest trends. It allows for more creative shapes, materials, and embellishments and more glamorous styles, as well as multiple collections within one season. Men, on the other hand, are much more conservative and buy mostly wallets, cardholders, key fobs, and fewer bags, but with a very specific purpose like work, leisure, or travel. They are much less driven by concepts and much more inclined to buy a good quality durable piece that lasts a long time and looks classic instead of trendy. Men require bags, or small leather goods with a sturdier make. This means that a menswear accessory designer will concentrate on traditional features, like leather quality, more conservative colors, and understated hardware. For a men's group, a designer would create fewer fashion groups driven by patterns and bold elements and more driven by texture and materials (Figure 7.2).

Designing for the Right Season

Always keep in mind what season you are designing for and understand the differences for each particular market. Each season deals with different elements and requires specific materials for the main body, trims, handles, and hardware. Apart from trends, which may dictate brighter colors and patterns, colder seasons are usually the time to use leather and sturdier materials that can withstand a bit more cold, while warmer conditions permit lighter fabrications and natural materials like straw and cotton canvas. Summer handbags and SLGs usually include a wider array of embellishments and brighter colors. Shells, beads, and stones are usually used for summer styles. Prints are also affected by seasonal changes. Tropical fish and flowers are more characteristic for summer or holiday months, while furry animals are usually seen in winter styles. Naturally, the concept and the brand identity affect these decisions, and product can vary from company to company, but it is important to recognize the impact of weather on every single piece that comes out of your hands and make educated decisions

FIGURE 7.2 These examples of accessories from a single brand, Louis Vuitton, were created for different customers and with different functions in mind but preserve the brand identity. The bags and briefcase (above) are geared toward more traditional, conservative customers who need classic shapes for everyday use and prints that cannot be dated to a specific collection so easily. These bags can be worn season after season and would look timeless. The wallet and agendas (right) are geared toward customers who are looking for functional items but need the most current print update. The yoga mat and its bag and the skateboard case (bottom) satisfy the specific needs of an active person but can easily be recognized as Louis Vuitton products, bearing signature LV logo prints. Clockwise from top: Courtesy of WWD; Courtesy of WWD; Courtesy of WWD/Thomas Iannaccone; Courtesy of Louis Vuitton/Michael Brunn; Courtesy of WWD; Courtesy of WWD/Mitchell Feinberg; Courtesy of WWD; Courtesy of WWD.

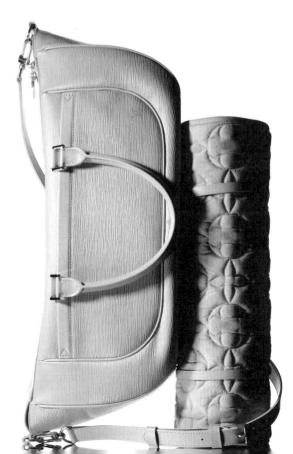

INTERVIEW WITH MARIE HAVENS FROM MEND

Marie Havens in Gulu, Uganda, and some of the preliminary designs for the Fall/Holiday 2009 MEND handbag line. © Marie Havens.

ANETA GENOVA: Tell us a little bit about yourself.

MARIE HAVENS: I'm a designer and photographer based in New York City. I moved here at 17 to study fashion design at Parsons The New School for Design—where I graduated with honors and the distinguished Designer of the Year award. I have worked within the fashion and photography fields for over a decade—traveling the world from Europe, Asia, and Central America to Mexico, Australia, and Africa. I am currently the design director of MEND, the new accessories division of the media-based nonprofit movement Invisible Children. I also collaborate and consult for celebrity photographer Patrick McMullan, a ten-year working relationship that includes photographing events and designing his top-selling photography book and exhibition: *so8os: A Photographic Diary of a Decade*. As a result, my design and photography work focuses on extremes in society, which greatly parallels my life and experiences in both New York City and Africa.

AG: How did you get involved with MEND?

MH: I grew up with Jason Russell, the co-founder of Invisible Children, so he was very familiar with my love for both philanthropy and design. Around 2005, I was working on business in China, and upon leaving Hong Kong, I had the unique opportunity to meet Jason in Uganda and see firsthand this war-affected country. It was an extreme and life-changing event for me. Upon return to New York City, I was asked to design accessories for Gap and Bono's first Product Red line and thereafter was so moved I wanted to get involved. I began working for Invisible Children in 2006, when the initial development for MEND began, but it took over three years of design and development until we officially launched on November 2, 2009.

AG: What is the concept of MEND?

MH: MEND is both a fashion brand and an educational program dedicated to educating and providing employment for the women of Northern Uganda. Years ago, a relationship existed between vendor and consumer. You knew who your money was going to and saw how it was impacting their life. Doing business involved much more than acquiring a product; it involved building a relationship. With that idea fading behind assembly lines and mass-production, MEND is inspiring a fashion mutiny by encouraging customers to ask, "Who made your bag?"

Formerly abducted girls return home, often with children, only to be rejected by their villages. Even though free, there is nothing for them. MEND offers them a way to repair what was lost. The women proudly sew their name in each handmade bag. Not only do these women create fashionable and functional bags with pride, but this employment allows them to provide for their families.

Through MEND, the life of the consumer is seamed with the life of the tailor. It is simply a process, rarely if ever seen in the fashion industry.

AG: What is the process of design and development for the handbags?

MH: The initial process is very similar to working at any design house in terms of inspiration and developing concepts to creating technical packages and sourcing materials. However, the primary differences revolve around the designer's character and resourcefulness. Creating this type of brand requires more research (due to often limited resources), heavy development and additional production time. As a designer working in Africa, I have learned to be more flexible, patient, and think "outside-of-the-box" but in the end, the rewards and end product have a much higher satisfaction rate for me. Ultimately, a finished MEND handbag has great power and symbolism, and I can go to bed each night knowing that MEND has left a positive contribution to the world—among a vast sea of mass-produced products.

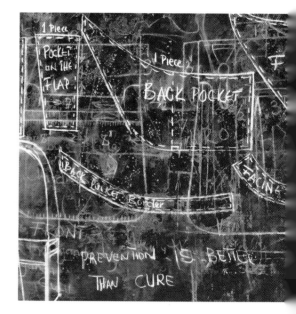

Work in progress. Every pattern piece is drawn on a blackboard for easy demonstration and discussion. © Marie Havens.

The MEND work facilities in Gulu are equipped with simple but sturdy machines and have plenty of space and light. © Marie Havens.

AG: Who are the people of MEND?

MH: MEND has a sewing facility with 13 women, one pattern/fabric cutter, one technical manager, and one production coordinator—all based in Gulu, Uganda. All the women are former sex slaves, abducted very young and tortured for years by Joseph Kony's rebel army. Now they are all free and rehabilitated and have been given full-time employment.

AG: How does working in Africa differ from manufacturing in Asia or even Europe?

MH: I have worked and traveled to sewing factories all over the world. What makes Africa quite different is its current lack of key resources (hardware, fabric, materials, sewing equipment) more readily available throughout Asia. All can be shipped; however, one must be aware of delays and the possibility of missing or late packages while working throughout Africa. It just requires a "built-in" cushion within your production deadlines. In general, it requires more flexibility and more research in regards to the shipping of materials and product. However, there are many positives to working in Africa as it's a new manufacturing destination, and one can create a unique type of fashion environment with limitless possibilities. MEND thrives in Africa because of this freedom and diverse approach.

AG: How do you distribute the product?

MH: We sell the majority of bags online (through www.invisiblechildren.com) and additional bags are sold at retail locations and gallery spaces.

AG: How does MEND contribute to the trend of global sustainability?

MH: MEND is paving the road for a new fashion approach. We are slowing down the production process, creating new seasons, creating a personal connection between the consumer and the seamstress, and ultimately raising the bar for Africa by introducing a high-quality and very personal product.

AG: What advice do you have for graduating fashion/accessory designers?

MH: Take your time to discover yourself as a designer, find inspiration in life, take time off (breaks from fashion are extremely important), and instead of focusing on a specific designer to work for, focus on the company's approach to protecting the "quality of life" for both yourself and all people involved in the creative process. Remember, a company who "turns out" product with a mass-produced approach will ultimately care very little about their factory, their seamstresses, your role, and your well-being.

The women who work on the MEND bags have a renewed purpose in life and an opportunity to provide for their families. They feel empowered through their work and proudly sew their names in each handmade bag. © Marie Havens.

FIGURE 7.3 Layouts with seasonal accessories. Each one of these layouts contains items specific for seasons from summer to fall and holiday. Think about how color, texture, and fabric determine the look and feel of each item. Colorful straw and tie-dye point to summer collections. Sparkly rhinestones and floral motifs suggest a resort collection, while darker colors, and the suede and crocodile textures point to fall/winter collections. From left to right: Courtesy of WWD/Thomas Iannaccone; Courtesy of WWD/George Chinsee; Courtesy of WWD/Charles Masters.

using that information. Figure 7.3 shows some examples of accessory layouts based on seasonal design concepts.

Questions to Keep You Focused

As you already learned, the design process starts with identifying a concept, researching ideas and inspiration, and then sketching the collection. Here is a summary of the basic design elements and some questions that will help keep you focused on creating a great collection:

- What is the brand identity?
- Who is the customer?
- What season are you designing for?
- Does the handbag collection match a clothing line or does it stand on its own?
- What are the purpose and function of the bags?
- What is the main material?

- What are the design details to be carried throughout the whole collection?
- Do you need to develop a print?
- Is there a decorative stitching or trim that can be used as an important element throughout the whole collection?
- Do you need to develop new hardware, or is there a classic one that will be used with a different finish (for example, shiny nickel, matte gold, or antique brass)?
- Do you need to create a new closure?
- Is there lining, and what would it be?
- Do you need to pick or develop a special print for the lining?

These questions should help you organize your thoughts and push you to explore different design options while sketching.

Sketching Handbags and SLGs

Sketching for the design process is different from creating illustrations for a presentation and drawing flats for the tech packs. It is important to understand that in each stage of the process, you need to master different techniques in order to become an excellent designer. No matter what company you work for, you will be required to draw sketches that represent the design idea as clearly as possible. Here is what you need to master in each stage of the design process.

Concept Drawings

As soon as the concept is chosen, a designer needs to start sketching ideas. The initial sketching is usually done with pencil in a sketchbook or on loose paper. This is the simplest form of free style drawing, meant to help get the concept thoughts on paper and focus on some initial ideas. Every designer has a different way of drawing, and there is no right or wrong way of doing this part. The most important thing at this stage is to be comfortable and prolific and get as many ideas as possible on paper so that the best ideas can crystallize.

Figures 7.4–7.7 show initial loose sketches, representing the design ideas and different drawing styles of various designers.

FIGURE 7.4

Quick concept sketches by Reed Krakoff for Coach. For the initial stage of getting your ideas down on paper, you can omit drawing details that are not important to the overall concept.

Courtesy of Coach.

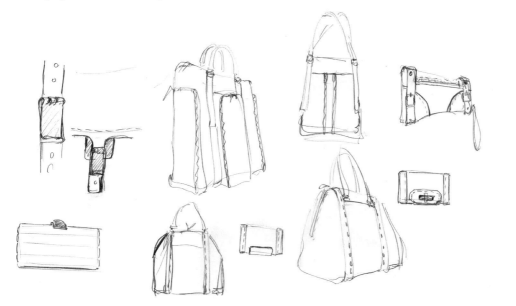

FIGURE 7.5

Loose concept sketches from the sketchbook of handbag designer Gabriella Zanzani.

Gabriella Zanzani.

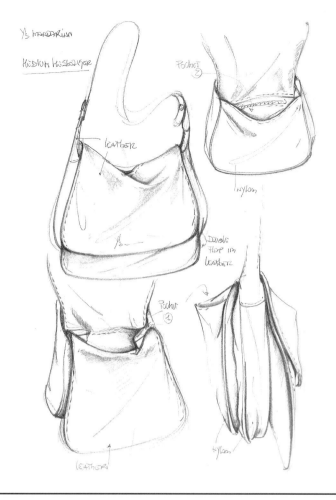

Y.s MANDARINA

MEDIUM MESSENGER

Pocket
3

leather

Nylon

Double
Flap in
leather

Pocket
3

Nylon

LEATHER

Nylon

Presentation Sketches and Illustrations

In the next stage of showing and presenting the design ideas in a meeting to the design team, to a director, or to a design VP, it is much more important to have beautiful sketches with ample visual information and possibly some necessary notes. In these meetings you are selling your ideas to the person who will decide whether to go forward with your designs or not and a beautiful presentation will make that choice easier. Illustrations are used to represent the overall idea, main shapes, patterns, and trims. These illustrations can be drawn by hand or created with the help of software like Photoshop or Illustrator. The pattern, texture, proportions, and design details should be rendered as in the intended design. Some details can be exaggerated, and others can be omitted so the illustrations look more beautiful and represent the concept ideas in the best possible way. Full figures carrying or using the product can be added to better illustrate the customer. Such images can also be used effectively for design meetings, buyer presentations, and ad campaigns. While it is fun to see the product in use on a figure, certain details can be obscured, so it is not recommended to use those illustrations in a tech pack, where the visuals serve a different purpose.

HAND SKETCHES

Hand-drawn illustrations are an obvious choice for representing the concept and mood of the overall idea, because they can be created easily with simple tools like markers but they could be more difficult to alter compared to computer-drawn illustrations, since you would have to redraw the whole illustration from scratch every time. If you need the bag in a different color or in multiples it might be easier

FIGURE 7.6 Maria Pia Capitano draws multiple views of the same bag and uses pencil to create realistic shading. Maria Pia Capitano for Fratelli Rosetti.

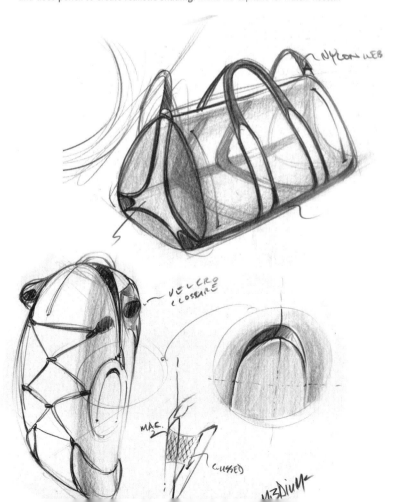

NYLON WEB

VELCRO
CLOSURE

MAG.
2

CLOSED

MEDIUM

FIGURE 7.7 Coleman Horn also sketches his designs with pencil and creates three-dimensional shapes with shading and an internal view to show the construction. Coleman Horn.

just to work in Photoshop. Hand illustrations add a touch of flair to any presentation, and most designers favor this technique. This is where individual style can shine and add to the liveliness of the design. Various rendering techniques can be used, from paints to markers and pencils, but most designers use mixed media as it is the most flexible and powerful way to get the message across.

Figures 7.8–7.21 are examples of the unique styles of several designers in their hand sketches, showing the accessories alone or held by full figures. Notice how different drawing styles represent the brand identity of each label or designer as well as the mood of the concept.

COMPUTER-AIDED ILLUSTRATIONS

Good knowledge of Photoshop or a similar program and a skillful hand can create a stunning presentation with drawings of the designs, full or partial figures holding product and backgrounds featuring patterns and design elements. With the aid of a computer it is much easier and faster to fill in different colors and repeat patterns, and create signs with appropriate fonts. A texture or a specific color can be scanned in and then overlayed in a specific part of the design to create a realistic interpretation of the final design. Once the sketches are created they can be altered very quickly and printed multiple times to represent the whole collection. Skillful designers can use actual photographs as a starting point or highlighting techniques on an existing sketch to create a realistic view of a concept vision. For these reasons many companies and designers use Illustrator or Photoshop to create the full presentation or parts of it.

FIGURE 7.9
Illustrator Steven Broadway draws bold fashion figures with dynamic strokes. The handbag design is presented on a figure and paired with other accessories. This creates a better overview of how a customer could wear this design. Such illustrations would be used for a presentation or an editorial in a publication. Steven Broadway NYC.

FIGURE 7.8 **This Giles Deacon sketch, featuring a full figure wearing various accessories, is perfect for a general presentation. You can see how accessories work within the whole outfit, but because it is impossible to observe any particular details, this would not be used in a tech pack.** Illustration by Giles Deacon.

FIGURE 7.10
This illustration by Kenzo mixes hand illustration collaged with a photographed face and creates an interesting dynamic. Antonio Marras for Kenzo.

antonio marras

FIGURE 7.11
Illustrations of full
figures holding bags,
rendered in marker
by Ivy Kirk. Ivy Kirk.

FIGURE 7.13 Handbag sketch by Gabriella
Zanzani drawn by hand, then colored in
Photoshop. Gabriella Zanzani.

FIGURE 7.12 Illustrations of handbags rendered in marker by Ivy Kirk. Ivy Kirk.

FIGURE 7.14 A Christian Siriano design
for Payless rendered in mixed media. Christian
Siriano design for Payless.

FIGURE 7.15 Hand sketches with realistic shading can show main shapes and details, serving as an effective presentation without rendering
of specific color, texture, or pattern. Maria Pia Capitano for Fratelli Rosetti.

CLOSED VIEW

GHURKA

EMBROIDERED LOGO

OPEN VIEW

NAME
ADDRESS
PHONE
EMAIL

LUGGAGE TAG: CANVAS, LEATHER, ANTIQUED BRASS

FIGURE 7.17 A sketch of Ghurka's 2009 Arena bag creates an artistic look with realistic details. © Ghurka.

FIGURE 7.16 Pencil sketch of luggage tags by Brianna Allen as part of a student homework assignment, prompting her to design for a famous brand. Brianna Allen.

FIGURE 7.18 Concept illustrations from the Rebecca Moses Heart Soul Style collection. Accessories are represented with very few construction details; accent is on the overall look. Courtesy of WWD/Sketch by Rebecca Moses from the Rebecca Moses Heart Soul Style collection.

FIGURE 7.19 Mixed media illustration of a handbag by Gabriella Zanzani with ample design details. Gabriella Zanzani.

FIGURE 7.20 Diane Von Furstenberg sketch for Michelle Obama. Handbag rendering shows pattern, but few other details. Courtesy of WWD/Sketch by Diane Von Furstenberg.

FIGURE 7.21 A realistic illustration featuring a wealth of details for the accessories by Oscar de la Renta. Courtesy of WWD/Sketch by Oscar de la Renta.

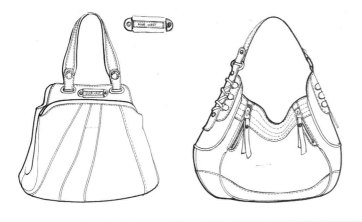

FIGURE 7.22 Flat sketches for a tote bag (left) and a hobo bag (right) used in a tech pack. These sketches would be used on the front page of a multipage tech pack to show just the overall shape and design details. The same sketches with added measurements would be used on the spec page to show the patternmaker and sample maker how to construct the final bag. Courtesy of Nine West.

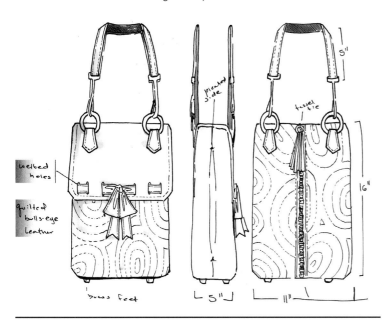

FIGURE 7.23 Hand-drawn bag flats corresponding to a design in Figure 7.12. Ivy Kirk.

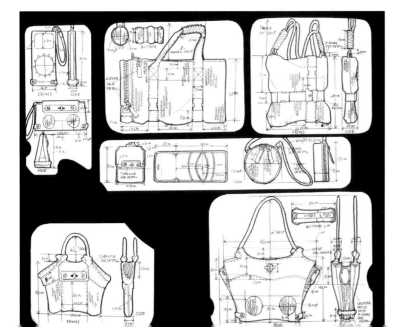

Flat Sketches

In the last stage of the design process, when tech packs are created and sent out for prototyping, sample making, and production, the most effective tool is the black-and-white flat sketch. Accessories are drawn flat by hand or in Illustrator or Photoshop. Usually the outline of the silhouette is created with the thickest line, the inner seams are drawn with a thinner line, and the stitching line is represented with the thinnest dotted line. A flat sketch represents the design idea as clearly as possible, and every single design element should be drawn with great detail. Each style should be drawn in multiple views: a front or three-quarter view plus back, top, and bottom. Side views might be required if there are important details that can't be viewed from any of the other sketches. Most bags, wallets, agendas, checkbook covers, and other small leather goods also require a detailed inside view, with exact placement of pockets, compartments, closures, brand name plates, and decorative stitching. Print patterns can be indicated only partially to give the basic idea. Drawing flats is probably the most painstaking part of sketching, but it is the most important part of the design process. If you master flat sketching as a tool to get your ideas on paper, you are well on your way to be a professional.

The flat sketches in Figures 7.22–7.27 represent various views of handbags with all details needed for a tech pack.

FIGURE 7.24 Hand-drawn flats with technical information and measurements by Clara Yoo. These flats have been arranged in a layout on a blackboard for a student competition presentation. The same sketches were used in making the actual sample, which won her first place in the CFDA design competition in 2008. Clara Yoo.

FIGURE 7.25 Some designers like Sabato Riccio from Italy are extremely good illustrators and create realistic sketches with all design details, which can be used for either presentations or tech packs. Riccio's résumé includes designing accessories for Dolce and Gabbana and Hugo Boss. Sabato Riccio.

FIGURE 7.26 Flats can be drawn in color to show the contrasting fabrics or textures used in a design, as in these three views of a handbag hand-drawn by Melinda Albert for an Italian design company. When drawing different views of an accessory it is a good idea to depict them all in the same size and align the bottom part below the main view, the side and back view next to it (right). This way design details correspond to each other and make it easy to understand how the whole piece functions. Melinda Albert.

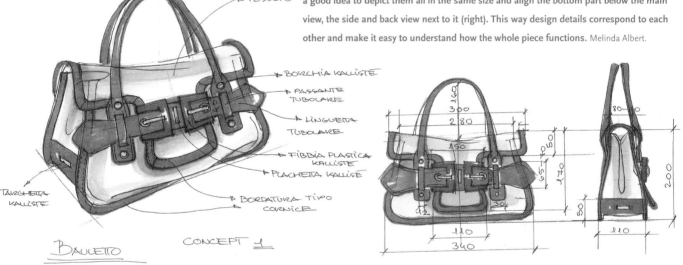

FIGURE 7.27 In these flat sketches Han Josef, men's accessory designer for Cole Haan, provides separate color swatches instead of coloring the bags (left). This technique can be used when the whole bag is one color. Han Josef.

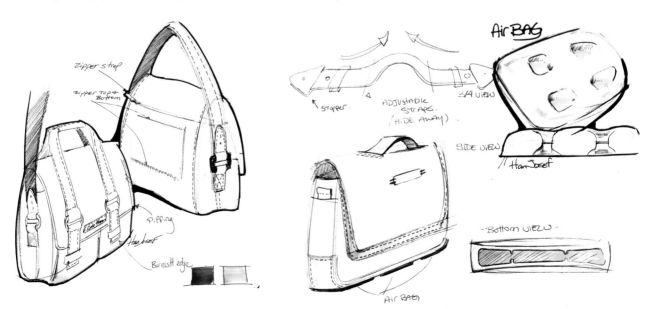

INSIDE SPEC PAGE

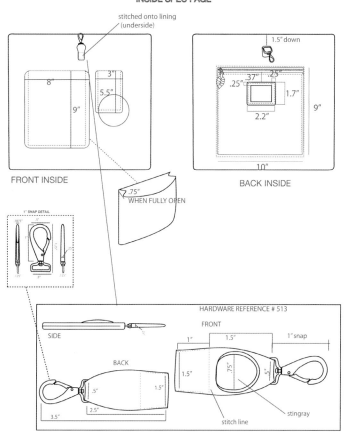

stitched onto lining
(underside)

8"
3"
5.5"
9"

FRONT INSIDE

1.5" down
.37" .25
.25" 1.7"
2.2"
9"
10"

BACK INSIDE

.75"
WHEN FULLY OPEN

1" SNAP DETAIL

HARDWARE REFERENCE # 513

FRONT

SIDE

BACK

1"
1.5"
.75"
.5"
1" snap

1.5"
.5"
1.5"
3.5"
2.5"

stitch line

stingray

DETAIL PAGE

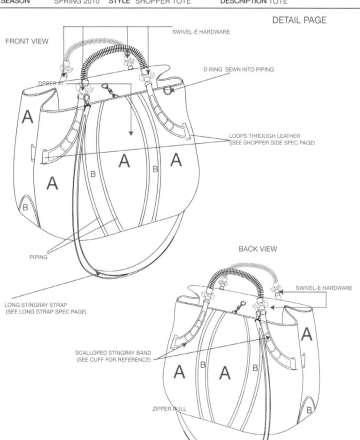

FRONT VIEW

SWIVEL-E HARDWARE

D RING SEWN INTO PIPING

ZIPPER #1

LOOPS THROUGH LEATHER
(SEE SHOPPER SIDE SPEC PAGE)

A A A A B A B

PIPING

BACK VIEW

LONG STINGRAY STRAP
(SEE LONG STRAP SPEC PAGE)

SWIVEL-E HARDWARE

SCALLOPED STINGRAY BAND
(SEE CUFF FOR REFERENCE)

A B A B A B

ZIPPER PULL

In some companies, designs are rendered directly on the computer with programs like Illustrator or Photoshop. Illustrator is usually used for more technical drawings that require vector-based techniques (Figures 7.28 and 7.29), while Photoshop is a bit more flexible in creating a multidimensional sketch through various filters and shading techniques. Illustrator is possibly the fastest and easiest way to create flats and fill them up with color or repeat pattern (Figure 7.30). You can easily create half of the sketch and mirror it onto the other side. Most designers have an existing library of basic silhouettes and can alter them quickly into a brand new design. Photoshop's advantages lie in the various filters and the ease of scanning and manipulating textures as well as drawing with a pen and tablet. You can easily create a more realistic sketch and even create three-dimensional objects. These sketches are usually used to show what the final product will look like without actually making a sample. In both programs, it is fast and easy to add and change colors and add or remove texture. This is the quickest way of altering images. With the help of Photoshop, you can scan a photograph of a real bag or a wallet, for example, and change its texture or color without having to redraw it. Generated or scanned textures can also be used in swatches accompanying a flat (Figure 7.31). Here are some examples of computer-generated sketches (Figures 7.28 through 7.31).

FIGURE 7.28 These flats demonstrate the attention to detail that is necessary for a flat sketch used in a tech pack. Different materials are represented with alphanumeric indication. In this case, A stands for calf leather and B for exotic skin. Khirma Eliazov.

SPEC PAGE

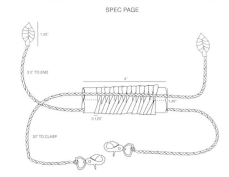

FIGURE 7.29 Flat sketches with a detailed sketch for the handle (top) and a photo of the finished handle (bottom) from the archive of Khirma Eliazov handbags. Khirma Eliazov.

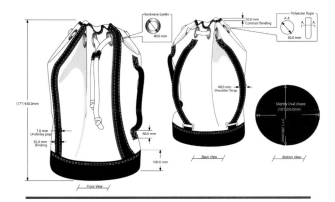

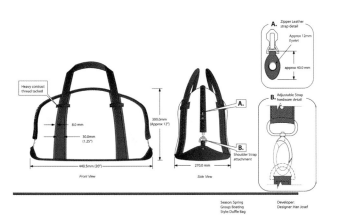

FIGURE 7.31 Designers often use an alphanumeric color coding system to indicate color blocking or pattern or material positions. In these computer-generated flats by Kristina Gress, the color and material swatches are clearly indicated and shown on the same page. Kristina Gress.

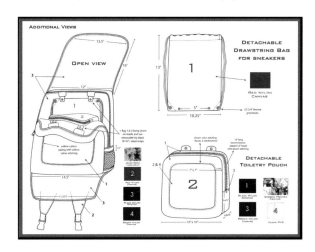

LEATHER LAPTOP CARRYING CASE
COLOR AND MATERIAL DETAILING

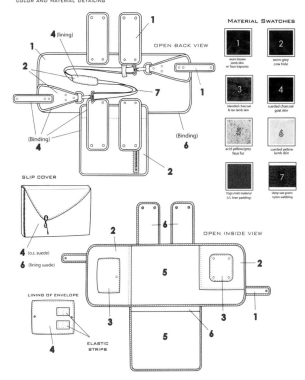

FIGURE 7.30 Computer-rendered flat sketches (left) by Han Josef showing close-ups with measurements of important details that appear small in the sketch. CAD sketches allow great precision and are the preferred method of drawing for hardware like zipper pulls and closures. They are also effective for rendering not just various textures but also their movement. Han Josef.

FIGURE 7.32
A presentation from
the Coach design team
reflecting the array of
products for a given
concept in a season.
Courtesy of Coach.

Presenting the Collection

This is the time and place to create a beautiful presentation that gets the concept ideas across and also speaks to the overall brand identity. At this stage of the design process it is important to know the company design history and the customer details and to create a presentation that is innovative but is also a part of the global vision for the company. Such a presentation needs to fit in the overall look and feel of the brand philosophy as does the Coach presentation in Figure 7.32. It contains everything from concept sketches, illustrations, and inspiration photographs to finished examples of actual product.

Creating such presentations takes a lot of practice and in most cases, when you are starting as an assistant designer, you will be helping to prepare such presentations and gaining the experience to understand what is required for your particular company. The following sections describe what you need in order to create a beautiful presentation. A designer may use all or only some of the following visuals.

Collages

A collage of inspirational images is typically used to represent the concept of the collection and the customer lifestyle. This part of the presentation varies wildly from company to company, but is an important element in making the idea understandable by all. A collage of beautiful images speaks louder than words and can transform your ideas from paper to reality. It makes the product more realistic in terms of use by the consumer. The scale of the presentation depends on many factors, and so the collage can be a single page in a sketchbook, a full wall of mixed media images, a large movable board or a complete room of tears, illustrations, fabric swatches, and actual samples. The more texture or actual objects are added to a collage the better it looks. You should use actual fabrics, yarns, hardware pieces, and even leather to represent your ideas. Layering all the above pieces will create a rich and engaging presentation.

Lifestyle Showroom Presentations

Large companies like Ralph Lauren, Nine West, Coach, and American Eagle are famous for creating enticing visual presentations in different stages of the design process. They include mostly inspiration images, sketches, illustrations, and possible design details like hardware pieces. The design stage might include actual samples and mock-ups, and the final presentation includes the finished prototypes arranged in a showroom with appropriate furniture, art, and design pieces. The Ralph Lauren company regards these presentations so highly that they actually have a special creative team that works on such presentations for all divisions. For each new season the showroom is repainted, new graphics are created, and furniture is brought in to recreate the lifestyle of the customer. Handbags and small leather goods are presented in an atmosphere that represents the concept to the very last minute detail. The benefit of such detailed presentations translates into a greater understanding of the concepts and entices buyers to purchase the product with confidence.

PROJECT

Designing a Collection of Handbags and SLGs

GOALS

To give you practical experience in designing and sketching a unique group of handbags and small leather goods, based on the compiled research.

ASSIGNMENT

Keeping in mind the final concept, season, colors, and, of course, customer profile, design a handbag and small leather goods collection with 10 to 15 pieces. Include various shapes that represent a well-merchandised collection. Sketch all design ideas as a finished presentation in a technique of your choice.

8
_____

TECH PACKS AND MANUFACTURING

for Handbags and Small Leather Goods

_____

CHAPTER EIGHT describes the technical responsibilities of a designer of handbags and small leather goods. After reading this chapter, you will be able to trace the manufacturing process for handbags and small leather goods and understand how to use spec sheets and tech packs to communicate with manufacturing teams.

THE JOB OF AN ACCESSORY DESIGNER starts with being creative and thinking of great ideas that are perfect for his or her customers and continues through a variety of other responsibilities. Researching, sketching, and presenting a collection are just some of the tasks he or she needs to address every day. Before it gets to the store and the hands of a loving owner, each design style needs to be sent out to the factory and produced. Therefore, each designer must be clear on all measurements and design details and be able to complete the appropriate paperwork for each style to instruct the manufacturer. The level to which a designer is involved in creating the tech packs varies from company to company, but technical knowledge itself is a must.

Spec Sheets and Tech Packs

Before each bag can be made, it needs to be carefully drawn, measured, and explained in a technical package. This information is carefully compiled and filled in a single page, called **spec page** or **spec sheet** or a lengthy tech pack. This document explains in great detail what the handbag looks like, how it is made, and what it should be made of. It contains sketches and notes on design and stitching details, colors, materials, hardware, closures, and so on, and it has pictures of references for any of the design components.

A manufacturer or a sample-maker needs to see an exact explanation of how every little detail will be created, what it should look like, and where it should be positioned. It is surprising how every little feature can be interpreted in a completely different way from the original design if it is not explained properly. A handbag tech pack consists of the following:

- A clear sketch of the design
- A list of materials to be used for each component

- Colors for each specific component
- Clear notes on any specific details like topstitching, measurements, logo placement, embellishments, and finishes
- Exact measurements for every single detail
- Close-up pictures or detailed drawings of design details, hardware, and inner structure with pockets and compartments
- Reference pictures of samples being sent to the factory and accompanying notes explaining them

Tech packs are created for every single style to be made, every season, and every year. Each company has its own template for a tech pack that it uses according to its needs and requirements. Figures 8.1 through 8.3 are examples of spec sheets from different designer brands.

Sketching for Tech Packs

As we discuss in Chapter 7, sketches for tech packs are different from illustrations or concept sketches. This particular flat sketch is usually black and white and needs to represent the accessory as realistically as possible and

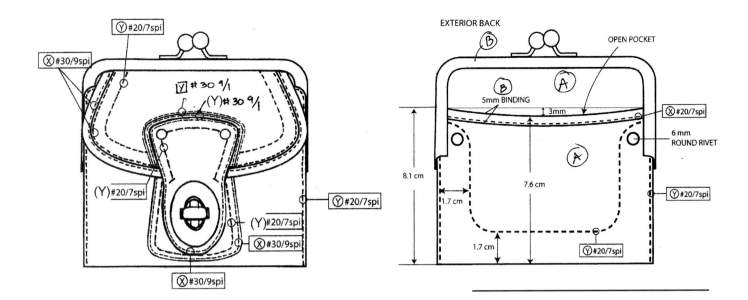

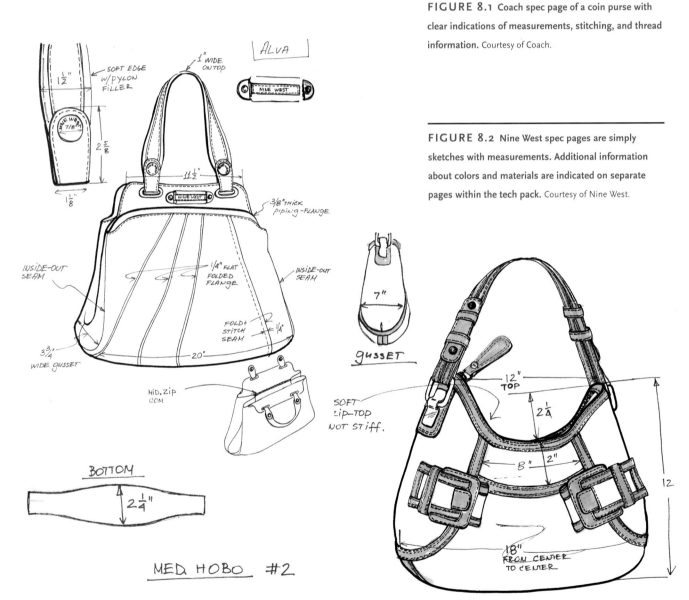

FIGURE 8.1 Coach spec page of a coin purse with clear indications of measurements, stitching, and thread information. Courtesy of Coach.

FIGURE 8.2 Nine West spec pages are simply sketches with measurements. Additional information about colors and materials are indicated on separate pages within the tech pack. Courtesy of Nine West.

LADIES: HOBO

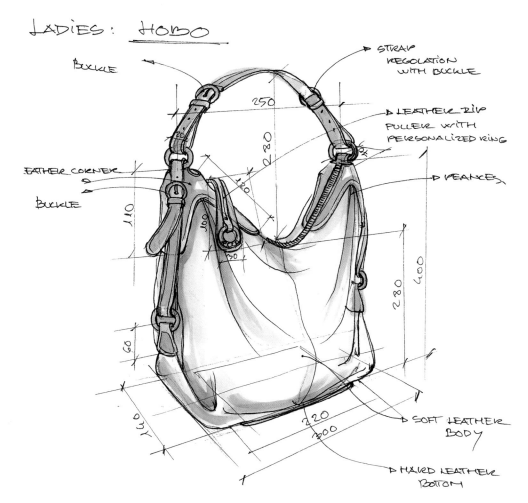

BUCKLE

250

STRAP REGULATION WITH BUCKLE

LEATHER ZIP PULLER WITH PERSONALIZED RING

LEATHER CORNER

BUCKLE

PIANCES

110

280   400

60

280   400

SOFT LEATHER BODY

220
200

HARD LEATHER BOTTOM

MESSENGER

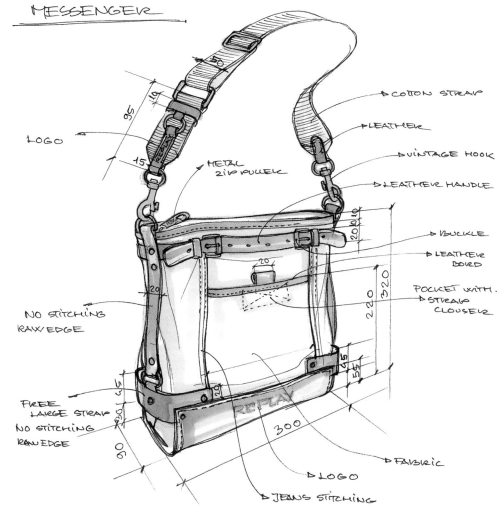

LOGO

50

95   10

15

METAL ZIP PULLER

COTTON STRAP

LEATHER

VINTAGE HOOK

LEATHER HANDLE

BUCKLE

LEATHER BAND

POCKET WITH STRAP CLOSER

320   280

20

NO STITCHING RAW EDGE

20

45
55

FREE LARGE STRAP
NO STITCHING RAW EDGE

30

REPLAY

300

60

FABRIC

LOGO

JEANS STITCHING

FIGURE 8.3

Handbag designer Melinda Albert shades her flats to show volume and neatly organizes all information evenly spaced around the sketch. If both sides are constructed the same way, then a three-quarter view, as in this sketch, is sufficient. Separate sketches would be drawn for all inside views though. All additional information about colors and materials is prepared on a separate page and can be grouped together for the whole collection. Melinda Albert.

needs to include all construction details. Some shading or a different color could be used to indicate a contrast color or texture (Figure 8.2). For handbags and small leather goods, all measurements are noted on the sketch with clear indication for every single detail.

List of Materials

On each tech pack, the designer needs to identify what every component will be made of. If a handle is made from plastic or wood or covered in leather or embellished with a trim, this is where you explain what material you want to use and how it should be used. There are so many different ways a sketch can be interpreted that you cannot leave anything to the imagination. You can add notes with arrows to each section or indicate with alphanumerical indications (Figure 8.4) and make a list of them or a chart on the side. The list should include lining or any other trims used in the design.

Colors

Each designed style is usually produced in more than one color. If there is more than one color within the body, the trims, or handles and hardware, then the spec sheet has a section where color combinations are listed with specific instructions on how they work together. You need to be very precise and clear with the placement and designation of each color, especially if you have multiple color combinations. The sketch itself is usually drawn in black and white with an alphabetical or numerical indication of where different colors go. The initial sample is made in one color or color combination.

FIGURE 8.4 A detailed list of all materials and actual examples or photos of them need to be included in each tech pack for every style. This materials page by Kristina Gress shows a very organized numerical method of indicating materials (above). An example of a hardware and materials page for a tech pack (below). Kristina Gress.

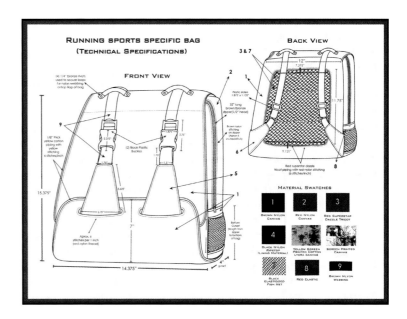

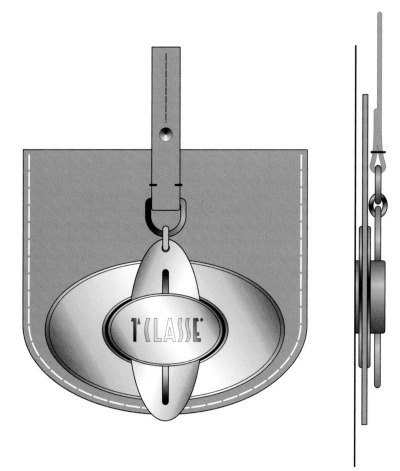

FIGURE 8.5

More precise sketches
of trims or hardware
pieces with exact
proportions are usually
created in Illustrator,
as this example
from Melinda Albert.

Melinda Albert.

Notes and Descriptions

For a designer, it is clear what the finished
accessory should look like but those seeing
the design for the first time need some notes
and descriptions to explain the sketch.
Once you have conceived the idea, it is easy
to forget that other people cannot see it as
clearly as you do and cannot guess every
detail. Manufacturers know a variety of ways
to produce a handbag or any other accessory
and want to know which technique you need
to use and what are the exact measurements
of every single element. This section should
be edited very carefully to have accurate
comments with precise measurements
and short but clear explanations. General
abbreviations can be used if they are accepted
as commonly used between the design team
and the manufacturer. See Figures 8.1, 8.2,
and 8.3 for examples of added notes to each
sketch.

Close-Ups

A close-up of a complicated design or
application element should be provided in
addition to the overall sketch. It can be a
drawing or a photograph showing in greater
details a particular component and how it
works. You can do as many close-ups as you
feel necessary to demonstrate how each detail
should be made or what it should look like.
Close-ups are usually drawn a bit bigger to
allow for more details and can be drawn by
hand or in Illustrator (Figure 8.5).

Mock-Ups

A mock-up shows dimensions and general
shape as well as changes or additions of new
elements without actually making a proto.
It is an excellent way to send a reference
to the sample room, because all printouts
and drawings of details added to the mock-
up are in actual size and are accompanied
with additional notes on any details and
directions (see Chapter 4, the section "Proto
Development," for a description of mock-ups).

Mock-ups are necessary in order to
represent the design idea as realistically as
possible. If you are presenting a style that
was already created in the previous season
but want to change a few small details you
can just add those details onto the existing
body. Adding actual patches, zippers, or other
real elements work just as well as adding a
sketched detail. Sometimes you might sketch
a few different options and overlay them
and present each one of them as options.
The sketches can be plain black and white or
computer aided to match the color, texture,
and design details.

Sample References

It is a common practice in the accessory
industry to use an existing sample as a
reference of how the new one should be made.
A pocket from a vintage sample or a buckle
from luggage can be an excellent resource

MONICA BOTKIER

A born and bred New Yorker, Monica Botkier began her career in the fashion industry in 2003 as a fashion photographer, shooting for fashion magazines and advertising campaigns. For her, handbags were a true love. She always collected leather and used it to cover her portfolios, but when she sketched a handbag design and had it made, editors and models started asking to buy one. Botkier started taking small orders and developing new styles.

A casual dresser herself, Botkier feels that a handbag should be sexy, functional, and edgy and should dress up an outfit. She creates statement bags which are not too heavy, have lots of exterior pockets, and have a long enough handle drop to be carried comfortably. One of the best features of a Botkier bag is a key chain that is really long so the wearer will never lose her keys. With her eye for detail, and a knack for key functionality, Botkier took over a niche in the fashion industry, an approachable designer brand. Inspired by her own urban chic and busy downtown Manhattan lifestyle, she designs high-quality handbags and small leather goods and consistently introduces new materials, intricate details, and custom hardware. The product execution is on the level of a luxury designer brand and the quality is superb, but the price points are lower than Prada and Dior. Botkier goods are made at a Korea-based factory that works with some of the biggest names in the industry and has 30 years of experience. It allows Botkier to create custom hardware and quality workmanship at an affordable price.

Creating about 40 different silhouettes every season, Botkier has established a devoted fan base in the United States and around the world. The handbags are sold at numerous stores throughout the country as well as at botkier.com. Barney's New York, Fred Segal, Harvey Nichols, and Neiman Marcus are just a few of the famous U.S. stores that carry her handbags and wallets.

In July 2007, Monica Botkier was recognized for her contributions to the world of accessory design and became a member of the esteemed Council of Fashion Designers of America. For Spring 2008, in celebration of Botkier's five-year anniversary and all of her accomplishments, the designer launched an extensive collection of footwear made in Italy. Her aim with that collection is also luxury and comfort.

Botkier bags and shoes are now a favorite among fashion icons like Angelina Jolie, Jessica Alba, Rachel Bilson, and Sienna Miller, who love her vantage point of marrying luxury with utility.

Monica Botkier. Courtesy of WWD/ Steve Eichner.

The Botkier bags have signature shapes that are easily recognized by its loyal customers. Pictured here is the limited edition Bianca bag in gold python. Courtesy of WWD.

for the sample maker and the manufacturer. Sometimes it is difficult to explain everything with words, or it is not enough to draw what you need to use. A sample can provide an easy and clear reference. In addition to sending the sample, it is always a good idea to take pictures of multiple angles and views and include those on the tech packs with notes of how those samples should be referenced and which parts should be used.

Manufacturing Process

The manufacturing process for each particular handbag is different but there are some main steps that can be summed up in an overview as follows:

- Design
- Procuring all components: leather, fabrics, trim, hardware
- Pattern drafting for sample development and final production
- Prototyping/sampling
- Correcting samples and finalizing all details
- Creating steel dies for factory production
- Cutting all pieces
- Preparing cut pieces by adding appropriate stabilizers, "stays," or foam padding
- Applying edge paint to finish raw edges and buffing them prior to sewing
- Gluing, applying decorative elements such as embellishments, trims, rivets, snaps, pockets, outer components, logo plates, embossed and debossed elements
- Sewing the main construction of the outer body
- Adding closures
- Sewing lining and inner pocket components
- Closing the bag
- Buffing, cleaning
- Adding tags, additional trims
- Wrapping
- Boxing

Design

Depending on the company, the design process can be done in-house or at the manufacturing facility. We already discussed the design process in depth, but it is important to remember that all design details need to be clearly explained before the handbags go into the manufacturing process. All problems and changes need to be identified, corrected, and finalized in the prototyping stage. Once the handbag style is in production, it is too late to correct any mistakes. By this time, all leather and all other components are in the factory, and deadlines are fast approaching. Any delay can be fatal for the brand.

Procuring All Components

Each handbag requires a variety of components in order to be completed. Special trims or hardware that require development of molds need to be preplanned well in advance so they can arrive on time for sample making and production. The designer normally selects each component and might also be involved in ordering them, unless there is a product manager that works within the design team. Larger companies have a trim department that develops hardware and components with the designers and then orders all necessary pieces for prototyping and production. Even if you are not responsible for the actual orders, it is important to understand what components are needed and how long it takes to develop, so that a realistic timeline can be established. The following components may come from different factories and thus require special arrangements (Figure 8.6).

- Stiffeners
- Custom made hardware
- Frames
- Zippers and other closures
- Trims

Pattern Drafting

Patterns are essential to creating a beautiful product. Pattern drafting relies on exact measurements, and a small mistake can change the final product dramatically. Your job as a designer is to give accurate measurements to the pattern maker (Figure 8.7). Each sketch you create needs to have exact measurements of every single detail that will be made. They can be tweaked after the first sample, but it is essential to start out with realistic and complete measurements.

Samples

The sample stage is the time to try out ideas and make changes. Your design ideas are coming to life, and it is the first time you see them come into reality. You, as a designer, get to evaluate the look and the feel of the finished handbag and how it fits in the overall concept and collection. During this process you have time to present the finished proto in front of the design director or VP of the company and get feedback on the overall direction of the brand. This is the perfect time to evaluate the workmanship; the quality of the leather; and all the little details like stitching, color combinations, and hardware. All of those decisions should be finalized in this stage.

FIRST PROTOTYPE

The first prototype is an important step from a design concept to actual production. This is the only step where you get to try out your ideas and see what works and what doesn't. If you submitted clear sketches and exact measurements on the spec sheet, you will get a good first proto (Figure 8.8). It is important to pick and work with an excellent sample room or a factory. It makes all the

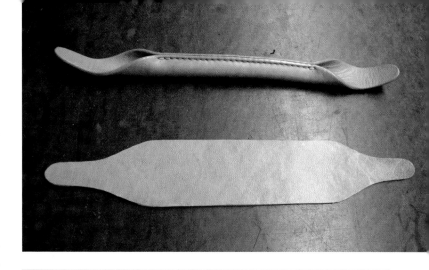

FIGURE 8.6 Handles can be created from the same material as the main body or they can be ordered from a different manufacturer. Courtesy of Aneta Genova.

FIGURE 8.7 Paper patterns are created by hand for each style on oak tag paper. They can be used as is for manual cutting of the pieces for the first sample. Later on, when all corrections have been made, they are used for creating the steel dies. Courtesy of Aneta Genova.

FIGURE 8.8 Handbag prototype from a design by Maria Pia Capitano for the Italian brand Fratelli Rosetti. Maria Pia Capitano for Fratelli Rosetti.

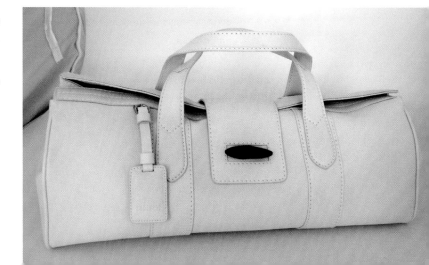

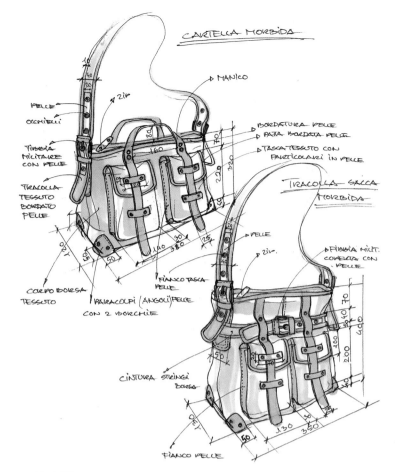

stitches, decorative elements, maybe even have two different shapes of pockets made on the sample proto. The first proto can be made just to test the overall idea if it is something brand new, or it can be made from the actual material if the idea has already been tested.

Once you receive the completed piece your responsibility is to examine all aspects of the finished design, take detailed notes on any corrections and communicate them to the sample room or manufacturer. At this point you might have to draw directly on the finished proto in order to correct placement or show any changes. Here are some techniques with which you can show changes without drawing directly on the proto:

- Use masking tape to cover the area that needs corrections and then draw on the tape.
- Draw any design detail on a separate piece of paper and then attach that to the appropriate spot.

If you developed alternate design details like pockets or trim, you can interchange them and see which one works better with the finished shape. Keep in mind that you need to look at all details inside and out and inspect every single thing: lining, trims, functionality of closures, hardware finishes, stitch quality, print if there is one, overall shape, and anything else that looks wrong or disproportioned. Once the corrections are submitted, the next step of the process is getting a correct second proto, which can be used for sales meetings and presentations.

SECOND PROTOTYPE

The second proto is the result of all the corrections from the first one. It should be as close as possible to the final product in shape, size, material, hardware, and design elements. It can be used in a showroom for sales meetings if it is approved and as perfect as a production sample.

FIGURE 8.9

Spec sheet (top) and a top of production sample (bottom) for an O.X.S. bag by Melinda Albert.

Melinda Albert.

difference between an excellent sample that is even better than your design and a disaster. An experienced sample maker would tell you if you are missing any measurements or details and will not interpret anything without consulting you. He or she will ask questions and follow directions well to achieve maximum quality. In this stage, you can try out a couple of different techniques,

TOP SAMPLE

Each company works in a different way, but in general, if you had the prototypes made in a sample room and the actual production is in a different factory, you would require your factory to create a sample for you (Figure 8.9). If you are not changing factories but salespeople required some minor changes to the second proto you showed them, you would require a new sample to be made. That would allow you to make sure the factory is executing the changes correctly and you would see whether the new changes actually work well and look good. The top sample should be as good as the production goods. It is a perfectly finished and executed piece that serves as the best example possible. This step can be omitted altogether if there is no need for it.

Creating Steel Dies for Factory Production

After all pattern pieces are finalized, each one of them—no matter how small or large—gets a steel die made for it (Figure 8.10). This allows the use of large press and automated cutting. Steel dies are costly and can easily add to the overall bill but are necessary for large production runs and repeat styles. They repeatedly produce an even, smooth edge for every single cut pattern piece and can be used indefinitely or until they are damaged.

Cutting Pattern Pieces

Simple pattern pieces can be cut by hand (Figure 8.11), but most manufacturers use the created dies or an automatic computerized cutting system. Each piece needs to be cut precisely to the shape of the specs of the pattern, avoiding any blemishes or defects of the leather. If the pattern piece is being cut from fabric, then it is important to place the grain or print correctly so it complements the final design.

FIGURE 8.10
Every single pattern piece gets a steel die made for it. Even though they are costly and bulky, they are integral to styles that are made over and over again and ensure a perfectly cut pattern every time. Courtesy of Aneta Genova.

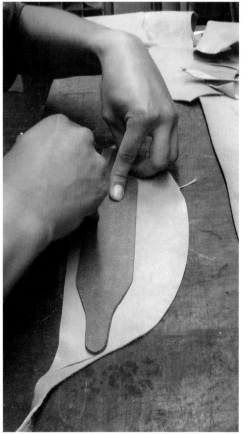

FIGURE 8.11
Skillful worker cuts a pattern by hand. Some simpler pieces or patterns for the first sample can be cut by hand to save on the cost of dies before all changes are made and the design is finalized. Courtesy of Aneta Genova.

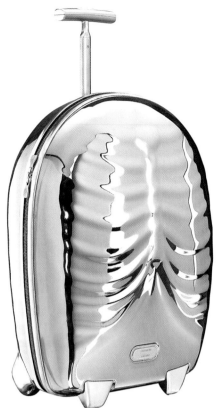

FIGURE 8.12

Luggage from the
Samsonite Black Label
by Alexander McQueen,
utilizing a molded body.
Courtesy of WWD.

FIGURE 8.13 Accessories like this one
need a layer of padding under the surface material.
Courtesy of WWD.

Preparing Cut Pieces

When developing the idea, the designer needs
to determine and explain the overall feel of the
shape. If it is a slouchy soft bag, it might not need
any additional support except for a lining. If it is
a structured bag, it might need some stabilizers
or stiffeners applied in order to hold the desired
shape. Some hard shapes as in Figure 8.12 might
require a cardboard or molded plastic inner
support in order to create and hold the overall
structure. Some quilted bags (Figure 8.13) or
wallets might need a layer of foam or other filling
to create a soft, padded feel. It is important for a
designer to explain what is desired for the final
accessory or try out a variety of solutions within
the sampling. Once all materials are chosen
and ordered, any further changes will delay the
manufacturing process.

Buffing Edges and Applying Edge Paint

Edges need to be buffed before being painted.
That smoothes away any inconsistencies after
sewing the layers of leather together and helps
an even distribution of the edge paint afterward
(Figure 8.14). Each exposed edge of the handbag

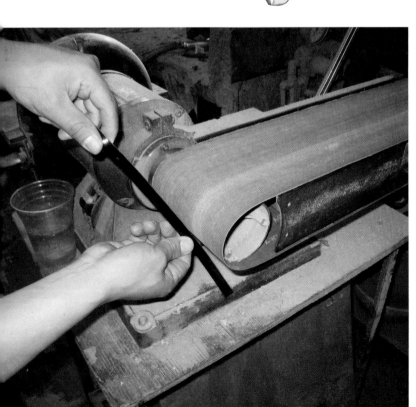

FIGURE 8.14 Edges of a strap are buffed to achieve a smooth finish before
they are painted. Courtesy of Aneta Genova.

could be painted with flexible paint in matching or contrasting color to give it a nice finish. Paint can be applied in multiple layers by hand with a single brush (Figure 8.15) or by machine with a rotating applicator.

Adding Trims and Logos

Each company has a developed logo and uses it on the product in various ways. Accessories, especially handbags, can carry a lot of hardware and trims, and they are a great way to present the logo in a stylish way. Hardware can be developed in various shapes to represent the brand and the current concept. The logo can be displayed externally or hidden inside the item (Figure 8.16). Embossing (raising the image higher than the rest of the surface) or debossing (lowering it below the surface) the logo directly on the leather is an elegant way to introduce the logo (Figure 8.17).

Applying Trims and Closures

Planning the stages of applying all elements depends on the design itself. Once all pattern pieces are cut and the edges are painted it is time to look at all pockets, pocket flaps, trims, and closures. Most external elements should be added before the overall body is sewn together. Once the overall shape is put together it might be impossible to have good access to all parts of the accessory in order to apply all other elements. Magnetic closures and snaps might also require additional support to the part where they will be applied. A bit of additional interfacing can help avoid wear and tear and increase the longevity of the accessory. Elements like rivets and grommets can be applied after the overall piece is

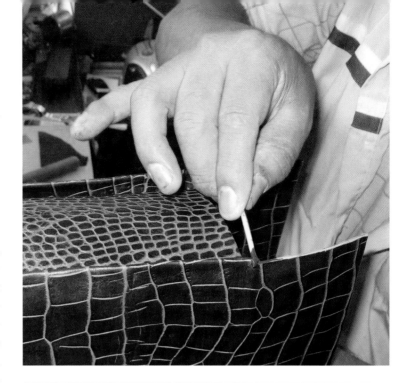

FIGURE 8.15 Edge painting can be done by hand or with a machine. Either way, it requires great precision so the rest of the accessory does not get damaged by the paint. Courtesy of Aneta Genova.

FIGURE 8.16 Embossing the inside of a wallet presents the logo and brings awareness to the brand but does not create bulk in a wallet that needs to be as flat and functional as possible. Courtesy of WWD.

FIGURE 8.17 Metal plates with the designer's logo can be used with a metallic tape, gold pictured here, to create a lasting contrasting effect. The metallic tape when pressed with the logo plate leaves a metallic debossed impression of the logo. Courtesy of Aneta Genova.

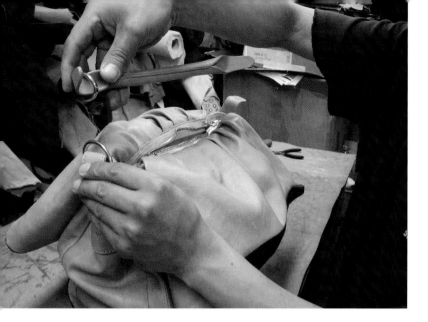

FIGURE 8.18 Some trims, closures, or handles can be added toward the end of the sewing process. In this case, a handle is added (left) and the zipper is top-stitched (right) after the body is sewn together. Courtesy of Aneta Genova.

FIGURE 8.19 A handbag being sewn on a post bed leather machine. Courtesy of Aneta Genova.

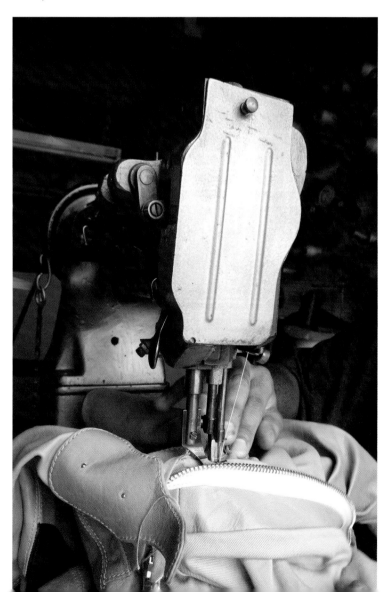

finished, but it is important to consider every element first and have a plan for every step of the process (Figure 8.18).

Sewing the Main Body and Adding Lining

Sewing together all the pieces and constructing the overall body depends on how complicated the design is. Here are some of the sewing machines involved in the process (Figure 8.19). They are made specifically to handle multiple layers of leather and heavyweight fabric:

- A flat bed industrial machine is used for all basic sewing and joining pieces within a flat construction or large openings.
- A post bed, or cylinder bed machine, is used for more difficult construction where the needle needs to get into small openings or narrow slits. Each one of the last two machines has a much smaller bed that allows the needle to reach deep into the cavity of the accessory and complete difficult seams.

Before the lining is added, some edges and seams might have to be pushed outward to their final shape and softly hammered. Leather can be stretched a bit to allow for even distribution and some of the seam allowance can be cut out or sliced to fit better around corners. Lining is usually sewn separately and inserted inside the accessory after the outer body is created and all trims are applied. All inner pockets and compartments are added before it is dropped inside the outer body. There are various ways of attaching the lining, and finding the right one for each particular design is an important part of the design process. It can be sewn to the top edge of the bag or connected to the zipper tape on the inside. Each designer needs to consider what is the best possible way to do that with respect to the overall design. In some cases the lining is an integral part of the design as a decorative element. Various wallets, for example, open to uncover a whimsical or luxurious lining, which only adds to the quality of the accessory.

Finishing Operations

The last steps of the process involve checking all functioning closures, pocket flaps, drawstrings, and zippers; removing any dirt, scratches, and marks; conditioning the leather; buffing; brushing; and polishing. After those steps, all labels and tags are added, and the accessory gets packaged for shipping to the stores.

Communicating with Factories

Designers and assistants might be required to communicate with the factories on a daily basis. At each stage of the process, from creating a first prototype to actual production, many questions arise, and designers need to be available and ready to answer them. Be prepared to work on a few different seasons at the same time. Usually there are multiple collections from different seasons and at different stages that you need to be aware of. It is extremely important to employ your best organizational efforts and keep your records in excellent order. You should have labeled binders with sketches and paperwork for each style that is in the making. Keep detailed notes of each meeting, and file them in the proper binder under the right style.

Factories and designers communicate through e-mail and phone on a daily basis. Working with overseas teams spread from the Far East to Europe makes it a bit harder to follow up with the answers on time. While you might be just getting to work, your factory contacts might already be facing the end of the day and could have pressing issues that need your immediate attention. If you are well organized, you will be able to find your references quickly and resolve problems immediately. If you have to look through a pile of paperwork and have somebody on the phone from around the globe waiting for you, it might be wise to rethink your efficiency and work on your organization skills. You need to have a system in place and file all sketches and paperwork as soon as you are finished with them. Never pile up work to be filed later.

A Visual Review of the Creation of a Handbag

All pattern pieces are cut out and ready for assembly.

For a simple open construction, the accessory can be sewn on a flat bed machine.

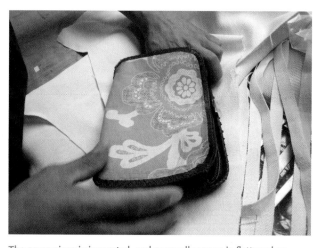

The sewn piece is inspected, and seam allowance is flattened or hammered. The colorful canvas fabric on the outside serves as an interfacing and stabilizer.

The soft inner part of the clutch is completely finished and it includes all inner pockets. This lining has one compartment and one side pocket.

A plastic molded shape is used for the overall frame of the bag. It consists of two identical parts hinged at the bottom with a decorative closure on top.

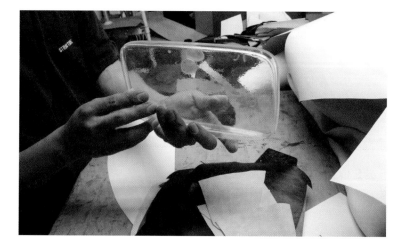

FIGURE 8.20 A series of photos following the making of a clutch with a hard plastic case as a base, beginning with the cut pattern pieces and concluding with the finished sample. Courtesy of Aneta Genova.

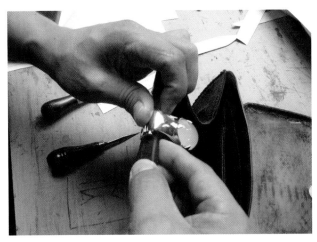

Exotic skin is glued onto the outside part of the molded plastic, and the inside is covered with a strong adhesive in preparation for attaching the lining. Notice that the top closure is already attached by clamping an inner and an outer piece through the shell. On the outside, you see the decorative piece while the magnet on the inside will be hidden in between the lining and the shell.

The closure is given one more test run before final gluing of the lining.

The leather lining is carefully glued onto the inside of the plastic mold to perfectly fit the shape.

The finished clutch has a sturdy shape covered in python skin with soft lambskin lining and an internal pocket. A semiprecious stone is added as a decoration to the closure to make the bag more valuable.

PROJECT

Creating Technical Flats

GOALS

To give you practical experience in creating flat sketches and tech packs.

ASSIGNMENT

Draw a black-and-white flat sketch for every single design you created in the project for Chapter 7. Draw multiple views for complicated handbags and close-ups where necessary. Add measurements and notes for all materials, colors, shapes, hardware, and design details.

DESIGNING

Footwear

Part Three

9

COMPONENTS
AND STYLES
of Footwear

CHAPTER NINE describes the different components of footwear. After reading this chapter, you will be able to identify the essential parts of a shoe as well as different types of shoe and heel styles for men and women.

THE FOOTWEAR INDUSTRY is like no other and requires full dedication and years of studying. Most people do not realize and will never see how many different components have to be put together to create one shoe. From picking the material for the upper to fitting together all the components like outsoles, heels, insoles, fillers, stiffeners, shanks, and so on, all coming from different sources, it seems impossible to create a shoe or boot on time and for the price that the market demands. And yet new collections, offering new variations of the basic footwear styles, appear every season, and they become highly prized possessions of happy customers. No wonder people in the footwear industry say that you need to be a bit crazy to torture yourself through the process every time. And yet, professionals in the industry seem to have so much love for the final product that they consider it worth all the "trouble."

Footwear Components

The most basic structure of a shoe is an upper and a sole, but that would be a very simple shoe. Depending on the type of shoe, there are numerous other components. The reality is that there are so many components that for each one of them, there is a separate producer that designs, manufactures, and delivers them to the appropriate shoemaker. The process for each one can be as simple or as complicated as the design requires. In this section, you will become familiar with some of the most common and widely used components for men's and women's shoes. Naturally, there is a difference in the components used for dressy shoes as distinguished from performance shoes, as well as high-heeled shoes.

The most common components of a shoe are as follows:

- **Upper** Everything on the shoe above the sole—vamp, quarter, back, toe box, tongue, laces, lining. Depending on the style of the shoe, the upper can be cut from a single piece, or can be constructed from many pieces.
- **Vamp** Part of the upper, the vamp covers the top part of the foot between the toes and the ankle area or the instep.
- **Quarter** Part of a shoe's upper, which covers the sides and the back of the foot. It could be a separate piece sewn onto the vamp of a shoe.
- **Tongue** Part of the upper, the tongue extends under the laces or other closures to protect the foot.
- **Front and back stiffeners (counters)** Thin nonwoven shaped pieces attached in-between the upper and the lining at the heel or toe area to add some stiffness and structure.
- **Toe puff (cap)** A shaped, thick, nonwoven or metal reinforcement, added to the inside of the upper to provide stability, protection, and stiffness for the toe area.

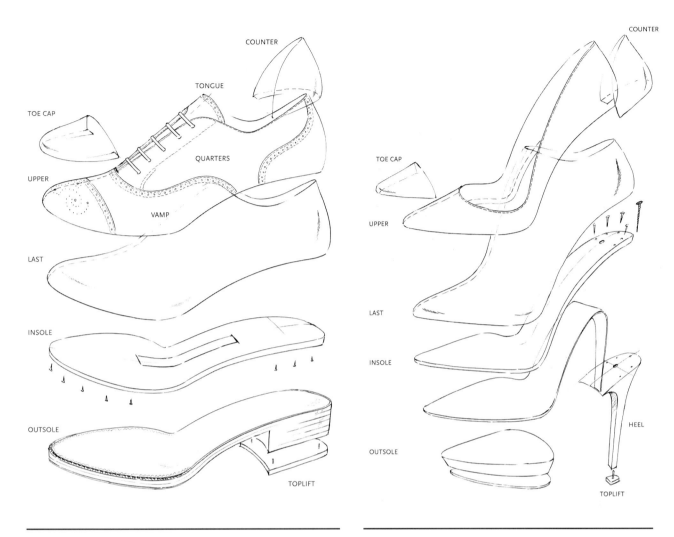

FIGURE 9.1 The basic shoe components for a men's dressy shoe with cemented construction. Danilo Giordano.

FIGURE 9.2 The basic shoe components for a women's high heel shoe. The outsole of this shoe also has a platform component. Danilo Giordano.

- **Insole** The insole is the inside part of the shoe, positioned above the outsole on the inside of the shoe.
- **Sock** A lining of sorts inserted in the finished shoe.
- **Shank** A metal piece positioned in between the heel and the outsole, sitting under the arch of the foot. The shank supports the whole foot and helps the overall structure.

- **Outsole** The outsole is the bottommost outer part of the shoe, which is in direct contact with the ground.
- **Heel** The outer part of the shoe that is placed under the heel of the foot. Shoe heels come in varying heights, shapes, and materials.

Figure 9.1 shows the components of a men's dressy shoe. Components of a dress shoe for women are shown in Figure 9.2.

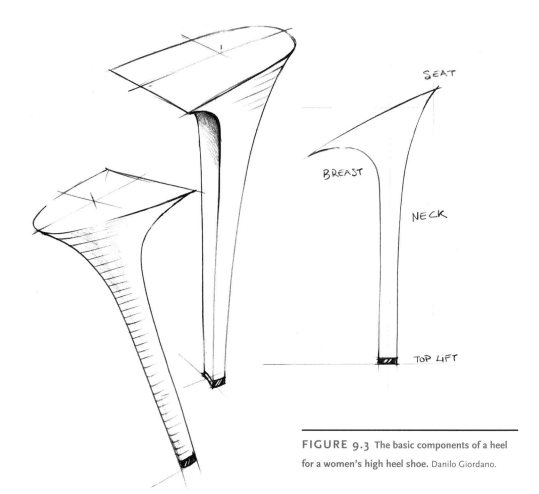

Heels

A **heel** is the support piece attached to the outsole of a shoe under the back part of the foot (Figure 9.3). The heel consists of the following parts:

- **Seat** The part directly under the foot.
- **Breast** The front part under the sole.
- **Neck** The back part of the heel.
- **Top lift** The bottom of the heel, touching the ground.

Heels can be made from stacked leather, blocks of wood, or man-made materials like plastic or metal. They can be created as part of the sole or attached (nailed) to the outsole of the shoe (Figure 9.4). Here are the basic types of heels:

- **Stiletto heel** Named after the stiletto dagger, this heel is thin and high.
- **French heel** (Louis heel, curved heel, pompadour heel) During the seventeenth century, King Louis XIV of France, who was only 5 feet 3 inches tall, had shoes with high heels specially made to increase his height. The trend caught on. In the 1800s, American women began copying Parisian fashion, including the high-heeled footwear known as French or Louis heels. Today, this curved, medium-high heel is used on women's footwear.
- **Kitten heel** A thin-based, low heel (usually 1.5 inches or less) is set in from the back of the shoe and has a little curve. More than just being a low heel, what makes a kitten heel is its placement and feminine shape. It starts as almost the full width of the foot and tapers toward the bottom into a very thin base cap. Audrey Hepburn popularized this heel in the 1950s.

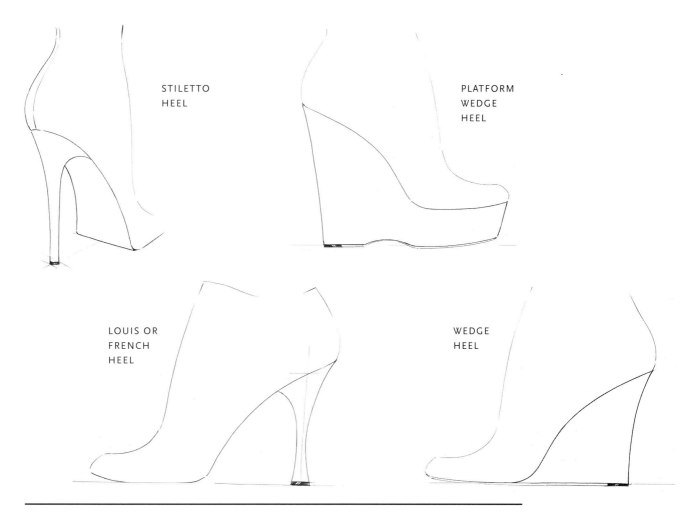

STILETTO
HEEL

PLATFORM
WEDGE
HEEL

LOUIS OR
FRENCH
HEEL

WEDGE
HEEL

FIGURE 9.4 Some common examples of heels for women's shoes. The modern version of the French heel shown here has a very slight curve compared to the original eighteenth-century French heel, which had a more exaggerated concave curve with a skinny middle part and a wider top lift. Danilo Giordano.

- **Wedge heel** A wedge heel is formed by a roughly triangular or wedgelike piece that extends from the front or middle to the back of the sole; it is used on women's shoes. On most shoes, the heel sits under only the heel of the foot, but a wedge heel runs under the foot, from the back of the shoe to the middle or front. It has a somewhat triangular, wedge shape, but not all wedges are high heels. In fact, wedge heels range from low to high; it's the shape and the length of the heel that classify it as a wedge. Many people confuse platforms and wedges. While shoes with wedge heels may have platform soles, the two features do not always appear together. When they do, they're considered platform wedges.

- **Platform wedge heel** A combination of the platform and the wedge heel creates an even higher heel. It allows the whole foot to be lifted an additional inch or two, and the actual height of the arch might not be as pronounced as in a traditional heel.

- **Cuban heel** The slightly tapered back and straight front of the Cuban heel can be seen most often on cowboy boots for both men and women.

Footwear Styles

Footwear has evolved over the centuries and nowadays, there are hundreds of styles and variations on styles, heels, and constructions.

In general, there are fewer men's shoe styles than women's. There haven't been many changes in men's dressy shoes since the beginning of the twentieth century. They are much more consistent in the variety of styles offered, and one can see the same design details with the same heel year after year with an accent on quality and workmanship rather than new ideas.

Women's shoes, on the other hand, are driven purely by trends and color. There are hundreds of styles in different heels, colors, and materials offered every year.

Here are the basic and most recognizable men's footwear styles.

Men's Shoes

The basic styles for men's shoes are shown in Figure 9.5.

- **Oxford** The oxford style is a low-cut, closed, leather shoe with lacing. The quarters with the lacing are placed under the vamp and topstitched on the vamp. The design of the shoe can be plain or brogued. The oxford originates from Ireland and Scotland, and the term varies from Britain to the United States. While in Britain a Balmoral is a particular type of oxford, in the United States, the term oxford is the general name used for both plain and brogued shoes. These shoes are mostly made of black or brown leather and are considered formal. Normally they have a plain front, but they can be decorated with cap-toes.
- **Derby** The derby style is a low-cut, closed, leather shoe with lacing. The tongue is part of the vamp, and the quarters are topstitched on top of the vamp. They are usually kept apart at the tongue.
- **Wing tip** The name for this style comes from the shape of the toe-cap. It resembles the spread-out wings of a bird or a W. This toe-cap design is usually applied to coarse leather, low-cut, low-heeled, closed, leather shoes with laces or loafers. It may feature a perforated pattern.

- **Brogue** Often called wing tips, brogues are low-heeled shoes, usually made from coarse leather with a punched design. **Broguing** is the hole-punching process, used to create decorative patterns, emphasizing the design and seams of the shoe, but modern designers experiment with varied hole sizes and sometimes a scattered arrangement for a more distinctive design. The brogue is believed to have originated in Ireland in 1791, worn by lower classes and also seen worn by Scottish Highlanders, who needed a shoe with good drainage for wearing in bogs. The original brogues, casual outdoor shoes for Scottish and Irish men are far from the modern dressy brogues of today. Nevertheless the term *brogues* is used largely for dressy or casual shoes that have a punched design and are usually wing tips.
- **Moccasin** A classic moccasin is a soft leather shoe constructed of two pieces of hide: a bottom piece which comes around and up the sides, stitched to a vamp (top part), which also serves as a tongue. They are usually adorned with leather fringe, embroidery, and/or beads. Moccasins originated from Native Americans and allowed the wearer to feel the ground while walking perfectly quietly.
- **Loafer** Loafers are low-cut, lace-less, slip-on shoes with very low heels. They are descendants of the moccasins, with an applied synthetic sole. Some of the most recognizable styles are the penny loafer, which has a slotted strap on the top front part of the vamp, and the tasseled loafer, which has tassels on the instep. Another popular and easily recognized style is the Gucci loafer, adorned with the signature metal horse-bits. A loafer with moccasin details has the distinctive gathered and hand-stitched upper look with or without laces.

OXFORD

DERBY SHOE

WING TIP

DRESSY LOAFER

BOAT SHOE

SANDAL

ESPADRILLE

FIGURE 9.5 Basic styles of men's shoes.

Danilo Giordano.

- **Boat shoe** Boat shoes, also known as *deck shoes* or *top-siders*, are made of leather and usually have a white rubber sole with a specific **siping pattern** (thin slits across the surface), which is specifically designed to provide traction on the wet deck of a boat. They usually have a moccasin construction and a decorative cord, running through the top of the upper.
- **Sandal** Sandals are open-toe and -heel shoes that usually have openings on the sides, too. The upper usually consists of multiple straps, which are attached to the sole and buckle around the ankle. Sandals vary greatly in design.
- **Espadrille** Espadrilles are slip-on shoes with a canvas upper and a woven sole, usually from rope or grass. They might have rubber reinforcements or a full rubber sole to prolong their life by improving resistance to wear and tear.

Men's Boots

Men's boots can be categorized by how high they extend on the leg. From lowest to highest, styles include ankle boots, low boots, and knee boots. Figure 9.6 show some examples.

MEN'S ANKLE BOOTS

The lowest men's boots end just above the ankle and are meant to protect it. The most common styles are as follows:

- **Chelsea boot** Chelsea boots have a low heel and are fitted right around the ankle. They have a plain leather upper and elasticized insets on both sides. Chelsea boots became very popular during the 1960s as a part of the Mod scene and have remained a classic style. A variation of the Chelsea boots, *Beatle boot* were very tight fitting with Cuban heels and pointy toes and zippers on the side. They were worn and popularized by the Beatles but are not so commonly worn anymore.
- **Derby boot** This boot has the construction of the Derby shoe but extends right above the ankle.

MEN'S LOW BOOTS

Men's low boots can be any style as long as they are higher than the ankle boot but lower than the knee. When making these boots, it's necessary to make a different last from the same style shoe because the foot travels a long distance through the shaft to get all the way in.

- **Cowboy boot** Cowboy boots have a pointy toe, extend to mid-calf, and have a Cuban heel. Traditionally, they are made of durable calfskin but can also be constructed from pigskin, horse, or kangaroo. They feature extensive decorative stitching and/or tooling. Originally intended to be functional footwear for cowboys and ranchers, this style has been reinterpreted by many fashion houses and today can be a fashion statement worn around the globe.

KNEE BOOTS

As the name suggests, knee boots come right up to the knees. They can be a variety of styles with a wide shaft or fitted with a zipper on the side or back. Almost any style shoe can have an extended shaft to become a knee boot.

- **Riding boot** Riding boots or equestrian boots, as the name suggests, are made to be worn while horseback riding. They are made of stiff calfskin or cowhide leather in brown or black and have a low heel to prevent the foot from slipping from the stirrup. They end right below the knee and are generally plain looking without decorative elements. The traditional hunt riding boots are black with a tan cuff at the top.
- **Wellington boot** These boots, nicknamed *Wellies*, have a very plain straight cut. Named after the Duke of Wellington, they were first worn by the military during the eighteenth century as Hessian boots. They became fashionable among the British aristocracy during the nineteenth century as a soft calfskin boot (see Chapter 1). They are still very popular as a rain or snow boot for both men and women and are usually made of PVC.

FIGURE 9.6

Styles of men's boots.

Danilo Giordano.

CHELSEA
BOOT

DERBY
BOOT

COWBOY BOOT

RIDING BOOT

WELLINGTON BOOT

Brian Atwood's signature style as a shoe designer is devoted to making women look elegant, lean, and fabulously sexy. He creates expertly constructed, irresistibly extravagant women's shoes, using only the finest luxury materials. He loves the instant transformation of a woman as she slips her feet into a pair of his shoes. He calls it "The Cinderella Factor." His shoes might not be magic, but Brian Atwood shoes have become a hit with fashion editors and top boutiques around the world.

Atwood's love for fashion and accessories was cultivated at an early age, while admiring his mother's impeccable wardrobe. He grew up with the desire to be creative and went on to study art and architecture at Southern Illinois University and fashion design at the Fashion Institute of Technology in New York City. His first foray into the fashion industry was as a model on the catwalks of Europe, but he continued to perfect his design skills and look for ways to enter the creative side of the industry. His efforts were rewarded in 1996, when he became the first American to be hired as a designer by Gianni Versace in Milan. He started working on the company's Versus line,

Brian Atwood. Courtesy of WWD/ Stefanie Keenan.

where he excelled in the accessory areas and was soon promoted to chief designer of women's accessories. This opportunity allowed him to master the intricacies of high-quality Italian shoe production, and he succeeded in creating a strong brand identity for the Versus accessories.

Looking to fulfill his love for shoes on his own product, Atwood took the plunge in 2001 and created his own label dedicated to gorgeous shoes made by the best manufacturers in Italy. He started using the most luxurious skins, jewels, and trims to create brazenly sexy shoes and developed a cultlike following from devoted starlets and fans around the world. The designer's talent was recognized in 2003 by the CFDA, who awarded him the Swarovski's Perry Ellis Award for Accessory Design.

In 2007, Brian Atwood was hired as a creative director and designated to revamp and revitalize Bally, the Swiss brand. The relationship ended in April 2008, when Bally was sold to Labelux Group, and the brand aimed to be more focused on its Swiss heritage, but his career has advanced through various collaborations. One of them featured a $2,915 over-the-knee platform boot with chain detail, designed with celebrity stylist Rachel Zoe. A larger partnership with Jones Apparel Group allowed him to

create, produce, market, and distribute B Brian Atwood, a new shoes and accessory line that is the contemporary counterpart to his high-end, luxury shoe business. The initial launch will commence in fall 2011, followed by the launches of B Brian Atwood handbags and jewelry in 2012. Launching a secondary line allowed him to adapt his design aesthetic and high-quality, sexy, modern footwear for a larger audience.

Currently, the globe-trotting designer splits his time between his design studio in Milan and his New York residence. He takes full advantage of working in Europe, where shoe design is considered an art, and creates his own fantasy with every new collection. He loves to "make someone dance a little longer, laugh a little harder, and of course look better." In a video interview on his own website, www.BrianAtwood.com, he reveals what inspires him and how he works:

> I design for the woman who loves to have fun with it, and I think that's what really makes me love what I do. I can just design and there are no barriers. When I start designing for any collection, I usually have a certain woman in mind. It could be a supermodel of the eighties like Gia or Lauren Hutton, and that being in my head starts the process for a sexy, feminine, and glamorous collection. I've also started designing handbags, just to complement the shoes, and they are just as luxurious and sexy. I work with silk velvet, handmade in Venice on an eighteenth-century wooden loom. Something like that for me is real luxury! I always love the hidden details; I don't always like it in your face! It's all about touching the fabric, touching the shoes, touch and the sensation while you are wearing them, and even the whistles you get while you are wearing my shoes. That's what I love.

Brian Atwood's sexy high heel shoes involve intricate work and some of the best quality materials. Courtesy of WWD/Geoerge Chinsee & Thomas Iannaccone.

Women's Shoes

Women's styles vary wildly and can have any height of heel. Here are the most popular styles (Figure 9.7):

- **Pump** The pump is the simplest shoe, but it is actually incredibly difficult to make. The upper hugs the foot and forms one line, and there are no straps or laces to help keep the shape. A pump usually has a wide open top that sometimes goes quite close to the toes, and it needs to maintain that shape through daily wear. The shape of the edge needs to be elegant and beautiful with the help of the inner support only.
- **D'Orsay pump** A d'Orsay style pump is a high heel shoe with the sides of the vamp cut out, revealing the arch of the foot.
- **Ballerina flat** Ballerina flats are inspired by ballet slippers. They have a flat sole with no heel or very low flat heel, closed toe, and a slipper-style construction. They are usually very low cut and show most of the top of the foot. They can go as low as showing the toes.
- **Mary Jane** A traditional Mary Jane shoe has a short, rounded toe box, and very flat heel. They are low cut and look like the shoes little girls wear, but a more elegant women's shoe might be at any heel height. The defining detail is the strap that crosses the middle top of the foot. Nowadays any height of shoe can have Mary Jane styling.

FIGURE 9.7 Styles of women's shoes and features that can be combined in a variety of ways. For example, a Mary Jane can have a flat sole or a high heel, a sling-back can have a flat sole, low heel, or high heel, a sandal can have any heel, and an espadrille can have a flat sole or a wedge heel, but any version has the woven rope sole. Danilo Giordano.

PUMP

D'ORSAY

BALLERINA FLAT

HIGH HEEL
MARY JANE

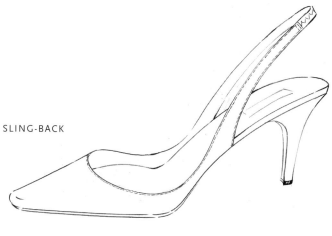

SLING-BACK

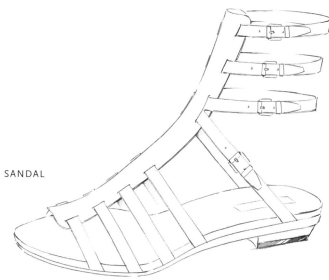

SANDAL

PEEP-TOE

- **Sling-back shoe** A sling-back shoe has a strap that wraps around the back part of the foot. It can have an open or closed toe and can be casual or dressy. The back strap can come from the sides of the vamp or could be tucked in between the insole and sole.
- **Ankle strap** An ankle strap shoe has a strap that wraps around the ankle. It could be a sandal or a pump and the straps could be tied or closed with buckles. As long as they wrap around the ankles they are called ankle straps.
- **T-bar shoe** The distinguishing characteristic is a T-strap at the front, connecting the upper to the ankle. T-bar shoes can be flat or have a high heel.
- **Sandal** A woman's sandal, like a man's, consists of a sole and multiple straps in various designs, which fasten around the foot. It can be a flat or a high heel. Roman sandals have been a popular style throughout the years. These lace-up sandals have multiple straps that cover at least the ankle; they usually go as high as the calf. They are named after the sandals worn in Rome, but similar designs were worn even in ancient Greece (see Chapter 1).
- **Peep-toe shoe (Open-toe)** Peep-toes have small openings at the front of the shoe that show part of the toes. The opening is usually a rounded shape that shows only part of the big toe and the second one. The openings do not show the whole toe line, as sandals do, for example. They can be sling-back or closed back.

- **Slide** Slides or slide sandals are shoes with open toes and open backs. They can have a single or multiple straps, but a true "slide" has no toe or ankle straps. They are very easy to slip on and off and can have any heel or no heel.
- **Clog** Clogs are worn by both men and women but are predominantly a women's fashion style. They are shoes with open backs and predominately closed toes, but could also have open toes. The heel is usually a thick wood or cork platform with or without some heel height.
- **Mule (Sabot)** A mule is a backless shoe with a fashion heel. It can have any heel from a stiletto to flat. It's basically a clog with a fashion heel.
- **Moccasin** Women's moccasins look like men's in construction, but as the fashion of the moment dictates, they can have a wide variety of surface designs and can be any height of heel, from a high platform to the usual half-inch flat sole.
- **Loafer** Women's loafers, like the men's, are low-cut, lace-less, slip-on shoes with a very low heel. Some of the most recognizable styles are the penny loafer, which has a slotted strap on the top front part of the vamp, and the tasseled loafer, which has tassels on the instep. The penny loafer in Figure 9.7 has a moccasin construction.

MULE

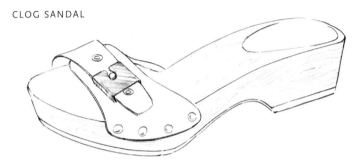

CLOG SANDAL

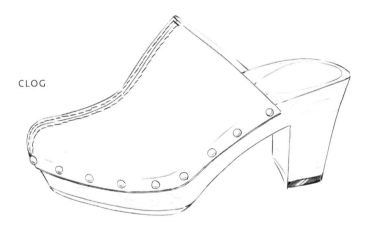

CLOG

MOCCASIN
LOAFER

ESPADRILLE

PLATFORM SHOE

- **Espadrille** Women's espadrilles are the same slip-on canvas shoes with a woven rope sole as the men's, but they can have a bit of a heel or a thicker platform. There are also some variations that resemble the d'Orsay style with cut-out sides on a platform sole.
- **Jelly** Jellies can be any style but are usually made as flat sandals or waterproof low shoes. They are made of PVC through injection molding. They are inexpensive and mass-produced, although designer companies like Chloe and Marc Jacobs have developed interesting variations of the original jellies that require complicated production methods and are much pricier.
- **Platform shoe** A platform shoe is defined by the thick sole under the front of the foot, not the heel. The sole is usually an inch thick or more and can be combined with a variety of heels, including wedge as a part of the sole, in which case it becomes a wedge platform (see Figure 9.4). The heel can also be separate, as shown in Figure 9.7. In the 1970s, platform shoes had very thick soles and wide heels. They were widely worn as a fashion statement and remain a symbol of the disco era.
- **Spectator shoe** The term *spectator shoes* is often used to define a shoe category, but in reality those are simply shoes with design that features two contrast colors. They might have pinked edges and punched or perforated details and wing-tip details. The most common color combinations for spectator shoes are black and white and brown and white. Nowadays they could have any combination of two colors and punched design.

Women's Boots

Women's boot styles can be categorized by the height of the shaft. A particular style can be further defined by identifying the style of the heel and other features. The four basic styles are (Figure 9.8):

- **Ankle boot** As the name suggests, an ankle boot just about reaches the ankle height.
- **Low boot** Low boots do not reach the knee. They end anywhere below the knee but above the ankle.
- **Knee boot** Knee boots reach the knee.
- **Thigh-high boot** Thigh-high boots go above the knee. Typically, to make this style easy to put on and comfortable to wear, the shaft is flexible and opens with a zipper along its full length or it is in part or fully made from a stretch material.

LOW BOOT

ANKLE BOOT

KNEE BOOT

THIGH-HIGH BOOT

FIGURE 9.8 Women's boot styles are named by the length of the shaft. Danilo Giordano.

Identifying Shoe Types and Heel Shapes

GOALS

To give you practical experience in identifying different shoes by their proper names and recognizing different heels.

ASSIGNMENT

For this project, you will need to identify different types of shoes and heels and find a visual representation in a current shoe design collection for every shoe and heel described in this chapter.

Look through the latest runway fashion shows and websites of shoe designers and find a match for every shoe that you see described in this chapter. Do not just search by name in a search engine like Google. Learn to look through the collections and identify the shoe styles by looking at them.

Create a presentation with printouts for every shoe style and heel shape.

10

CONSTRUCTING SHOES

CHAPTER TEN provides an overview of the footwear industry and the responsibilities of a footwear designers and technicians. After reading this chapter, you will be able to identify different types of shoe construction and describe advantages and disadvantages of each.

NOWADAYS, THE ART of making a shoe in the traditional way of handcrafting is getting lost in the demand for cheaper trendier shoes. In order to meet deadlines and create fashionable footwear, the designer needs to understand the full cycle of the complete process even though he or she is not involved in most of the steps. Fast-paced factories in the Far East are replacing the workmanship of generations of European cobblers, lastmakers, and other craftsmen and thereby lowering the prices and the quality for mass production. As a designer, you need to understand the process of the particular company you work for. Each company operates in a different way and has its designers involved in particular steps. Some might have to travel to the factories often while others might never go. Either way, it is important to know all the steps of the manufacturing process and what other people's responsibilities include. This knowledge will make you a better designer. Drawing a pretty illustration does not mean that you will receive a sample that looks like the initial sketch—unless you give the technicians all the necessary technical information.

The designer's sketch initiates the process of shoe creation; then the technician executes the prototype with the help of specialists representing each area of production. Pattern-maker, lastmaker, heel maker, and suppliers of all components come together to deliver each necessary piece in order to make one prototype.

The designer has the important task of the final aesthetic approval and the responsibility to deliver shoes that fit the brand's identity and the customers' needs. Understanding the components of the shoe, the basic styles and variations, the construction methods, and how each technician contributes to the shoe-making process will help you become a better designer. Using this knowledge will make you an irreplaceable designer.

A high-quality pair of shoes goes through the hands of more than a hundred people before it is completed. There are so many components and so many steps in the process of making a shoe that it is comparable to manufacturing a car. Even though a variety of high-tech computerized machines have been invented to aid in the process of manufacturing, the human hand is still irreplaceable.

Shoes have evolved into highly sophisticated hybrids of comfort and technology and have become extremely complicated to manufacture. While elegant high heel shoes are always in fashion and might never disappear, high-tech athletic footwear is here to stay for the long run, too. Running and walking shoes go hand in hand with science and have evolved well beyond anything we could imagine. They can track your heart rate and measure the distance you have passed. Some shoes with injection-molded soles require expensive computerized machinery and chemical compounds that need a team of experts in each field. The job of a designer is just the first step in a long and complicated process before a beautiful creation can come to life. To become a successful footwear designer of high-quality handcrafted shoes or high-tech athletic or any other footwear requires immense knowledge and years of training.

Responsibilities of Designers and Technicians

Designers for different footwear or fashion companies can have different responsibilities, depending on the size of the company and the structure it has adopted. In a smaller privately owned company, there could be just one designer working with a couple of assistants and overseeing a wide array of steps of the process. In some larger corporate settings, teams are strictly structured in a very particular hierarchy that works for the specific company. In some companies, a designer will source, sketch, and communicate with the factories; in others, the designer will only conceptualize, sketch, and present the ideas, and then production people will take over the responsibility of overseeing the sample making and production process. That's not to say that if you worked in one kind of environment you couldn't move to another. In reality, designers move from larger to smaller brands and back, but most people tend to specialize in a particular part of the process. Here are the basic titles and responsibilities that can be found in most shoe design teams.

Designer

A designer is usually a graduate of a fashion design or shoe design school and is responsible for researching the current trends, selecting materials and hardware, conceptualizing ideas, and designing the shoes and possibly other components like soles and heels. Various titles from Assistant to Senior Designer and Design Director can give more or less responsibilities and creative power to a designer within the company.

Depending on what kind of company the designer works for, the main concepts can be driven by the main clothing line and thus all shoes would be designed to go with the current clothing collection. In this case, the designer must communicate well with the clothing design team and follow the appropriate themes, colors, and fabrication. In other cases, where the brand manufactures a variety of accessories like handbags, small leather goods, and hats, the shoes will be designed in concept groups driven by the overall identity and direction of the brand. Usually there are multiple groups developed for each season. In this case, a designer is responsible for developing mood boards with individual concepts for each group.

It is important for a shoe designer to sketch very well, as that is the only way to present the concept and shoe ideas to the rest of the design and merchandising team, the sample-makers, and the manufacturers. Most designers sketch their ideas on paper, but some of the technically savvy designers would actually draw on the last for a more realistic shoe look or at a later stage in the design process.

Another designer responsibility is to approve the first prototypes and participate in fittings. A designer might have to approve the design of an upper on the last without the heel, before the final prototype is created or he might see a proto made from a similar material if the actual material is too expensive to waste. The designer corrects any mistakes and hands off all paperwork that is needed in order to proceed with the manufacturing. Some designers are in constant communication with the factories, following production and answering questions, while others leave that to the production team.

Designers usually travel on a development trip to make sure samples are done correctly until all issues are cleared and the actual orders for production are written. Until then designers comment on lab dips, wash finishes, stitch quality, outsoles, and so on. And even after bulk production is manufactured, designers still look at at least one sample to make sure it looks good.

In some companies, a designer also needs to work closely with the merchandising team in order to have knowledge of which styles, colors, and heel heights sell better and which ones do not. This helps the designer understand the customers of his brand and create shoes that will keep selling. A designer usually also presents the latest collection to the merchandisers and hears the feedback firsthand. Following up with the visual teams and knowing where and how the shoes are displayed in the stores also helps a designer understand why and if certain styles sell better than others. In some cases, a designer might be involved in the PR or advertising photo shoots and give direction as to the concepts and themes of the collection.

Very often, footwear designers travel to footwear, textile, leather, color, and trend or component shows to follow the latest trends and see the latest innovations in each area. This helps bring new ideas to life and gives a good overview of the industry as a whole.

Lastmaker

In most cases, the shoe designer won't even see or meet the lastmaker, but this specialist plays a fundamental part in creating the actual shoe. The lastmaker makes the wood and then the plastic mold that is needed for every single pair of shoes manufactured. Each **last** is different according to the style and size, and a new last is needed for every single new design. The process is lengthy and can cause many problems in the final shoe if done incorrectly.

Patternmaker

The patternmaker will start the process of creating the upper for the shoes you designed. Patternmakers interpret the design sketch on pattern paper or draw directly on the last to see the three-dimensional shape of the shoe. After the patterns are finalized, an upper can be made and lasted to represent the design for the first corrections.

If you work with a sample maker in Europe, you will most probably work with a **modellista**. The modellista does all of the above functions of a patternmaker and is an experienced technician who knows very well the necessary measurements of the foot. The modellista can play with proportions to create a shoe that looks like the designer's sketch.

Heel Maker

The heel maker creates and manufactures the heels and ships or delivers them to the actual sample maker or manufacturer who is assembling the shoes. The process of creating the heels is very complicated as they are composed of many layers and must fit perfectly with the sole and the upper. The wrong height or width of a heel can throw off the whole design of the shoe.

Sole Maker

The outsole of each shoe is very telling of the overall function of the footwear. Dressy shoes have thin elegant leather soles, while athletic shoes have highly specialized performance soles. Naturally, the process of making them and the facilities where they are made are completely different, and so are the professionals involved. Leather soles might be carefully handcrafted one by one, while injection-molded soles are carefully created with extreme precision in a high-temperature environment by computerized machinery. Either way, the people involved in the process are highly skilled and train for years before they can perform the operations.

MINNA PARIKKA

Born in 1980 and raised in Helsinki, Finland, Minna Parikka always knew she wanted to design shoes and began sketching her ideas at the tender age of 15. She acquired a BA in footwear design at De Montfort University in Leicester, UK, and has spent the years since then perfecting her craft and traveling the world in search of inspiration for her creations. She launched the Minna Parikka brand in 2005 and now her shoes are sold in ten countries. She designs and lives in London and operates a flagship boutique in Helsinki as well as an online boutique at MinnaParikka.com.

All of her accessories are manufactured in the same Spanish family-run factory in Alicante, which for years has made shoes for established English designers Lulu Guinness and Nicole Farhi. All Minna Parikka creations are made of the finest leather, and are brimming with glamour, attitude, and edge. Parikka's parents had a passion for antiques, and she grew up in a house full of them. Secondhand furniture, antique shoes, vintage clothes all influenced her eclectic design style and taste. Combining her love for purity and the surreal, Parikka creates designs that pay tribute to the footwear of past eras and art. Her stylistically innovative designs include playful and seductive elements. Tassels, bows, and hearts enhance the strong aesthetic embodied by her work.

"I have had so many different styles. . . . I used to dress like a skater girl when I was 15. I even had piercings," says Parikka in an interview for MademoiselleRobot.com. "Then around 2000, I started dressing more electro-clash, it was right at the time. I don't regret anything. I like experimenting with my style. It is more fun that way."

From wearable to nine-inch high heels to boots that are made for much more than just walking, she designs and creates with passion and creates her own distinctive signature style: feminine, edgy, and quirky. There is no hint of the stark Scandinavian design typically associated with Nordic designers. She has lived and worked in London in recent years and enjoys the hectic life and the multitasking responsibilities of a young company owner. In a typical day she can go from administrative work to designing new shoes and then fly off to another country for a business meeting or an accessory expo, but she wouldn't have it any other way.

Currently the Minna Parikka brand is expanding to ladies' leather gloves and ladies' knitwear, all bearing her signature style and eclectic touch.

Minna Parikka creates playfully seductive shoes that are distinctly feminine. Pictured above is the Elvira shoe from the Fall/Winter 2009–10 collection. Minna Parikka Shoes.

2009
MINNA PARIKKA
1 LK / KL
SUOMI FINLAND

In 2009 Minna was honored with her very own stamp in her home country of Finland. The first-class stamp was issued on May 6, 2009, and features the "Starlet" lipstick red stiletto heels from the Spring/Summer 2009 collection. © Finland Post, Philatelic Centre.

Leather Supplier or Buyer

Some companies have a single person or a team of people in-house dedicated to the process of researching and buying all leather. Other companies rely on outside suppliers, and the designers order the leather from them. A good leather specialist provides quality leather and knows where each skin comes from, what conditions the animals were raised in, and what defects to look out for. The buyer or supplier knows the current trends in the fashion market and recognizes the most appropriate leathers for each company's needs. There are many ways of treating and dyeing leather, and many more trends come out each season. The role of the leather expert is to pick the best skins for the company based on quality and price point.

Seamstress

A seamstress for the shoe industry (this position is typically filled by women) is highly skilled in using the machinery designed specifically for the operation she performs. Since shoes are three-dimensional products with hard parts, different machines are used for sewing the upper from those used for lasting the upper onto the sole.

Assembler

As the name indicates, the assembler assembles the uppers with the soles, which is also called **lasting**. The upper is stretched over a last and attached to the sole with one of the processes covered later in this chapter.

Collaboration among the Designers and Specialists

Naturally, each company has its own structure, and responsibilities might overlap in certain areas and be even more split into smaller, specific roles in others. Nonetheless, the above structure gives you a guide to what you should expect in the footwear industry.

Always try to learn as much as you can about the specialists around you and how they can be helpful to you as a designer, as well as what they need from you in order to complete each design quickly and efficiently. Understanding your role in the overall process is the key to a successful career in the footwear design industry.

Types of Shoe Construction

As soon as an idea is conceptualized, a footwear designer needs to know and identify what type of construction should be used for that particular style and should reflect it in the flat sketch. Attaching the sole to the upper is a highly specialized process that requires different and expensive machinery for every single type of construction. Knowing what is the most appropriate construction type for each shoe as well as how it is done is imperative to being a successful designer. That knowledge also helps the selection of an appropriate factory for each style to be made, as factories specialize in particular types of constructions. Some work only on athletic shoes, others on dressy footwear, and are equipped only for particular construction types. Having the knowledge to choose the right construction for every shoe will give you a significant advantage in your career. Listed below are the popular shoe constructions used today.

Blake/McKay Construction

This is a one-stitch-only, high-quality process used primarily for high-end men's shoes (Figure 10.1). With this construction the sole is stitched to the upper by a single chain-stitch seam made directly through the insole from inside the shoe to the outside. No welt or glue is used. If the stitches are visible the shoe is not waterproof. If this process is used on rubber soles the holes close up as opposed to leather soles where they stay open.

The sole-sewing machine using this process was invented by Lyman Blake in 1858 and later perfected by Gordon McKay, who financed the construction of the first machine. It became the most successful shoe sewing machine of its time and the first important step in the process of sewing together soles and uppers. This process was widely used till the mid 1860s.

Nowadays the stitching can be done through an incision process, which allows for the stitches to be covered, and thus, the sole becomes waterproof.

Goodyear Welt Construction

This is an expensive, high-quality complex construction usually used for dress shoes. It is assembled with two seams and was invented by Charles Goodyear Jr. It is made by Goodyear welting machines, and the process was patented in 1877. With this process, the upper is sewn onto a narrow strip of leather called a welt and then the welt is attached to the outsole with a second seam (Figure 10.2). This allows for an easy repair and resoling of the shoes. Another advantage of this construction is that stitching moves and adapts to the foot, which ultimately creates very comfortable shoes. In addition, the cavity created by the welt is filled with cork material, which also has high flexibility and resilience and adds to the comfort of the shoes.

Stitched-Down/Ideal Construction

This construction is made with one stitching. It is very lightweight and flexible. The upper is lasted outward and then sewn onto the outsole. In a variation of this construction, the upper can be stitched to an insole and then cemented to an outsole so the stitches are inside and thus invisible. With this construction you see all layers on the outside edge (Figure 10.3). Since the different layers have different absorption capabilities, the edge should be painted or otherwise covered to prevent moisture from getting in the shoe.

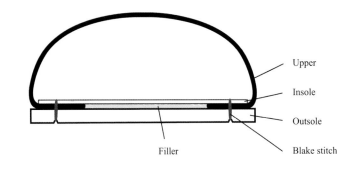

FIGURE 10.1 Blake/McKay construction. Courtesy of Aneta Genova.

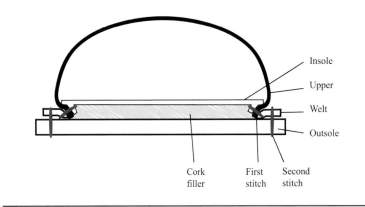

FIGURE 10.2 Goodyear welt construction. Courtesy of Aneta Genova.

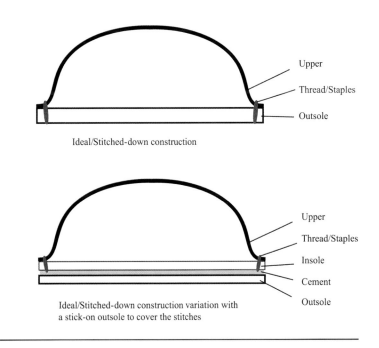

Ideal/Stitched-down construction

Ideal/Stitched-down construction variation with a stick-on outsole to cover the stitches

FIGURE 10.3 Stitched-down/ideal construction. Courtesy of Aneta Genova.

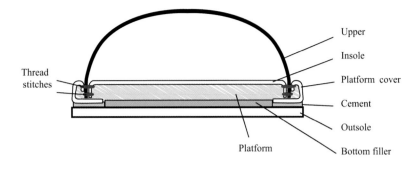

FIGURE 10.4 **California construction.** Courtesy of Aneta Genova.

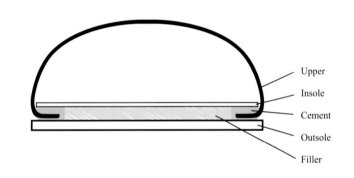

FIGURE 10.5 **AGO/cement construction.** Courtesy of Aneta Genova.

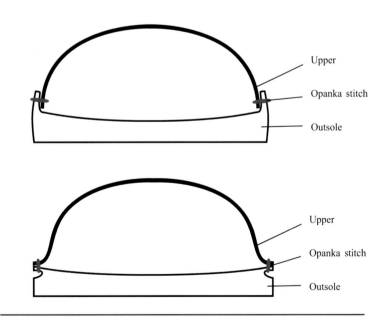

FIGURE 10.6 **Opanka construction.** Courtesy of Aneta Genova.

California Construction

This construction type was developed in California in the 1940s. The upper, the sock, and a thin strip of material are sewn together, then the last is forced in, the platform is attached to the bottom of the sock, the strip is pulled around the edge of the platform and glued under, and then the outsole is attached. The textile midsole and the cushion insole or an orthopedic sock makes this construction feel soft, and walking in shoes with California construction is very comfortable. This is an inexpensive, lightweight, and casual-looking construction (Figure 10.4). Nowadays, it is mainly used for casual women's and children's platform slippers and sandals.

AGO/Cement Construction

This process has no stitching involved and just bonds the upper to the sole with an adhesive, activated by heat and/or pressure (Figure 10.5). This construction is used for inexpensive lightweight dress shoes.

Opanka Construction

This construction is a one-stitch process, which attaches the upper and a sock liner to the outsole with an Opanka stitch and usually a heavy waxed thread. This is a casual construction that creates very flexible shoes (Figure 10.6). The thread allows the upper, outsole, and sock liner to move with the natural movement of the foot.

Moccasin Construction

The traditional process constructs moccasins from two pieces of rawhide with one handmade stitch. It is used for high-quality shoes, and an additional outsole and even an insole can be attached. The bottom piece forms the insole, vamp, and quarters. It is pulled up and attached to the U-shaped top piece or apron (Figure 10.7). This creates a lightweight and flexible shoe. The holes for the stitch are usually premade and the wrinkles on the sides can be smoothed by a machine. Loafers are usually made with moccasin construction.

Strobel Construction

This construction utilizes the Strobel stitch, named for its inventor. It is very light, gives great flexibility, and was created for direct injection soles and mainly for athletic shoes. With this method, the upper of the shoe is stitched to a sock liner with an overlocking Strobel stitch, then slipped onto a last and a sole is added by direct injection (Figure 10.8).

Molded Construction

Injection molding is another process for shoe manufacture, which has become very popular because of the ease of the process and cheap materials like rubber (Figure 10.9). Injection molding of shoes with rubber as soling material by the vulcanization process is probably the most popular. It attained recognition during the early 1960s when PVC (polyvinyl chloride) followed by PU (polyurethane) were developed for use as soling materials. There are several types of molded construction.

DIRECT INJECTION MOLDING

This construction has no stitching. Solid synthetic rubber or thermoplastic is melted and shot inside a mold. The shoe is placed inside on top of the injected sole before it hardens, and when the process is complete, the sole is attached to the shoe. This construction is used for production of high quantity shoes. A manufacturer could buy injected soles and attach them to an upper.

SLUSH MOLDING

This process is similar to the injection molding but uses a dry plastic compound, which is poured into a heated mold.

PVC MOLDING

Polyvinyl chloride is molded directly onto an upper. This construction is most commonly used for rubber soled canvas shoes, Converse All-Stars, for example.

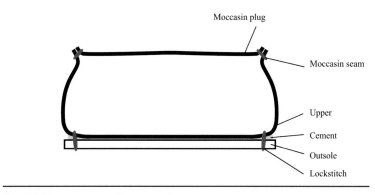

FIGURE 10.7 **Moccasin construction.** Courtesy of Aneta Genova.

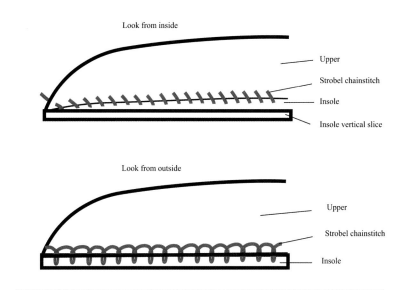

FIGURE 10.8 **Strobel construction.** Courtesy of Aneta Genova.

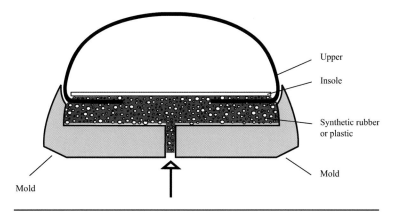

FIGURE 10.9 **Molded construction.** Courtesy of Aneta Genova.

FIGURE 10.10

Vulcanized construction.

Courtesy of Aneta Genova.

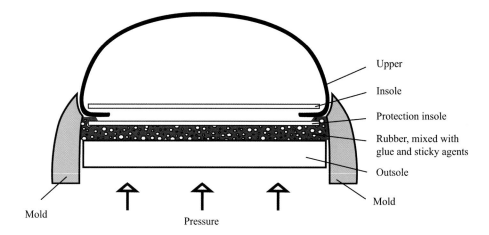

Upper
Insole
Protection insole
Rubber, mixed with glue and sticky agents
Outsole
Mold
Mold
Pressure

Vulcanized Construction

Vulcanization is the sequence or process by which the sole is stuck to the rubber (Figure 10.10). It is cheap and has no stitching. A natural rubber sole is wrapped around a fabric upper. The rubber is mixed with a sticky agent and pressed onto an upper prepared by a Strobel or California construction. All rubber components like a center-back logo label and toe decorations are added by hand before the vulcanization process when all the parts are bonded together. The shortcoming of this process is that only one color sole can be stuck. If there are additional colors in the outsole, they need to be lasted in advance. Usually if there is more than one color on a sole, it requires direct injection. This process works best with fabric uppers. If leather is used, the process requires an extra step to prepare the leather.

Turn Shoe Construction

The shoe upper and sole are stitched inside out and then turned right side out. This process hides the seam on the inside and is used for shoes such as slippers, ballet shoes, and baby shoes. The simplest variation, as in Figure 10.11, has just one seam, connecting the upper to the outsole. More complicated turn shoe constructions might involve more steps, as in Figure 10.11. In this case the upper is stitched to an insole and a welt, and then the welt is attached to an outsole. This is a process similar to the Goodyear welt construction but is much simpler and does not involve adding fillers.

Pegged, Riveted, or Screwed Construction

With this process the insole is nailed onto a midsole and screwed or pegged to an outsole. Then all three of them are riveted together. This is an extremely rigid and durable construction often used for army boots (Figure 10.12). Wooden pegs were used in the seventeenth and eighteenth centuries. In 1811, Samuel Hitchcock and John Bement obtained a patent for making shoes with wooden diamond-shaped pegs. They were used to attach heavy soles on shoes. They swelled when wet and created a waterproof sole. This is an outdated process no longer commonly used.

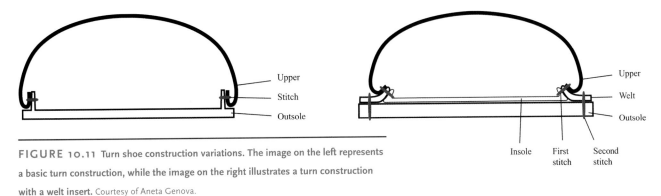

FIGURE 10.11 Turn shoe construction variations. The image on the left represents a basic turn construction, while the image on the right illustrates a turn construction with a welt insert. Courtesy of Aneta Genova.

FIGURE 10.12 Pegged, riveted, or screwed construction. Courtesy of Aneta Genova.

PROJECT

Defining the Customer Profile

GOALS

To give you practical experience in defining the parameters of customer profile, season, and functionality before designing a unique group of shoes.

ASSIGNMENT

You are preparing to design a footwear collection. For this project, you need to define the customer who will be buying the products, start looking for sources of inspiration, and researching a possible theme or a concept. You will identify the customer characteristics through visual means and build a collage to showcase them. Consider the following questions while searching for materials and building the customer profile:

- What is the age group and gender of your consumer?

- What is the purpose of the footwear collection (athletic, day casual, evening, and so on)?

- What competitive brands is the target customer wearing?

Compile various photographs, drawings, cutouts, and other images that answer these questions and visually represent your customer, and present them as a finished collage mounted on a board. The same can be achieved in Photoshop by layering digital photos or scanned materials in a cohesive presentation and printing it out.

11

INSPIRATION,
RESEARCH, AND DESIGN

for the Footwear Industry

CHAPTER ELEVEN explains how footwear designers conduct research, find inspiration, and translate their inspiration into design for uppers, heels, and the overall shoe. After reading this chapter, you will understand how to design a coherent, theme-based collection of shoes for a specific brand, customer, and season. You will also be able to compare the advantages and disadvantages of designing on paper versus on the shoe last.

THE PROCESS OF INSPIRATION FOR FOOTWEAR is similar to the one in any other accessory or clothing. The only difference is the variety of components that are involved in the making of a shoe. Getting inspired is simply an investigation into the world that surrounds us with the purpose of finding shapes and colors that bring new ideas. Inspiration has several purposes and serves many footwear professionals along the way. At the very beginning, the designers pick a theme as a starting point and design a collection. Then the same idea helps the merchandisers merchandise the collection, the buyers to select the proper styles, and the store display stylists to recreate the concept and present the shoes in the most appropriate way. At the end of the cycle, target consumers will buy the shoes because they fit with their lifestyle, and they can see the shoes fit into the current trends. For the process to unfold successfully, the concept should be very clear and focused from the outset.

Staying inspired throughout the whole process is important for a designer because it stimulates the imagination and helps create great product. At the same time, the components and the functionality of shoes are also important during this process. For the specific purposes of a footwear designer, the concept needs to provide design elements for each component of the shoes and for their functionality and the identity of the brand. As a footwear designer, you need to focus on each of the following key elements of a shoe during the process of research:

- Heel
- Upper
- Sole
- Hardware
- Embellishments

You must explore your sources of inspiration to discover texture, pattern, shapes, and materials for each component. You should be aware of all shoe elements during the research process and think of ideas for each one of them. Discover the main idea of the concept and then focus your research around it in order to gather all possible ideas that work for every element. Making an effort to stay inspired is what separates a student or an amateur from a professional designer. Waiting for inspiration is a luxury that a professional cannot afford. Looking around for materials and shapes to be implemented in the heels is a daily necessity. Searching for new leather treatments or new textiles and trims to be used in the uppers is a must. You should be creating new hardware shapes that can be implemented for buckles and closures in order to keep ideas fresh and original. Not all shoes can have a groundbreaking idea and shape like Alexander Fielden's futuristic wedge in Figure 11.1, and they certainly don't need to. While look and current trend are most important for some customers, functionality is key for others. Athletic shoes can also adhere to a metallic trend and have futuristic lines within the design as in Figure 11.2, but performance is their key driving force.

FIGURE 11.3 In these sketches, you can see how footwear designer Ann-Marie Mountford-Chu applies inspiration from feminine elements of vintage garments.

Ann-Marie Mountford-Chu.

Where to Look for Footwear Inspiration

Most footwear designers will tell you that they find inspiration everywhere: nature, city life, wildlife, art, museums, vintage shops, trade shows, color services, runway shows, or art shows. All of these sources can be used to create a footwear collection, but it is important to keep current on all trends in your design specialty and know what is happening specifically in the footwear industry.

Here are some of the sources you should go to when you are searching for new concepts for shoes.

Vintage Stores

Going to vintage stores and museums and looking for examples of workmanship always creates opportunities for discovering techniques that can be used. Garment design details, trims, and patterns can be applied to uppers. Hardware and closures can certainly be used in traditional or innovative ways on footwear (Figure 11.3).

Street Fashion

Some of the best ideas are seen on random pedestrians in the fashion capitals of the world as well as remote places where people do not adhere to the latest trends. Self-embellished shoes seen at clubs or on the street can give a great clue for color combinations and trims. Fashionable youngsters can give you interesting ideas on how to combine different materials or add on an unexpected detail to the upper of a shoe. With the invention of fabric markers and paints, many artistically inclined teenagers draw on their sneakers and create great designs. Athletic footwear companies certainly follow the trends with fashion styles, which are aimed toward the trendy customer who wears them to go out (Figure 11.4). Fashion sneakers can even be seen worn at award ceremonies.

FIGURE 11.4
Fashion sneakers often feature bright colors or metallic or exotic skins as shown in this style.
© Condé Nast Digital Studio/Joshua Scott.

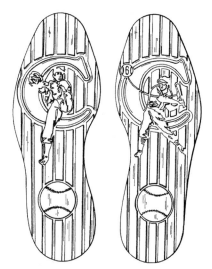

FIGURE 11.5

Baseball-inspired classic Keds shoes designed by Helene Verin. Helene Verin.

Sports

Creating a sport-specific shoe is one way of getting your idea out, but you could interpret it in many different ways. Even going to a sports game can bring you inspiration for creating a shoe or re-create some elements in the design of it. In Figure 11.5, you can see a patented design of a baseball-inspired shoe, which utilizes the stitch of a baseball ball.

Museums

Museums with rotating exhibits are not only inspirational but will give you a look into the history of footwear. Exploring paintings from different centuries will give you a vast wealth of knowledge and ideas for design details, trims, color combinations, and techniques of workmanship. Learning about the past will make you a better designer and add to your knowledge of heels and patterns. A collection of footwear can be a tribute to a famous person from the past, or it can be inspired by specific elements of design.

Marie Antoinette is one of those beautiful, charming fashion-loving queens that inspire multiple references in countless movies, costumes, and collections. A great example of interpreting her style in a modern collection is the Christian Louboutin shoe in Figure 11.6.

FIGURE 11.6

Portrait of Marie Antoinette by Elisabeth-Louise Vigée-Lebrun (above) and a modern shoe designed by Christian Louboutin who was inspired by her style (below).

Marie Antoinette (1755–93) with a Rose, 1783 (oil on canvas) by Elisabeth Louise Vigée-Lebrun (1755–1842) Chateau de Versailles, France/Giraudon/The Bridgeman Art Library; Courtesy of WWD/ Dominique Maitre.

Current Art and Design

Current art is not just about painting anymore. With mixed art media and art crossing over to the digital world, art fairs will keep you up-to-date on the latest techniques of artists and the direction of the art world. Elements from artists' work or the overall concepts can be used successfully for footwear inspiration. You can see an excellent example of an inspiration board for shoe design, based on the work of contemporary product designer Ross Lovegrove in Figure 11.7. Shoe designer Kerrie Luft explores the abstract forces of technology as sculpture in his work and translates those elements into her footwear design as seen in Figure 11.7.

For a complete list of inspiration sources refer to Chapter 6. All sources described in Chapter 6 can be successfully used for footwear inspiration. Just concentrate on how elements from anything that inspires you can be incorporated into the upper, heel, hardware, or even the sole or lining of the shoe.

FIGURE 11.7 The innovative design work of visionary Ross Lovegrove inspired shoe designer Kerrie Luft. Her mood board (top) is based on his digital, sculptural shapes, and the finished designs (bottom) show how she interpreted the design elements into the heels and the uppers. Kerrie Luft.

How to Use Inspiration for Footwear Design

Working with the different components of footwear, a designer needs to consider where each component is, what materials it is made from, and the shoe's specific function before applying the inspiration. The upper and the heel usually receive the most attention and thus are the elements that utilize best the inspiration of the current concept.

Inspiration to Design for Uppers

The upper of a shoe is the most visible element of a shoe and there are countless ways to explore design ideas in order to create an exciting design. Selecting different textures or creating your own is a wonderful way of achieving that. In Figure 11.8, you can see where an idea to use silver metallic paillettes came from and how it was implemented. The designer used paper cutouts to create a mock-up and show exactly how the shapes will overlap, where they would get stitched, and what the final design would look like. In the bottom two concepts, you can see the techniques that will be used to create surface treatment and how this idea will be implemented.

Drawing shapes from your inspiration images and experimenting with their lines is the best way of finding that perfect curve that fits the foot and creates a beautiful shoe. Shaping the opening of the shoe or creating cutouts drawn from the concept is one of the fundamentals of designing shoe uppers. A great example of that technique is the collection of shoes by Kerrie Luft based on flower and plant shapes. She uses blossoms with their stems and leaves as the starting point and draws a series of variations to find the perfect curves (Figure 11.9). Then she interprets them into seams and cutouts in the patterns of the shoe uppers. And finally, the designs are translated into actual shoes, inspired by the natural lines of flora, taking into consideration the shape of the foot.

FIGURE 11.8 Paillette-inspired ideas for shoes and a mock-up with paper by Ann-Marie Mountford-Chu reveal how she utilized the inspiration to design the uppers. Ann-Marie Mountford-Chu.

Inspiration
Nature Drawings

Notice how the stitch lines around the cutouts accentuate the curves and create even better visual reference for the flowing natural lines (Figure 11.9).

Various shapes can be used as inspiration and implemented into the pattern of the upper. An effective way to draw attention to the shapes is using contrast colors or different textures. This is a great way to implement the current color trends into the shoe design and use the latest development in textiles and leather finishes. Finnish shoe designer Minna Parikka is a master of using whimsical color combinations with contrast colors on feminine uppers. Her designs combine purity of overall shape with surreal playful patterns. Figure 11.10 shows a couple of her enticing and seductive plays on classic inspiration from wings and the movement of dripping liquid.

Using perforated or dye-cut leather is a great way to translate shapes from your inspiration directly to the leather of the upper. Creating your own design will customize your product and ensure nobody else is using that exact pattern. Nancy Geist is a seasoned shoe designer who implemented that technique in one of her collections. She carefully designed the laser pattern to fit perfectly in the shape of the upper and the liner. The scalloped edges create additional interest and details that cannot be achieved without careful design consideration (Figure 11.11).

Adding surface treatment like feathers, flowers or sequins is an easy way to create an interesting design and bring an upper of a shoe into the latest trend of the market. Figure 11.12 gives some examples of the use of variety of materials that add surface interest with three-dimensional objects.

FIGURE 11.9 An example of the natural evolution of the design process from inspiration (top) to sketching ideas (center) and creating an actual shoe (bottom). Kerrie Luft.

 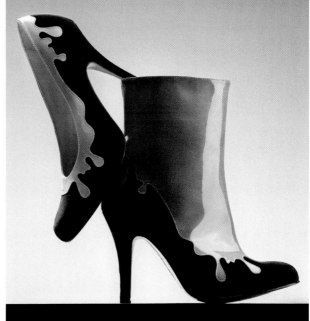

FIGURE 11.10 Minna Parikka uses smooth metallic leather and suede to create a contrast in texture and color within the wing design appliqué of the upper (left) and dripping liquid-like pattern appliqué (right). Minna Parikka shoes.

FIGURE 11.11 Custom designed laser-cut pattern upper (left). Nancy Geist.

FIGURE 11.12 Adding custom-made three-dimensional objects in complementing colors, or made from the same material as the upper, brings these shoes (below) into the chosen concept and makes them trendy and desirable. Courtesy of WWD.

FIGURE 11.13

FIGURE 11.13

This collage follows the development of an athletic shoe from inspiration to sketching, upper drawn on a last, to a rendered realistic sketch created in Illustrator. Han Josef for Reebok.

Creating a shoe for a specific purpose influences the upper immensely. An athletic shoe needs to deliver specific support and flexibility, and knowing the exact functions of the wearer, you can design an exquisite upper that looks as good as it performs. In Figure 11.13 you can see how the specifics of ballet, dancing, and gymnastics inspire a dynamic upper design.

Inspiration to Design for Heels

The heel of a shoe is an exciting component where you can experiment with a variety of different materials and can create very simple shapes or complicated sculptures. With new innovations in technology, manufacturing is capable of using new materials in unexpected ways and still achieve a great comfort level. As different customers pursue different goals,

designers always push the boundaries of beauty and comfort. The heel is probably one of the most controversial elements of a wardrobe and a reason for much pain, and yet heels are going higher and higher. Consumers are not always slaves to trends, but there are plenty of fashion-conscious women who like their heels as high and as interesting as possible.

Kerrie Luft is one of those innovative designers who pushes the boundaries and uses hand sketching combined with computer rendering to achieve her dream heel designs. The process starts with inspiration and drawings that reflect possible shapes (refer to Figure 11.7 and 11.9). Then she interprets the abstract silhouettes of nature and man-made shapes into possible design ideas for heels by drawing countless black-and-white sketches (Figure 11.14). At

FIGURE 11.14

Drawing many different design ideas and heel shapes is part of the process of implementing the abstract forms from the inspiration images to final product. Kerrie Luft.

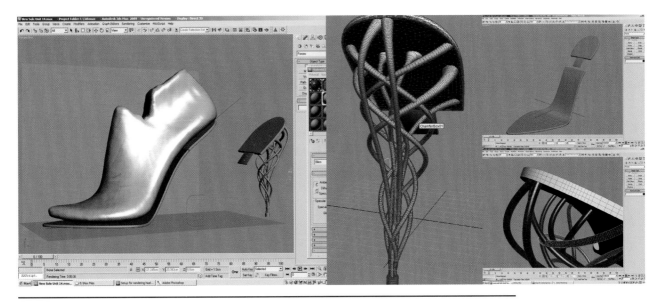

FIGURE 11.15 Two different views of heel development, a shoe shank and a view of how the last fits on the sole (left) and a close-up of the heel itself (right). These designs were developed with 3-D modeling software. Kerrie Luft.

this stage, a designer would draw a multitude of shapes to see as many variations as possible and select the best ones.

In this case, the abstract shapes are interpreted into fine lines that intertwine and create an airy heel. This design requires surgical precision in workmanship and is best developed with computer 3-D modeling software. Once some of the shapes are selected, Kerrie Luft works with software that renders 3-D objects and draws the heel shapes to see how they would look when finished. In Figure 11.15 you can see screen captures of the heel and shank, and a

rendering of the shoe and how the last fits, while Figure 11.16 shows the renderings of the heels, based on the above research and drawings, a finished shoe with the real heel, and a prototype of a new heel. The software allows the designer to rotate the object and see all possible angles of the finished object. With modern technology, abstract shapes become a reality much faster and allow designers to foresee problems and develop all elements of the shoe in a very short time and with great precision. You can see how the software creates a perfect representation of what the heels will look like.

FIGURE 11.16
Rendered heels (left) and a finished shoe (right) from footwear designer Kerrie Luft.
Kerrie Luft.

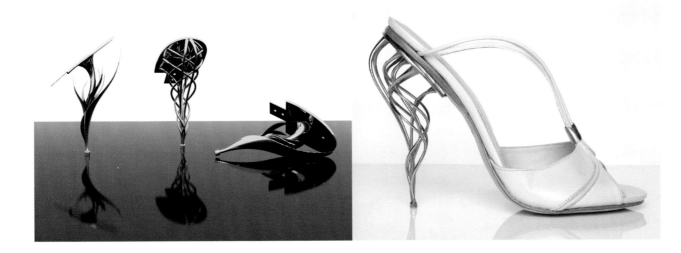

KERRIE LUFT

British footwear designer Kerrie Luft creates unique shoes embracing new technologies to bring to life her concepts and ideas. The sketches featured throughout this chapter are from her Fall 2009 collection called "Nouveau," which is inspired by the beauty of the Art Nouveau architecture in Paris. Seeing the curves of flowers caught in the lines of buildings and lampposts inspired the shapes for heels in her collection. She observed how cast iron was twisted into elegant outlines within staircases and doorways and sought to capture the natural lines in her designs. For this collection, Kerrie explored the field of Rapid Prototyping (automatic construction of physical objects from virtual computer-aided design (CAD), done layer-by-layer by a machine) to create the organic shapes derived from architectural forms and delicate plantlike forms. She created titanium swirls for some of the heels and solid leaf forms for others, marrying architecture, technology, and nature.

Kerrie Luft started her design career in Northampton, a small town in England famous for its vast shoe heritage and once-thriving footwear industry. During her second year of studying fashion design at the University College Northampton, a new major of footwear and accessories was added to the program, and she decided to enroll in it. Kerrie spent countless days searching through the archives of shoes at the Northampton Shoe Museum and developed her passion for shoes. She graduated with a honors BA in footwear design at Northampton, and interned at Lulu Guinness (see her profile in Chapter 6) and Patrick Cox.

After graduating, Luft moved to London to begin an MA in fashion footwear at the legendary Cordwainers, part of the London College of Fashion. That's where she perfected her design skills and began to create an identity as a contemporary footwear designer. She created her first footwear collection and graduated with distinction from Cordwainers in 2009. Since then she has entered a few competitions and became a finalist in the Fashion Fringe Accessories and Drapers Footwear Awards. Her "Nouveau" collection (see Figure 11.7) has been showcased in London at the Mall Galleries and Victoria and Albert Museum and as part of the LCF Pop-up-gallery at Carnaby Street.

She is currently gaining more industry experience and working on a business plan before launching her own label. She is aiming to develop a collection she can take to Première Classe in Paris and sell to boutiques all over the world.

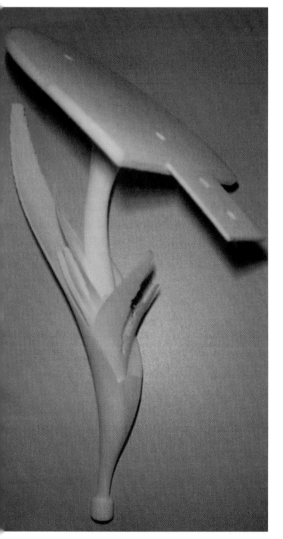

Heel prototypes developed through Rapid Prototyping for Kerrie Luft's "Nouveau" collection. Kerrie Luft.

Very often the inspiration is translated to the overall shape of the shoe, not just for the upper or the heel. In Figure 11.17, you can see how shoe designer Danilo Giordano takes curves from the shapes of seashells and applies them to all elements of the shoe. He draws directly on the photo, allowing himself to discover how the original form applies to the shoe. Different shells offer different possibilities, and after the initial quick sketches on the photograph, he starts drawing a variety of shoe designs with pencil. Different colors and textures can be used to reflect the realistic look of the seashells or to create a completely different look and feel.

Design and Sketching Possibilities

Different designers like to work in different ways. Some are trained and excel in old-school methods of doing everything by hand; others embrace the latest technology and can render every single design in Photoshop or a 3-D modeling design program. Neither way is better than the other, nor would either produce better results than the other. Many successful designers working one way or the other produce beautiful shoes. If you are starting your education now, consider trying a blend of both low- and high-tech approaches to design, and see whether you can achieve a balance with a combination of both.

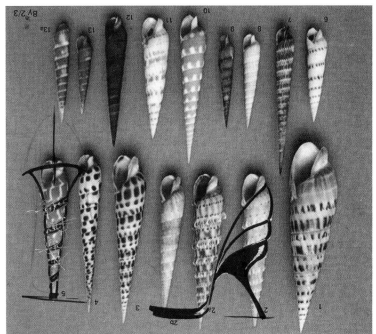

FIGURE 11.17
Natural seashells serve as inspiration for a women's shoe design by Danilo Giordano, who draws directly on photos of shells of various shapes (above). He then sketches the designs based on the inspirational photos (below).
Danilo Giordano.

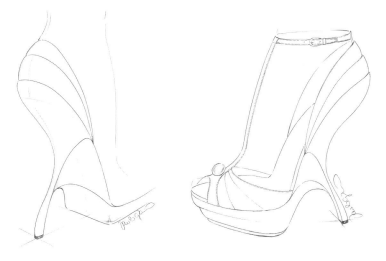

FIGURE 11.18 Doodle sketch sheet with a variety of shoe design ideas. Nancy Geist.

FIGURE 11.19 Nancy Geist and a patternmaker are creating a new lettuce-ruffle by hand and checking the proportion for closed toe versus open toe design. Nancy Geist.

The simplest and most natural way for a designer to start the design process is to start sketching different variations on paper. Some designers sketch big, others, small, and drawing media also range from an organized pretty sketchbook to loose sheets of paper or napkins. Design ideas strike at all times of day and night, and it is important to put your ideas on paper as soon as possible. That means that any surface can become a sketching ground. Most designers have an established habit of sketching in a particular way and for Nancy Geist that means drawing countless tiny sketches on a sheet smaller than a letter-sized piece of paper (Figure 11.18). These sketches could be confusing for other people, but for her they hold all necessary information until she is ready to go to the next step. Nancy is also one of those designer who prefer to get their hands "dirty" and work directly on the last to see how particular leather works and what kind of shapes it creates. Shaping the forms directly on the last gives an immediate satisfaction of seeing the actual material perform in real life, and you can make corrections and see what the shoe would look like in reality (Figure 11.19).

Another designer who works on her design ideas on paper is Nalini Arora. She sketches only a shoe or two per page, with many notes on various details and close-ups of important details. The group she sketched in Figure 11.20 is based on braiding. You can see how she creates different shoe styles by using this braiding technique in different parts of the shoe. In some boots, it wraps around the whole heel while in others, it is a trim at the edge of the opening or at the base of the heel. Sketching all variations helps her see the best possible designs and select the most interesting or functional ones.

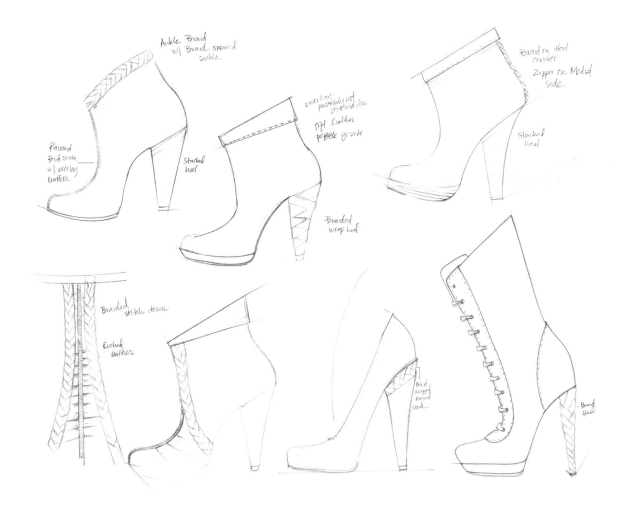

The following handwritten annotations appear on the sketches:

Ankle Braid w/ Braid around ankle

Raised Butt seam w/ overlay leather

Stacked heel

overlay possibly not stitched down

Soft Leather Pebble grain

Braided wrap heel

Braid on Heel counter

Zipper on Medial Side

Stacked Heel

Braided stitch down

Ruched leather

Braid wrap around heel

Braid Heel

The design of the shoe can be drawn straight on the last (Figure 11.21). Once the right last is developed, it is taped with masking tape, and the design of the upper is drawn with pencil. You can keep changing the design by erasing or retaping over the old one. Once all lines are finalized, you can cut out the unnecessary tape to reveal the final design. This method offers a realistic and immediate approach of seeing which ideas work and which don't.

Nancy Geist works closely with her patternmaker. After he tapes the last, she personally draws the shoe design of the upper and explains what kind of edges she would like to use: raw, folded, piped, and so on. Then the patternmaker removes the tape and extends it out on manila cardboard or pattern paper to be traced. He adds the seam allowances, mounts the margins, finishes the original pattern and cuts the first proof. Experienced designers like Geist prefer to work out their designs on a last to see how the human foot would affect the design. This method is preferred by anyone who does not wish to leave any details for interpretation. Some designers prefer to work out all or most of their ideas on the last and, after sketching the collection, make a specific trip to meet with the patternmaker and work on the shoe designs together for the first prototype. This is a precise and exact process that gives an idea of what the shoe will look like as soon as you draw it on the last.

FIGURE 11.20

Collage of black-and-white sketches by Nalini Arora. The defining element in this group is a braiding technique, and all ideas are worked out on paper.

Nalini Arora.

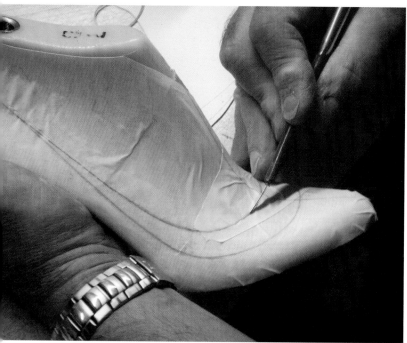

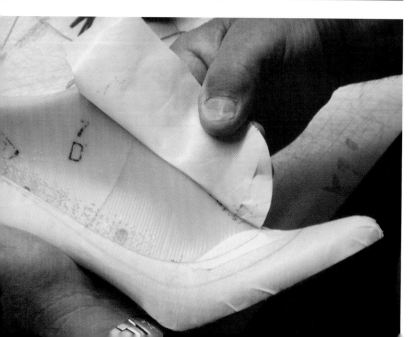

Design Process Overview

The design process is guided by a set of required elements, for which you gather information. It is about incorporating familiar design details in new ways to create an original idea, and it is a result of the knowledge, gathered from research and the defined concepts and direction. Once you have identified the concept, the season, and your customer or activity, the next step is to put your ideas on paper. You need to determine the materials you will be using for the upper and the heel and look at the inspiration for shapes. These two elements will lead you in the right direction to start sketching design ideas. In this stage you should use whatever technique works best for you. You can use pencils, pens, or markers or photocopy shapes and create collages to get different proportions or just doodle away until you feel that valid ideas are coming out.

Some designers go directly for a realistic shoe sketch in the right proportions with the right heel shape and upper design. Others sketch a variety of heels with the same upper until the shoe feels right. Others sketch a body to go with the shoes in order to get that overall feeling of the customer. There is no wrong or right way of approaching this process. The overall silhouette and the shape of the heel are usually the first thing that viewers will respond to. By designing an appropriate heel, you ensure that the shoe collection stays within the concept. Keeping in mind the design development elements, you need to keep sketching until you develop

FIGURE 11.21 Three steps in the process of design: drawing a design on a taped last for an upper of a pump shoe (top), cutting out the design (center), and removing the extra tape, revealing the final design to be traced by the patternmaker (bottom). Nancy Geist.

multiple ideas for the same group. The group is held together by the concept, the inspiration, shapes, materials, colors, and hardware, but it needs to have a variety of upper designs and heels.

If, for example, the group is held together by a historic theme, you need to stay true to that theme within the range of leather or fabric you chose and design hardware that will be used throughout the whole collection, but you need to provide a variety of heel heights and upper designs. That will ensure that customers who like flats and those who prefer high heels will both find a shoe that goes well with their wardrobe. Using the gathered information on historical shapes and looking at construction details, you can begin to analyze the elements you can use for your group and apply them in contemporary shoe designs that will appeal to your particular customer.

If the collection you design is inspired by a particular exotic skin, then you might create simpler upper designs that showcase the beauty of the material; again, you will make sure that you are sketching a good variety of different heels so you can accommodate different customers. But if you are designing a footwear collection based on function, the process starts with identifying the function and utilizing the latest technology of sole making and selecting upper materials most appropriate for that function.

Next come the details for each shoe. Designing one coherent collection also means that you develop hardware, stitching details, and embellishments, and you use them for every single shoe in that group. If you pick brass hardware, for example, then that is what you use throughout the whole collection. If you do not use consistent elements for each style, then you don't have a clear concept that can be followed in the next stages from merchandising to store display.

While you are designing the collection you need to keep in mind the following guidelines: brand identity, customer, and seasonal requirements.

Design Considerations

Identifying the customer and keeping the identity of the brand while designing is one of the main responsibilities of a footwear designer. Learning the history of the company and looking at past collections gives you the necessary information to identify the existing customers. For any future collections, the role of the designer is to understand the current trends and translate them into ideas that work for these customers. An established company does not want to alienate its current customers while trying to attract new ones, so the footwear designer needs to be able to work within these parameters. Looking at all current trends in footwear and clothing is necessary and provides a starting point for any collection. Regardless of what type of company you work for, current trends can be translated in one way or another to fit into the brand direction. Exotic leathers can be used in elegant high heels as well as athletic shoes. If the company has a lower price point, then the expensive skin can be replaced with a faux one. If you are designing for an athletic shoe company, it is quite obvious that you cannot present a crocodile high heel shoe, but what you should do is keep up with the trends, and if crocodile is in style, you can create a crocodile upper for the sneakers you are designing.

On the other hand if you work for an established lifestyle company like Ralph Lauren, which offers a wide array of products, you may get to design a variety of shoe collections that will satisfy different types of customers. We all need to wear an assortment of shoes according to our daily activities, and a customer who loves a brand will buy both the sneakers and the high heels from the same company. It is important to understand that when you are hired to design for a specific company, you need to immerse yourself completely in the identity of the brand. Learn its history and origins. Look at its collections from the very beginning of the brand. See what other designers before you created to keep the image and identity of the company, and then think how you can keep that image but offer a fresh new take on it. That's how you will be successful.

Design for the Right Customer

The lifestyle of the customer you design for is a leading factor in the decisions you will be making. That style might not match your own, but your job is to design for the consumer in your employer's target market. If you are not the target client or you do not actively pursue the activity you design shoes for, then you must learn as much as possible about their needs. If you are designing children's shoes and you don't have children, then it is necessary to study what children are interested in, as well as the shapes and materials used in their shoes. You should spend extra time looking at trend services for children and visit relevant expos in order to understand how they are different from any other consumer. The same philosophy applies to any athletic performance footwear. Nowadays technology has advanced so much that athletic shoes require extreme performance, targeted for each particular sport. Athletic footwear designers often come from product design or architectural backgrounds in addition to studying footwear and dedicating themselves to this segment of the business.

Always keep in mind that in addition to functional differences in their footwear, men and women have different needs and buy shoes for different purposes. Women buy multiple shoes to go with different outfits, and designers should present multiple collections within one season. This market is the most directional and conceptual and is driven strongly by the latest trends. It will allow you to be more creative with heels and embellishments than the men's market does, and you can design more glamorous styles.

Men, on the other hand, are much more conservative and buy fewer pairs of shoes and wear them more often, requiring a sturdier make. Men would not necessarily buy into the latest trends, especially if they are buying shoes for work. This is the segment, though, where custom-made footwear can be very expensive and specialized, and there are very few brands or single shoemakers providing that service.

Athletic shoes can be designed in two different groups: performance and fashion. The fashion group has become a lucrative business in the new century and gives a lot of freedom for experimentation and design idea implementation. Men and women buy trends in this category. Color and pattern can play a big role in the design process, with celebrities as a driving marketing force. Mega-brands like Nike or Puma produce multiple collections each season and reach a large customer base of all ages. Fashion sneakers have become an acceptable footwear for events and in many corporate work environments, and thus the market for them has grown explosively. They are easy to wear and fun to design.

Design for the Right Season

Always keep in mind what season you are designing for and understand the differences for the particular country you design for. Each season deals with different elements and requires different materials for the upper and possibly for the soles. For fall and winter, you need to utilize fabrications and leather that correspond to the conditions where shoes will be worn. That might include shearling, fur, and waterproof materials, as well as treatments to make shoes warm and comfortable during cold conditions. Summer shoes will include more bare styles like strappy sandals and lighter materials and also allow a much wider array of embellishments. Shells, beads, and stones are usually used for summer or evening styles of women's shoes. For summer collections, look for brighter colors and lighter materials. Usually the heels for women's shoes during the warmer months are impacted by the latest trends but there are some basic styles like driving shoes, espadrilles, and flats that emphasize on the upper much more than the sole.

Keeping Yourself Inspired

Looking for new sources on a daily basis is necessary for every designer. You need to make a conscious effort every single day to surround yourself with those physical or ethereal elements that keep you in the right mood. Music, art, current events, flora, fauna, people, those are all valid sources of inspiration. Cultivate the ones you understand and develop the ones you are struggling with. They are all useful starting points. What's important is to keep organized, collect the information, analyze it, and utilize it for the appropriate collection.

PROJECT

Creating a Mood Board, Color Story, and Materials Page

GOALS

To give you practical experience in researching inspiration materials and building a mood board.

ASSIGNMENT

Find sources of inspiration and compile research materials. Identify a concept for a footwear collection, research all possible sources, and find images that represent it best. Compile those images in a collage that gives enough information (design details, shapes, and overall direction) for designing the collection. Choose your colors and find appropriate swatches that represent them. Select materials and hardware to be used in your design collection, specifically for the upper and for the heels.

Create a presentation with a complete mood board, color story, and materials page.

12

SKETCHING, ILLUSTRATION, AND PRESENTATION TECHNIQUES

for Footwear

CHAPTER TWELVE offers many examples of presentation styles and techniques that are suitable for the footwear industry. After reading this chapter, you will understand how to visually organize and present a footwear collection using sketches and illustrations drawn by hand or by using the computer and mixed media.

SKETCHING FOR THE FOOTWEAR INDUSTRY involves very specific requirements related to the components of the shoemaking process. A good designer creates not only beautiful sketches that satisfy the eye, but also reveals construction details and the necessary information for the prototyping and manufacturing of a shoe. In this chapter, we will look at the specific needs for the different stages of the design process as well as the styles of several designers.

To begin the process, it is important to understand the difference between an illustration and a technical sketch. An illustration is a stylized version of a shoe and could just represent the idea or the overall shape, while a technical sketch has all design elements clearly represented. A flat or a technical sketch often offers multiple views to show details from all sides and represent all textures, seams, sole layers, hardware, and trims. An illustration is usually in color and can be done in any media, while a flat sketch is, in most cases, a black-and-white pen hand drawing or it is computer generated in Illustrator or Photoshop. In Figures 12.1 through 12.5, you can see examples of illustrations that give the overall feel for the colors, print patterns, trims, and hardware of the depicted shoes, but not much information about the actual construction or materials involved in the making. These drawings represent the main concept and the sensibility of the collection and are great for a presentation or an advertising campaign, but they are not meant to be used in a tech pack.

FIGURE 12.1

Hand-drawn illustration by Nancy Geist, demonstrating a loose interpretation of a shoe, without any construction details.

Nancy Geist.

FIGURE 12.2 (top left)
A marker illustration by
Stuart Weitzman.
Stuart Weitzman.

FIGURE 12.3 (bottom left)
Mixed media illustration by
Kenneth Paul Block. Courtesy of
WWD/Illustration by Kenneth Paul
Block.

FIGURE 12.4 (top right)
Illustration by Manolo Blahnik.
Courtesy of WWD/Illustration by
Manolo Blahnik.

FIGURE 12.5 (bottom right)
Watercolor illustration of a Pringle
shoe designed by Sigerson
Morrison. Courtesy of WWD/Sketch by
Sigerson Morrison.

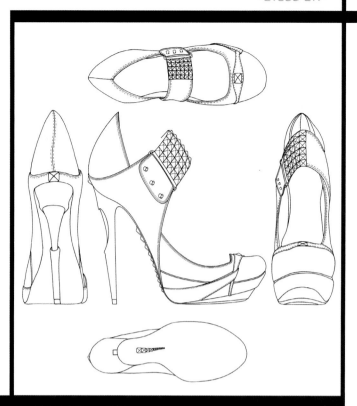

FIGURE 12.6 Computer-generated sketches of front, back, side, and bottom views of a shoe by Kristina Gress. Notice the more formal layout of these sketches, reflecting the designer's personal style. Kristina Gress.

The black-and-white sketches in Figure 12.6 represents flats drawn specifically for a tech pack. Each one of them shows the shoes in the right proportion and contains all design details needed for the prototyping and manufacturing of the shoes. The designer shows as many different views as possible in order to reveal all components of the shoe. These sketches can be drawn by hand or in a software program like Adobe Illustrator (Figure 12.6) or Photoshop. What's important is to create a clean sketch, showing how the shoe will be made.

The most common view to draw is the side view with notes and measurements. Figure 12.7 shows how detailed and descriptive these flats need to be. The designer needs to provide notes on overall measurements, stitching, and hardware size and finishes as well as placement. Every one of those notes adds to the tech pack and ensures a smooth transition from concept to real product.

Design and Sketching Styles

Most designers who work for a large company adopt the style that is already established or required for the brand. In general, designers naturally seek to work for companies that represent their sensibility and style of design and sketching, and companies usually hire designers and illustrators who demonstrate a style, compatible with the firm's design philosophy. Some designers are set on what type of customer they would like to design for; others can adapt easily and develop multiple portfolios with varied design ideas and style of presentation techniques. This is a very personal decision that designers need to make on their own. Most well-established companies have a system in place of what design sketches need to look like and already have a rich library of basic silhouettes that are used repeatedly, with the addition of new elements. Designers who work for such a

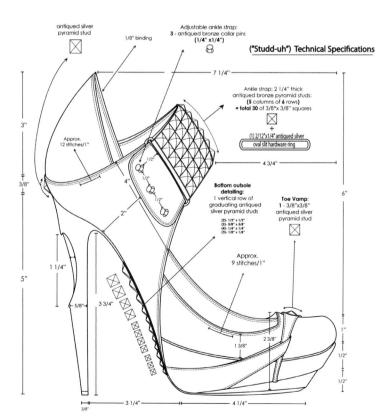

FIGURE 12.7 Computer-generated sketch with measurements and detailed notes by Kristina Gress. Kristina Gress.

company often utilize the existing silhouettes and adapt them to the new concept with new trims, hardware, or textures. Designers who are working independently or freelance for various companies have the opportunity to create original sketches and shine with a signature style. But even in this case, a designer already has a database of existing silhouettes and can revisit them and use them as a starting point for every new sketch. Your goal as a designer should be to create sketches that represent the design idea clearly and satisfy the sensibility of the brand you work for. If that happens to be your own collection, then you have even more of an incentive to present it in the best possible way.

Sketching with Purpose

Each part of the design process requires a different type of sketch. Some need more details; others need to be done quickly with less attention to details. It all depends on the purpose of the sketch. The following categories will help you understand what kind of sketch you need to create for each design stage.

Sketching the Initial Design Ideas

Within the first stage of the design process, the most important thing is to get the ideas down on paper. It doesn't matter how you sketch or what you sketch on, what's more important is to churn out as many ideas as possible. In this stage each designer has a different comfort zone and employs a different technique. Inspiration comes anywhere any time and so it is important to carry a sketchbook and draw ideas as they come. Some designers use loose sheets of paper and draw as many ideas as possible without particular order; others draw one shoe per page on letter-size paper and carefully craft every detail in almost real life size. Seasoned shoe designer Nancy Geist draws a multitude of tiny sketches, each no bigger than an inch and adds notes and photographs or tears that represent the inspiration or specific design details. You can see an example of her doodle sheets in Figures 11.18 and 12.8. Even though her sketches

FIGURE 12.8 Doodle sheet with multiple shoe ideas from Nancy Geist. Nancy Geist.

FIGURE 12.9

Hand-drawn sketch
of a shoe by Danilo
Giordano. Danilo
Giordano.

are tiny and might seem incomprehensible for other designers, they work perfectly well for Geist and help her get all her design ideas on paper, so she can start the design process. Other designers like Danilo Giordano and Sabato Riccio work in a much larger scale. Each of them draws a single shoe per page and carefully works out every detail in a black-and-white pencil drawing. As they draw their sketches, they add realistic proportions and shading (Figures 12.9 and 12.10). Either of these two sketches could be directly inserted in a tech pack and would be ready to go to the manufacturer.

Sketching for Presentations

When your design ideas are finalized and you are ready to present your work, you need to create some beautiful sketches that bring the attention to the best features of the design and their most important functionality. Depending on how you drew your sketches in the previous stage, you might be able to just photocopy and color up your initial sketches, or you might have to create new ones. For a presentation you don't need to be very technical, but you do need to show as many details as possible, as well as the real colors, patterns, and textures of the finished shoe. A presentation can be created for your superiors, like the design director or VP of design, or it can be aimed at merchandisers or buyers for the line.

If you are presenting your ideas in front of a design or creative director or anybody who needs to evaluate the design details and styles, concentrate on the shoes themselves and show large various views of the shoes in realistic color and texture. You might have to show multiple colors or different color combinations of the same shoe so the right styles can be selected. You can draw one shoe per page and simply line up all styles together, or you can show them on the feet as in Figure 12.11. You can create frames or layouts that complement the concept, but very often for a design meeting, the simpler

FIGURE 12.10

Hand-drawn sketch
of a shoe by Sabato
Riccio. Sabato Riccio.

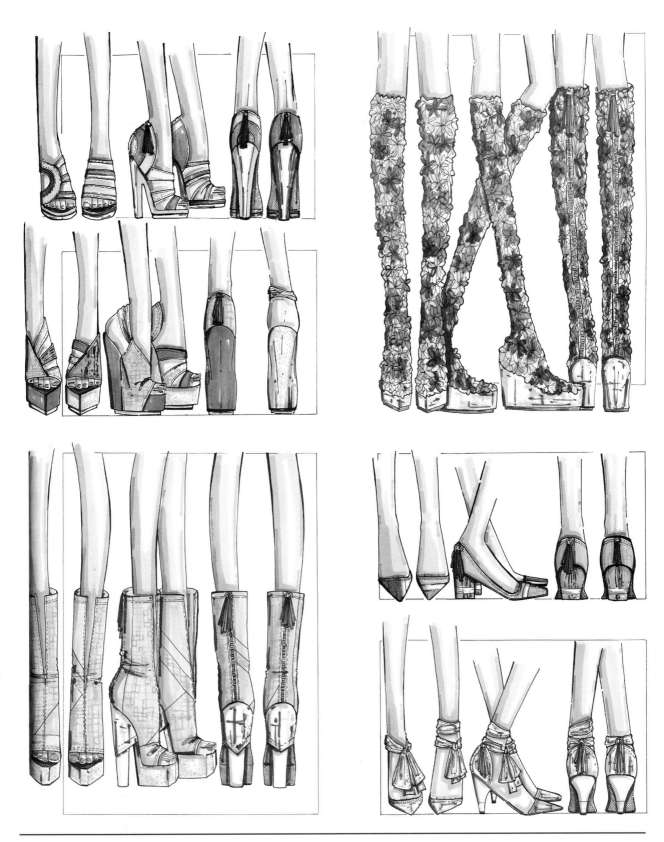

FIGURE 12.11 These sketches are a part of an accessory collection, designed by Ivy Kirk, a fashion design graduate from Parsons The New School for Design, who was a finalist for the Cesare Paciotti Shoe Design Competition in 2009. Ivy Kirk.

FIGURE 12.12
Presentation by Ivy
Kirk (left), which brings
together clothing and
accessories from the
same collection and
shows how they work
together. Ivy Kirk.

FIGURE 12.13
In this sketch by shoe
designer Nalini Arora
(right), the figure
is kept in black and
white with minimal
detail, while the shoes
are in color. This helps
keep the attention on
the footwear while
presenting it as it
could be worn on a full
figure. Nalini Arora.

clean presentations with large single shoe views are most effective.

If you are presenting the full collection to merchandisers or buyers, you might show the shoes themselves and accompany those with some fashion figures wearing the shoes and dressed in appropriate outfits that complement the concept of the collection. This can help anybody who is not familiar with the collection visualize how the shoes work in the scope of a whole outfit and who the target customer is for each concept behind every group.

This is the stage where you can be imaginative and create some interesting layouts. You can experiment with different borders and backgrounds and bring shapes and colors, from a print developed for this collection or a texture that is dominant in the group. Feel free to cut and paste on foam board and create dimension within your presentation. You can use fine quality paper or create your own background from leather or materials used in the collection. A presentation should wow the audience, but it also should not stray from the concept, and

it shouldn't overwhelm the actual product. Most effective presentations help the product look as good as possible without distractions that can take attention away from it. Figure 12.11 shows simple but successful layouts that consist of different views of the same shoes as they would look when worn. What makes these layouts attractive is the simple idea of a fine line border and legs that extend in natural but varied poses. Each composition is similar enough to create a cohesive presentation, but also different enough to make it interesting.

Including the legs in the presentation or adding full figures gives a better idea of the actual size and proportion of the shoes than images of the shoes alone. If the shoe collection is part of a bigger brand that also makes clothing, it is a great idea to include fashion pieces from the clothing collection. If they are designed to be sold together in the store, this is a great opportunity to showcase how accessories and clothing work together to complement each other. Figures 12.12 and 12.13 are great examples of that practice.

FIGURE 12.14

Flat sketches of shoes for a tech pack from Nine West Footwear Corp. Courtesy of Nine West.

FIGURE 12.15

These flats by Ivy Kirk were created for her winning presentation but they contain the technical information and were aimed at the prototyping stage of the design process.

Ivy Kirk.

Sketching for a Tech Pack

Some designers sketch very clear, clean drawings of shoes that are ready to be input into a tech pack, but most need to be redrawn. Flat sketches for tech packs are usually black and white and need to have all design details clearly drawn (Figure 12.14). Not all measurements of an upper can be determined from the sketch, but proportions need to be realistically indicated for all elements on a shoe, including upper, heels, and all trims and hardware. Make sure you draw topstitching where it belongs, paying attention to whether it is single or double and drawing it correctly. If small details are missing from the flat, they will be missing from the finished shoe, too. Patternmakers who review the tech pack and look at the sketch should be able to make a prototype with very few or no questions about the style and design of the shoe. You should add notes and alternate views of complicated details or anything that is not clear from the overall sketch (Figure 12.15).

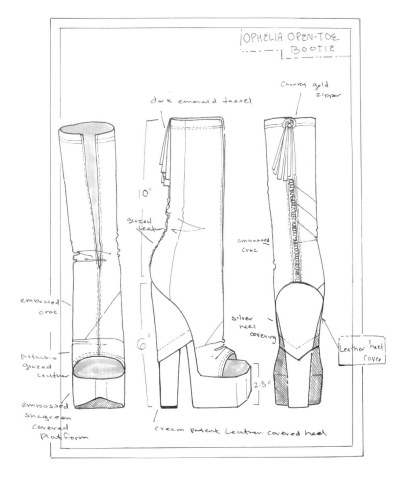

OPHELIA OPEN-TOE BOOTIE

dark emerald tassel

Chunky gold zipper

glazed leather

embossed croc

10"

embossed croc

pistachio glazed leather

silver heel covering

embossed shagreen covered platform

6"

Leather heel cover

2.5"

cream patent leather covered heel

FIGURE 12.16

Han Josef for Cole
Haan tech drawings
of construction, sole,
and overall design for
a wingtip men's shoe.

Han Josef for Cole Haan.

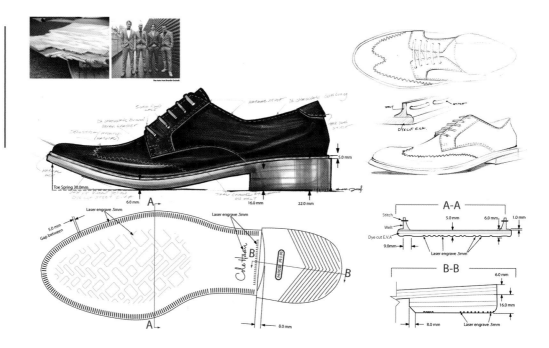

A footwear designer should offer interior views of construction and if possible color-code the most important elements of the sketch. In Figure 12.16, Han Josef offers a great layout of a step-by-step detailed sketch, showing the technical points of the design for this men's wingtip shoe. Notice how he shows colored and black-and-white views of the same shoe from different angles. Han designed the surface pattern of the sole and drew the actual pattern with all measurements clearly written with arrows pointing to every single detail, so the manufacturers can develop the sole from this sketch. Note that on the colored sketch there are notes on trims, shoelaces, and colors, as well as the lining. All measurements are clearly indicated and named appropriately. As you can see on this sketch, there is a blend of handwritten notes and ones added in Adobe Illustrator. A designer should be able to utilize different media and find the best tools for every single task. Some elements are better drawn by hand, while others require the precise hand of a designer skilled in using design software. You should strive to acquire as many different tools as possible and use the most appropriate for each task.

No matter what the tool or the technique of drawing, the purpose of the flat sketches for tech packs is to show all possible views and give all necessary information to make the designed shoe. If necessary, you can reuse the same sketch multiple times and give different information on each one. One can provide measurements, while the other can offer a guide to all the different colors and materials, used in the shoe model (Figure 12.17).

Orthographic views (Figure 12.18) are necessary when the design is really complicated. Creating the flats for every view shows the continuation of design details and explains how every detail is made.

For a flip-flop or an athletic shoe, the call out for measurements and materials is the same as in an elegant high heel. Orthographic views are even more important when the sole pattern is custom designed as in Figure 12.19. The three-dimensional ridges, cutouts, or embossing and debossing not only need to be drawn but also carefully drafted with exact measurements for height, width, and depth of the pattern. Multiple sketches are needed if, for example, the upper is the only thing that changes but the sole is the same. The same

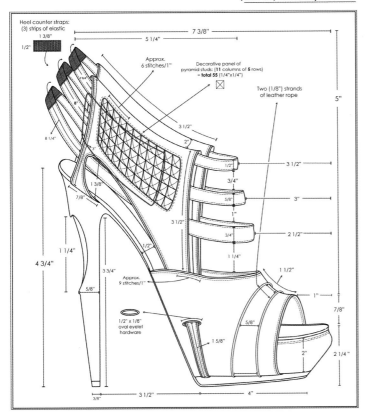

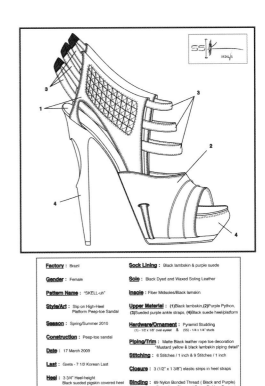

Heel counter straps: (3) strips of elastic
1 3/8"
1/2"

Approx. 6 stitches/1"

Decorative panel of pyramid studs: (11 columns of 5 rows) = total 55 (1/4"x1/4")

Two (1/8") strands of leather rope

7 3/8"
5 1/4"
5"
8 1/4"
3 1/2"
2"
3 1/2"
1/2"
3/4"
5/8"
3 1/2"
1"
3/4"
1 3/8"
7/8"
1 1/4"
4 3/4"
3 3/4"
1 1/4"
Approx. 9 stitches/1"
5/8"
1/2" x 1/8" oval eyelet hardware
5/8"
3/8"
3 1/2"
4"
1 5/8"
2"
1 1/2"
1"
7/8"
2 1/4"
3 1/2"
3"
2 1/2"

Factory : Brazil	**Sock Lining** : Black lambskin & purple suede
Gender : Female	**Sole** : Black Dyed and Waxed Soling Leather
Pattern Name : "SKELL-uh"	**Insole** : Fiber Midsoles/Black lamskin
Style/Art : Slip on High-Heel Platform Peep-toe Sandal	**Upper Material** : (1)Black lambskin,(2)Purple Python, (3)Sueded purple ankle straps, (4)Black suede heel/platform
Season : Spring/Summer 2010	**Hardware/Ornament** : Pyramid Studding (1) - 1/2 x 1/8" oval eyelet & (55) - 1/4 x 1/4" studs
Construction : Peep-toe sandal	**Piping/Trim** : Matte Black leather rope toe decoration "Mustard yellow & black lambskin piping detail"
Date : 17 March 2009	**Stitching** : 6 Stitches / 1 inch & 9 Stitches / 1 inch
Last : Greta - 7 1/2 Korean Last	**Closure** : 3 (1/2 x 1 3/8") elastic strips in heel straps
Heel : 3 3/4" Heel-height Black sueded pigskin covered heel	**Binding** : 69 Nylon Bonded Thread (Black and Purple) Petronious Glue and Barge Rubber Cement

Notes : 2 1/4" Covered Platform (Cork and Foam)- black suede
STRAPS :(3) purple straps woven through 2 side piece uppers
Pyramid Studding detail breakdown: (55) total 1/4"x1/4" studs
(25) - gun metal black (10) - antiqued silver finish
(10) - antiqued bronze finish (10) - antiqued copper finish

FIGURE 12.17 In these Illustrator drawings by Kristina Gress, the same drawing is used twice to show measurements (left) and other information about the construction and materials (right). Kristina Gress.

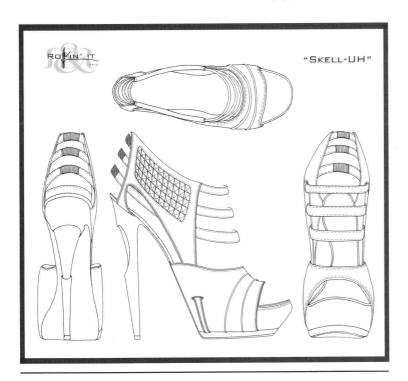

"SKELL-UH"

FIGURE 12.18 Orthographic views of a high heel shoe by Kristina Gress.

Kristina Gress.

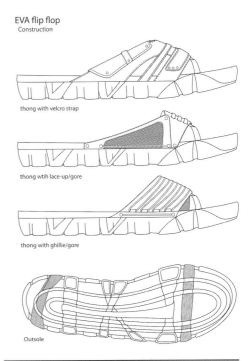

EVA flip flop
Construction

thong with velcro strap

thong wtih lace-up/gore

thong with ghillie/gore

Outsole

FIGURE 12.19 Illustrator sketches of flip-flop variations by Kristina Gress. Kristina Gress.

For someone who makes her living designing shoes, Nancy Geist has surprisingly few of her own. The reason? Her passion-fueled perfectionism. "I walk into a shoe store and I say, 'That shoe is great, but I would change this, and I would change that,'" she says. Her quest is to create perfect luxury pieces that consumers want to wear every day, and as a designer, she has an eye for even the most subtle details. Her career started in 1989, working as a creative director for Bally, but her passion for shoes is more deeply rooted.

She graduated from the Art Institute of Chicago in 1983 and started working as a shoe designer, traveling to Europe to develop new styles of shoes. Working for various companies she learned all aspects of the business and in 1993, gathered the funds to start her own company. In 1996, her footwear designs for a ready-to-wear designer won the Italian Trade Commission's prestigious Michelangelo Award. Fast forward to 2000, the first Nancy Geist boutique opened at the highly trafficked corner of Spring and Mercer in New York City's SoHo neighborhood.

Meticulously handcrafted by artisans outside of Venice, the Nancy Geist collection is sleek and mischievously glamorous. Adamant about quality and wearability, Geist also crafts the slightly less expensive nancynancy line near Venice. Sophisticated, yet girlie, there is a shoe, sandal, or boot for every whim, drama, or occasion, satisfying her customers' shoe lust without breaking the bank.

Her most recent line is Butter, the brainchild of Geist and longtime business partner and friend, Lee Riech. Originally vintage-inspired, Butter has evolved into a flirty, feminine line inspired by Hollywood but made for everyday glamour. The contrast between Geist's personality and the creations that emerge from it are what make the Butter line so fascinating. Outside her Fashion Avenue studio, Geist lives an eclectic life. She is a garden enthusiast with a love of rock 'n' roll, and she teases that her "rowdy music collection can beat that of any teenage boy," yet Geist, like any other woman, has a profound love for all things femme, and Butter designs are a tribute to that aspect of the female spirit. Geist is a no-frills woman whose inner diva emerges in her frilled-up, ruffled-up designs. Since its debut in 2007, Butter's recipe for success has evolved from the perfect peep-toe pump to chic, collectible skimmers and flats. Devout followers of Butter praise the line for its wearable styles and impeccable, of-the-moment details. Geist and Riech are dedicated to creating timeless shoes that can be reimagined each season, while still maintaining superb quality and perfect fit.

What makes Geist's creations truly amazing is the fit. She is one of the last designers to really invest energy into achieving perfect shape and proportions in her shoes. "My shoes always look better on the foot," she says. Once slipped on, each shoe appears to have that perfect Cinderella effect. "We aren't living in such a darling time anymore," Geist explains. "There isn't a car waiting for us every time we go out, and sometimes we need to run in our heels." Butter reflects this modernized approach to fashion that demands a shoe be both functional and fabulous.

In an interview in her office in New York's fashion district, Nancy Geist described her design process at the beginning of her career and how she uses sketching today.

ANETA GENOVA: The first thing that strikes me about your sketches is that they are *tiny*! Your average initial shoe sketch is about an inch or smaller. Why is that?

NANCY GEIST: I am constantly thinking up new shoe ideas and rarely have much paper on me.

AG: Have you always sketched like this?

NG: I have to admit, that I have been very lucky. For the first 10 years of my career I never had to present my work to anyone. I would leave for Italy with tiny doodles taped in my notebook and one summary sheet where I would outline my key pieces. I would extrapolate from those when I started sketching on the lasts. There was no formal approval process, company design direction, or committee decisions. There was just the critique at the end when I presented the finished sample line, so there was never a need for large presentation sketches.

AG: Nancy, you are known for your original heels and toe shapes. How do you achieve those?

NG: Of course for a new custom heel or toe I create precise 3-D sketches on vellum and grid paper. With those you *do* need to have a clear idea before you present your ideas to a master artisan. I always spend time working in Italy at their side, as they carve and sand and file the first last and heel. I am always there to direct even the tiniest modification.

AG: You went to the Art Institute of Chicago to study sculpture. How did you decide to go from sculpting to shoe design?

NG: In school I took an accessories class with one of the original masters Andrea Pfister, who was a guest lecturer from Italy. He couldn't speak English, but he didn't have to; when he pulled out tiny wooden heels, scraps of lizard, and a piece of wood form, shaped like a foot . . . well, it all became clear. The tactile nature of all those components, all the choices needing to be built into something curvaceous, sensual, harmonious, and wearable! Well . . . I was smitten.

AG: And how do you feel about design today?

NG: In 2000, for my signature line, anything was possible. Working in the same factories as Gucci, Prada, and Manolo Blahnik, I could indulge in difficult, even revolutionary constructions and techniques without worrying much about price. I worked with amazing technicians and being a sculptor and builder myself, I was not afraid to dirty my hands. There was great trust built between us. And then came the euro! With the new exchange rate and competition with China, I had to start looking at things from more of a business perspective and create more affordable shoes.

AG: Do you still travel extensively?

NG: I used to travel five months a year; currently it is down to maybe three months because I do present my sketches/ideas to my colleagues and partner before a trip, but for 80 percent of my samples, I still sketch directly on the last. That's what gives Butter its signature flirty feel, and the Nancy Geist touch.

AG: What advice do you have for students today?

NG: There is nothing that beats a Saturday afternoon with the patternmaker twisting, folding and gluing, going through trial and error, and searching for new ways and new looks. I hope future designers have the urge and chance to be present and touch all materials in a sample room setting versus only sketch and use cad-cam. As in food and wine, beauty and newness come from the kitchen and your own hands.

Promotional material for the Nancy Geist brand. Nancy Geist.

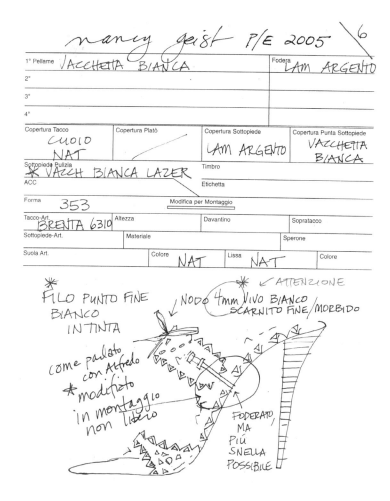

1° Pellame VACCHETTA BIANCA			Fodera LAM ARGENTO
2°			
3°			
4°			
Copertura Tacco CUOIO NAT	Copertura Platò	Copertura Sottopiede LAM ARGENTO	Copertura Punta Sottopiede VACCHETTA BIANCA
Sottopiede Pulizia ✱ VACCH BIANCA LAZER		Timbro	
ACC		Etichetta	
Forma 353		Modifica per Montaggio	
Tacco-Art. BRENTA 6310	Altezza	Davantino	Sopratacco
Sottopiede-Art.	Materiale		Sperone
Suola Art.	Colore NAT	Lissa NAT	Colore

your ideas clearly, a situation that emphasizes how important it is to draw clear pictures of your ideas, which cross the language barriers. A picture is worth a thousand words.

Sketching Techniques

The sketching technique is a personal choice for each designer and might be influenced by experience, education, or the company one works for. While there are countless ways to represent a shoe design idea and different techniques work well for different purposes and stages of the design process, we'll look at the two most basic ones, hand sketches and computer-generated sketches.

Hand Sketches

Hand sketching is the most common, easiest, and fastest technique for getting the design ideas on paper. All you need are a pen or a pencil and a piece of paper. Your job is to create many and varied ideas in a short time and to do so in a way that others can see and understand your thinking. A good pencil hand sketch fulfills both of these requirements. An experienced designer can visualize the ideas and create the details while drawing the shoe, and every new sketch can offer variations on the concept of the collection. Figures 12.21 through 12.23 are hand drawings that reveal design ideas by Danilo Giordano, Sabato Riccio, and Coleman Horn.

Computer Sketches

Software programs like Photoshop and Illustrator have become a staple in the fashion industry and most fashion companies require knowledge of these programs. They are certainly not a substitute for the hand sketch, but simply offer more tools to create your work. You can sketch by hand and then scan and color the design in Photoshop or you can create a brand new design idea from scratch. With the help of a pen and tablet you can easily have the feel of a drawing pen in your hand and sketch, as you would normally do with a

FIGURE 12.20

Tech pack for a shoe with a laser cutout upper by Nancy Geist.
Nancy Geist.

practice can be used to represent different color, texture, or material combinations.

If you have a long-standing relationship or work closely with the patternmaker as designer/owner of Butter shoes Nancy Geist does, you can have a looser sketch in the tech pack, knowing that you will be there in person to answer any questions and guide the process. Figure 12.20 shows a sketch in a tech pack that indicates all elements of the shoe, and has enough notes to support the design, but it is not necessarily a beautiful presentation sketch. In this case, the sketch gets the most important ideas to the patternmaker and presents the idea of the components. Note that while working with factories in foreign countries, you might have to learn some of the basic terminology of the native language in order to communicate

FIGURE 12.21
Hand-drawn sketches
by Danilo Giordano.

Danilo Giordano.

FIGURE 12.22
Hand-drawn sketches
by Sabato Riccio.

Sabato Riccio.

FIGURE 12.23 Hand sketches of athletic shoes by Coleman Horn explore different views of the shoe in motion (left) and a static side view (right). Coleman Horn.

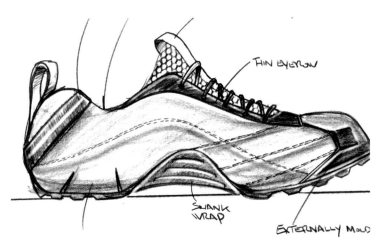

THIN EYELON

SHANK WRAP

EXTERNALLY MOLD

EVA flip flop
Construction

FIGURE 12.24 Sneaker sketches created in Illustrator by Amanda Blackwell. Amanda Blackwell.

FIGURE 12.26 This computer-generated sketch by Kristina Gress is the colored version of Figure 12.19. Kristina Gress.

pen or pencil. The ease of utilizing a variety of tools and the speed of coloring is unmatched by any hand technique. You can easily repeat the shoe silhouette and color it in dramatically different ways within minutes. The computer-generated sketches in Figures 12.24 through 12.26 demonstrate how different designers use computers to draw their shoe ideas.

Rendering Techniques

When it comes to rendering colors and textures, designers have different opinions on how they should be done. Painting with a brush could have similar results to coloring in Photoshop, but using software and printing the illustration would never produce the texture of the actual paint and the surface of the paper. Using only markers could be quick and dynamic but will not achieve the depth of a computer rendering, where shading or filters can create realistic textures. A mix of markers and pencils is a great way to make the sketch more dynamic, but

FIGURE 12.25 Sketches of high-heeled shoes created in Photoshop by Benyam Assefa. Benyam Assefa.

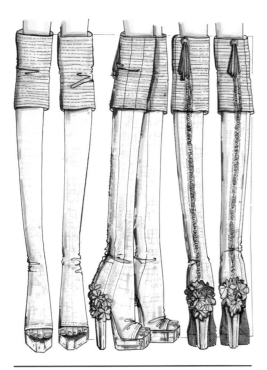

FIGURE 12.27 This marker illustration by Ivy Kirk was used in a presentation for a shoe design competition, but it has plenty of details to be used in a tech pack. Ivy Kirk.

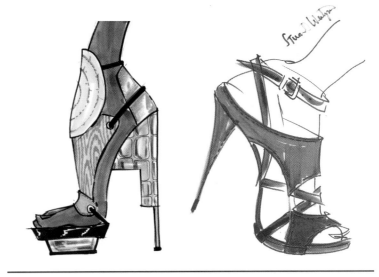

FIGURE 12.28 Both Steven Broadway's sketch (left) and Stuart Weitzman's sketch (right) of a women's high heel shoe are drawn in markers and demonstrate a quick and dynamic style of drawing. These sketches can be used for a publication or a presentation. Steven Broadway; Stuart Weitzman.

nothing compares to scanning and using the real exotic skin and then introducing color to it. Keep in mind that all of these techniques are simply tools that are interchangeable and most designers use a combination of them to achieve the best possible results. Consider what result you need to achieve, whom the presentation is geared toward, and what the budget is. If your expertise lies in marker rendering and you've never worked in Photoshop, then don't approach that tool unless you have the proper time to become educated. Rather work with what you do best. Figures 12.27 through 12.30 represent a variety of styles from designers and illustrators, including sketches using markers, paint, and scanned and recolored skins and textures.

FIGURE 12.29 Varied shoes with spikes, painted by illustrator Kevin Blow. This illustration does not reveal all design details, but it strongly conveys the main concept and is great for a presentation or a print publication. Kevin Blow.

FIGURE 12.30 Utilizing scans of real exotic skin creates a realistic feel and makes for a wonderful presentation. Using an appropriate background ties the designs to the overall concept of the collection and creates a cohesive presentation. Kristina Gress.

FIGURE 12.31 The mixed media shoe drawings by footwear designer Han Josef give a realistic feel and plenty of construction information. They are perfect for a design presentation. Han Josef.

FIGURE 12.32 Mixed media shoe illustrations by footwear designer Nalini Arora utilize markers, pen, and pencils and are created during the design process. Nalini Arora.

Mixed Media

Mixed media is the most common method of drawing fashion accessory illustrations. It offers the most flexibility in expressing different textures and surface treatments. Mixing markers or paints with pencils gives a lot of depth to the drawing and creates a powerful presentation (Figures 12.31 through 12.35).

You should practice various techniques until you discover which one is most comfortable for you, but being able to draw with various media and in various styles might also prove beneficial in this ever-changing creative environment. Creating a style of your own is just as important as being flexible. The responsibilities of footwear designers vary from company to company, and being able to adapt to the style of the brand you work for would make you a valuable asset as a designer.

FIGURE 12.34
Christian Louboutin shoe sketch, as seen in a Barneys window, is not intended to give any technical knowledge. It is best used in a presentation or a window display.
Illustration by Christian Louboutin.

FIGURE 12.35
Even though this mixed media illustration by Colin Robertson is somewhat distorted, it still gives plenty of design details and information and can be used within the design process or a tech pack.
Colin Robertson design for Charles David.

FIGURE 12.33 Mixed media shoe sketches by Italian footwear designer Edgardo Osorio give a stylized version of his designs and are best used in a presentation. Edgardo Osorio.

PROJECT

Designing and Illustrating a Shoe Collection

GOALS

To give you practical experience in designing a unique group of shoes, with the purpose of developing, sketching, and presenting the collection and possibly constructing one of the designs. This project can be an excellent portfolio piece.

ASSIGNMENT

Keeping in mind the final concept, season, colors, customer profile, and mood board, design a unique footwear collection. Sketch a group of about ten styles in various heels in a well-merchandised collection. Create illustrations for three to five styles as a presentation in a technique of your choice. Alternatively, if lasts are available, tape a last and create a shoe design on the last.

13

TECH PACKS AND MANUFACTURING

for Footwear

CHAPTER THIRTEEN describes the technical responsibilities of a footwear designer. After reading this chapter, you will be able to trace the manufacturing process for footwear and understand how to use spec sheets and tech packs to communicate with manufacturing teams.

FIGURE 13.1

The standardized form
used for all styles
within the Nine West
company relies on a
chart for indicating the
colors for each detail
of the shoe's design.

Courtesy of Nine West.

AS WITH OTHER ACCESSORIES, the job of a shoe designer doesn't end with sketching and presenting the collection. Each design style that is approved needs an accompanying tech pack in order to be sent to the factory for production.

Details of a Tech Pack

The most important role of a tech pack is to provide sufficient information for each shoe that is to be made. A manufacturer or a sample maker needs to see an explanation of every little detail and what it should look like in order to produce a pair of shoes that matches the designer's vision. It is surprising how every little thing can be interpreted in a completely different way from the intended design if it is

STYLE SPECIFICATION SHEET

ON   NINE WEST

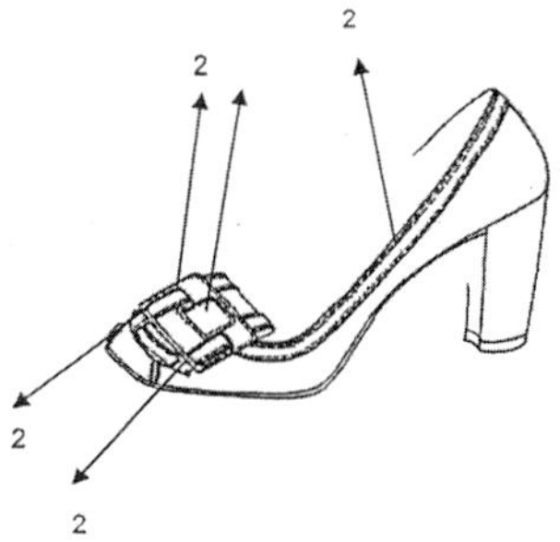

Style	PUGNOSE	DATE	
Last		Stitch	SELF
Heel		Counter Pocket	
Construction		Sock/Logo	ANT BRASS
Factory		MATERIAL INFO:	
Country			
Entry/Delivery			
Revision Date			
Version			
Season	0923		
Customer			
Reference #			
Total Pairs			
Width required			

Comments:

INK EDGES DARKER FOR #2

Pair/Size	Color/Material	Material/Reference	Lining/Color	Sock Lining/ Color	Insole Binding	Sole/ Color	Sole	Edge Color/ Mid Sole Color	Ornaments/ Finish	Heel
6.5	ORIGIN BERRY	1- LB TOP 2- NEW CHEROKEE CH	DEL KID SOFT CAMEL	DEL KID SOFT CAMEL	G3000 MATCH 1	TR DK BROWN			ANT. BRASS	STACK MATCH SOLE
6.5	ORIGIN AUBERGINE	1- LB TOP 2- NEW CHEROKEE CH	DEL KID SOFT CAMEL	DEL KID SOFT CAMEL	G3000 MATCH 1	TR BLK				STACK MATCH SOLE
6.5	ORIGIN FOREST ✓	1- LB TOP 2- NEW CHEROKEE CH	DEL KID SOFT CAMEL	DEL KID SOFT CAMEL	G3000 MATCH 1	TR DK BROWN				STACK MATCH SOLE
8.5	BLACK	1- LB TOP 2- NEW CHEROKEE CH	DEL KID SOFT CAMEL	DEL KID SOFT CAMEL	G3000 MATCH 1	TR BLK				STACK MATCH SOLE
8.5	ORIGIN BARK ✓	1- LB TOP 2- NEW CHEROKEE CH	DEL KID SOFT CAMEL	DEL KID SOFT CAMEL	G3000 MATCH 1	TR DK BROWN			✓	STACK MATCH SOLE
	ORIGIN PEONY	ʺ	ʺ	ʺ	ʺ				ʺ	ʺ

not explained properly. Here is what a footwear tech pack consists of:

- A clear sketch of the shoe
- A list of materials to be used for each component
- Colors for each specific component
- Clear notes on any specific details like topstitching, measurements, logo placement, embellishments, and finishes
- Exact measurements for every single detail. The page containing all measurements and specifications for the shoe design is often referred to as a spec page or spec sheet.
- Close-up pictures or detailed drawings of all of the above
- Reference pictures of samples being sent to the factory and accompanying notes explaining them

Tech packs are created for every single style of shoes to be made, every season, and every year. Even though each company has its own specific template for a tech pack that it uses for every design, in order to make a distinction between the different seasons and concepts, some companies might have a different header for each separate group. This can be a concept-specific header or a graphic design that spans the whole background or simply a title that changes with each season and collection.

Figures 13.1 through 13.6 are a few examples of pages from tech packs used in the industry.

The following sections describe the segments that need to be included in a technical package. Each one brings important information to the manufacturing process.

AN   NINE WEST

Style	nwFucshia	DATE	3/3/2009
Last		Stitch	SELF
Heel		Counter Pocket	
Construction		Sock/Logo	BLACK
Factory		MATERIAL INFO:	
Country			
Entry/Delivery			
Revision Date			
Version			
Season	0924		
Customer	Wholesale		
Reference #			
Total Pairs			
Width required			

Comments:

PLATFORM AS 1

PIPING AS LINING

Pair/Size	Color/Material	Material/Reference	Lining/Color	Sock Lining/Color	Insole Binding	Sole/Sole Color	Edge Color/Mid Sole Color	Ornaments/Finish	Heel
8.5	(A) 1- FAWN 2- TRUFFLE 3- MINK 4- CAMEL	SOHO SUEDE	UNIKA DORE KID HR CH INT BRASS	UNIKA DORE KID HR CH INT BRASS	AS 2	COR-INTO CUOIO BIRRA	DK NATURAL	ANT BRASS	AS 3
6.5	(B) 1- GRAPE 2- RASPBERRY 3- HEMATITE 4- VIOLET	SOHO SUEDE	UNIKA DORE KID HR CH INT BRASS	UNIKA DORE KID HR CH INT BRASS	AS 2	COR-INTO CUOIO BIRRA	BLK	ANT BRASS	AS 3
6.5	(C) 1- PETROL 2- PEACOCK 3- FIR 4- QUARTZ	SOHO SUEDE	UNIKA DORE KID HR CH INT BRASS	UNIKA DORE KID HR CH INT BRASS	AS 2	COR-INTO CUOIO BIRRA	BLK	ANT BRASS	AS 3

FIGURE 13.2

This spec sheet and
sketch were created in
Illustrator by Kristina
Gress, a graduate of
FIT. Kristina Gress.

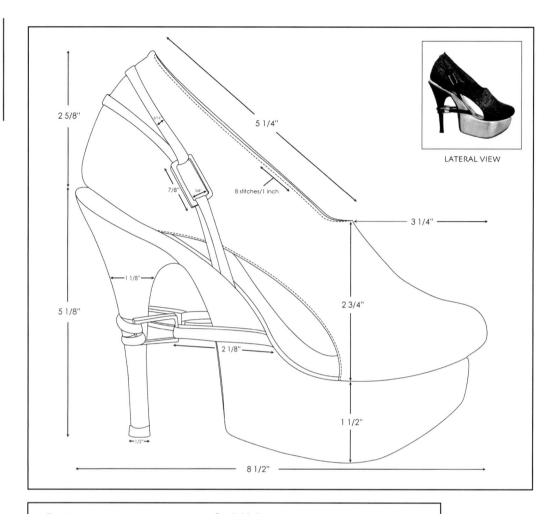

LATERAL VIEW

Factory : Brazil

Gender : Female

Pattern Name : "Ssik Designs"

Style/Art : Cut-out, High-Heeled,
Platform Pump

Season : Spring 2009

Construction : Platform Pump

Date : 12 December 2007

Last : Greta - 8 1/2 Korean Last

Heel : 3 1/2" Heel-height
Black Pigskin Covered Plastic Heel

Sock Lining : Silver Metallic Kidskin Leather

Sole : Black Dyed and Waxed Soling Leather

Insole : Fiber Midsoles

Upper Material : Black Pigskin w/ Shimmer
Sparkle Finish

Hardware/Ornament : Four 7/8" x 3/8" Steel
Rectangle Rings

Piping/Trim : Shiney Black Satin Decorative Rope

Stitching : 8 Stiches for every 1 Inch

Closure : Slip-on , Open-lip Upper

Binding : 69 Nylon Bonded Thread (Black and Cream)
Petronious Glue and Barge Rubber Cement

Notes : 1 1/2" Covered Platform (Cork and Foam)
Satin rope draped around heel: 2" from top lift of heel
Measurement at Bottom of heel : 1/2" across
Total Vertical Measurement : 7 3/8"

FIGURE 13.3

The handwritten first page of a tech pack by Aimee Kestenberg for the Australian company Sass and Bide, includes sketches of the shoe, reference photos of various details, and callouts providing specs and other information. Aimee Kestenberg for Sass and Bide.

FIGURE 13.4

The front page of an athletic shoe tech pack was created in Illustrator by accessory designer Coleman Horn. Coleman Horn.

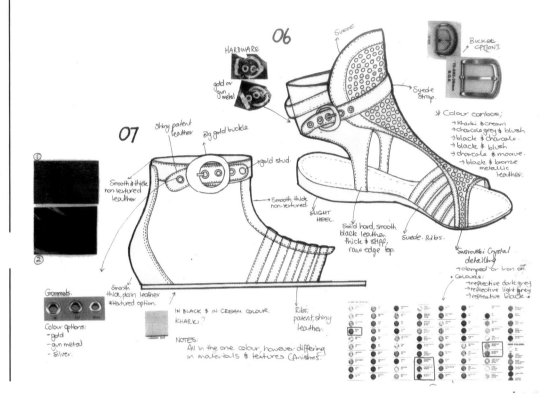

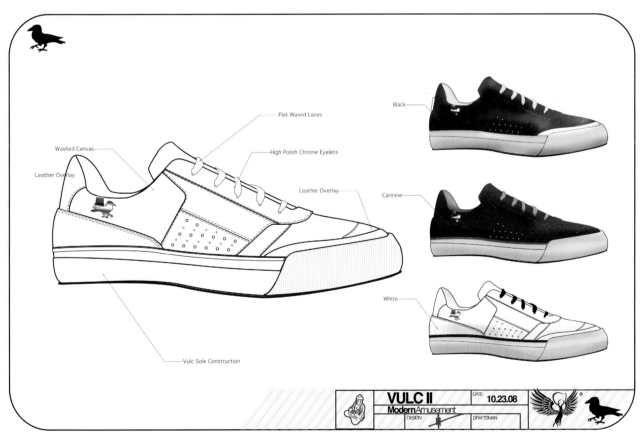

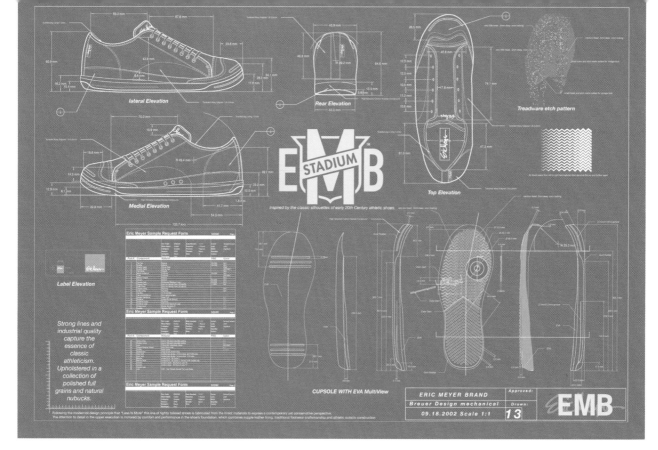

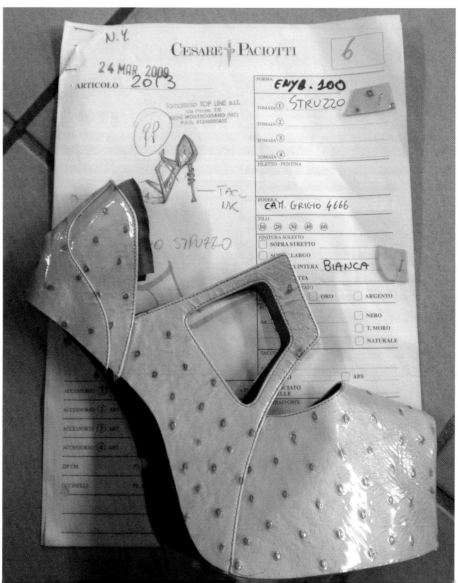

FIGURE 13.5
Spec page (above) of a
tech pack for an athletic
shoe created by Coleman
Horn, freelance designer
for EMB. Coleman Horn.

FIGURE 13.6
A Cesare Paciotti tech
pack front page with a
completed upper (right).
Cesare Paciotti.

Flats

As explained in Chapter 12, flat sketches for tech packs (also called flats) are different from illustrations or concept sketches. These flat sketches (Figure 13.7) are usually black and white and represent the shoe as realistically as possible with all construction details in correct proportions.

Figure 13.8 shows various shoe sketches by Han Josef, footwear designer for Cole Haan. He has a lot of technical knowledge and understands the footwear construction very well, so every time he sketches, he builds a shoe with all of its components. He draws in perspective, starting with the sole and the heel, and then builds the upper, the hardware, and the embellishments on top of it. Looking at his work is like looking at a construction diagram of a shoe. Every detail is clear, and it is easy to add measurements for

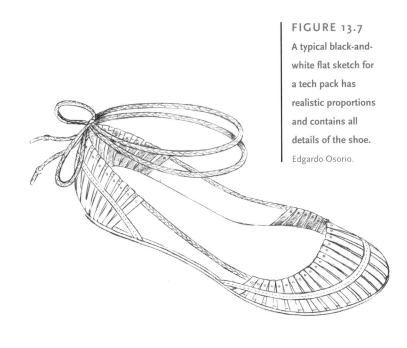

FIGURE 13.7

A typical black-and-white flat sketch for a tech pack has realistic proportions and contains all details of the shoe.

Edgardo Osorio.

FIGURE 13.8

Various views are necessary to show the design details for each shoe. Han Josef for Cole Haan.

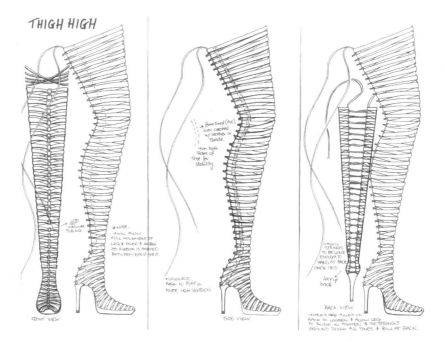

THIGH HIGH

FRONT VIEW

SIDE VIEW

BACK VIEW

FIGURE 13.9

Multiple view close-up
of a lace-up high heel
by Aimee Kestenberg.

Aimee Kestenberg.

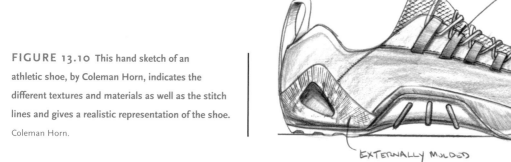

SPECTRA
LACE

ADJUSTABLE
(GHILLY (WEBBING)
LACE SYSTEM

CLIMBING
FOREFOOT

EXTERNALLY MOLDED

FIGURE 13.10 This hand sketch of an
athletic shoe, by Coleman Horn, indicates the
different textures and materials as well as the stitch
lines and gives a realistic representation of the shoe.

Coleman Horn.

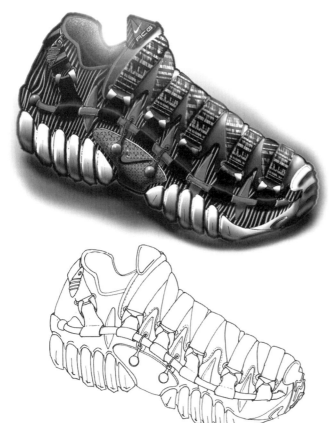

every component. This sketch and Figure 13.9
are both excellent examples of how a designer
needs to draw multiple views of the same shoe
to show all details.

Figure 13.10 is a side view of a hand-sketched
athletic shoe. A complicated athletic style like
this one might require indication of different
textures and materials. Some designers prefer
to draw by hand (Figure 13.9); others prefer
the ease and clarity of a software program like
Adobe Illustrator (Figure 13.11). As long as
all details are clear and understandable, both
techniques are valid.

FIGURE 13.11 Using a computer software program
like Adobe Illustrator is an excellent way to draw a
black-and-white sketch or to add texture and shading for
a realistic effect. Coleman Horn.

CESARE PACIOTTI

Cesare Paciotti was born in Civitanova Marche, Italy. His love for all accessories was nurtured at home by his parents Cecilia and Giuseppe Paciotti, who owned a local shoe factory and manufactured high-end shoes. Giuseppe Paciotti founded the company in 1948 and started production of a men's footwear collection called Paris. It was made by hand from start to finish. He was extremely detail oriented and personally supervised every step of the process. Giuseppe's passion for design transferred to his children, Cesare and Paola.

As a teenager, Cesare Paciotti had a passion for music. He loved the Rolling Stones, Jimi Hendrix, The Doors, and Patti Smith and felt that they pushed him to expand his creativity by playing the organ. His love for art drove him to attend one of Italy's most renowned colleges, DAMS in Bologna. Upon graduation, he traveled around the world and explored London, Paris, New York, Los Angeles, Tokyo, New Delhi, and Dubai. He observed foreign cultures and their use of color and developed a strong sense of style that defines his work even today. He returned to his hometown with a desire to transform his experiences into designs.

He took over his parents' company in 1980 and launched his first men's collection calling it simply Cesare Paciotti. Combining his craftsmanship and creativity with the management skills of his sister, he developed revolutionary men's shoes that completed an outfit in an elegant and unique manner. His provocative designs have earned him tremendous recognition worldwide. Having established friendships and collaborations with noted Italian designers Gianni Versace, Dolce and Gabbana, Romeo Gigli, and Roberto Cavalli, he is always open to explore new ideas.

His current collections include a women's line, inspired by a strong, sophisticated, elegant, modern woman. The desire to experiment with new innovative techniques and materials led to an investment in a new factory dedicated only to the ladies' collection. The new 4US unisex line of shoes is the most evident result of that investment. It is a line of footwear entirely dedicated to sport and leisure activities.

Following its tradition of handmade, high-quality goods and attention to detail, the Cesare Paciotti Company continues to grow in new venues. Nowadays, the company's product lines include handbags, eyewear, clothing, and jewelry and continue to use avant-garde materials and innovative shapes to manufacture unique and glamorous accessories. The company, employing more than 250 people and about 1,200 collaborators who work on external projects, produces more than a million pairs of shoes a year.

Cesare Paciotti in his design studio, fitting and correcting new styles. Note the lasts with pencil drawn styles on his desk. In 2008, Cesare Paciotti sponsored a shoe design competition for Parsons The New School for Design and a select few students had their designs manufactured by the renowned design house. In the top right photo, Paciotti himself is holding a winning design by Ivy Kirk. Her illustration is pictured in **Figure 12.27.** Courtesy of Cesare Paciotti.

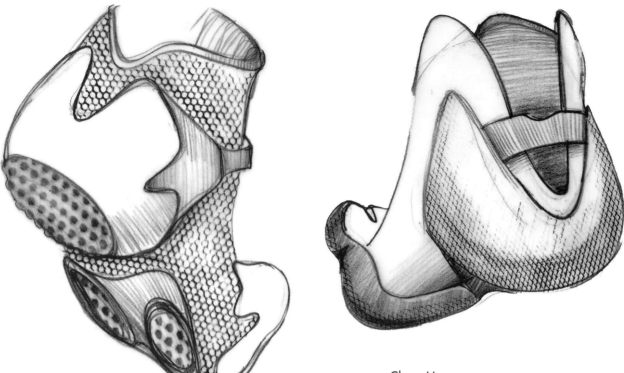

FIGURE 13.12 **Back views of athletic shoes by Coleman Horn, showing close-ups of textures and design details.** Coleman Horn.

FIGURE 13.13 **A Nine West Footwear Corp. shoe flat sketch for a tech pack, with a close-up of the "pug nose" detail.** Courtesy of Nine West.

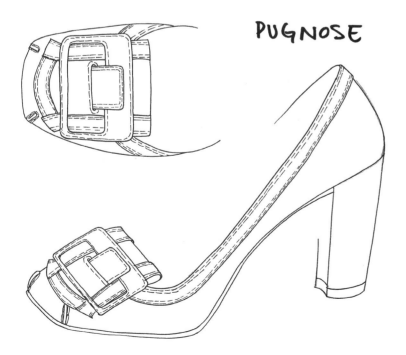

PUGNOSE

Close-Ups

A close-up of a particular texture, complicated design, or application element should be added in to the overall sketch. The shoe can be drawn at an angle or in movement (Figure 13.12), or the design element can be drawn separately from a different view (Figure 13.13), showing in greater details how it works. You can do as many close-ups as necessary to demonstrate how the shoe should be made or what it should look like.

List of Materials

On each tech pack, the designer needs to identify what each component will be made off. The heel could be plastic or wood, for example, or covered in leather or wrapped with braided rope or embellished with rhinestones. This is where the designer explains what material to use. There are so many different ways a sketch can be interpreted that you cannot leave anything to the imagination. The upper can be leather, or it can be a treated fabric that resembles leather—or a fabric that is selected for its own appearance. Whatever material is desired, it needs to be clearly explained.

Colors

Each designed style that will be produced is usually made in more than one color combination. Sometimes there is more than one color within the upper, heel, or embellishments. Each tech pack has a section where color combinations for upper, heel, sole, thread, sock liner, and other details are listed with specific instructions on how they work together. Specs need to be very precise and clear, with the placement and designation of each color, especially if there are multiple color combinations.

Notes and Descriptions

For the designer, it is clear what the shoe should look like, but everybody else who sees the design for the first time needs some notes and descriptions to explain the sketch. Once the designer has conceived the idea, it is easy to forget that other people cannot envision it as clearly and cannot guess every detail. Manufacturers know a variety of ways to produce shoes and want to know which technique to use and what the exact measurements for every single element are. That includes heel height, strap widths, and so on. This section should be edited very carefully to have accurate comments with precise measurements and short but clear explanations. General abbreviations can be used if they are accepted as commonly used and have the same meaning for both the design team and the manufacturer.

Sample References

It is a common practice in the footwear industry to use an actual sample as a reference of how the new shoe should be made. A heel from a vintage sample or a buckle from luggage can be an excellent resource for the sample-maker and the manufacturer. Sometimes it is difficult to explain with words or not enough to draw what you need to use. A sample can provide an easy and clear reference. In addition to sending the sample, it is always a good idea to take pictures of

multiple angles and views and include those in the tech packs with notes on how and which parts should be used.

Manufacturing Process

The manufacturing process for each particular shoe type is different from others, but there are some main steps that can be summed up in an overview.

- Designing
- Prototyping (usually on a wooden last)
- Making the last for production (plastic multiples in sizes)
- Gathering all components: leather, fabrics, outsoles, insoles, shanks, toe puffs, heels, stiffeners, fillers, hardware
- Clicking, cutting patterns for production—automated or manual
- Adding stiffeners and stabilizers
- Closing the upper/sewing uppers/lasting
- Adding the outsoles
- Sewing or next stage, according to construction method
- Painting edges
- Buffing, cleaning
- Checking quality (Chanel machinery to X-ray high heels)
- Adding tags and trims
- Wrapping
- Boxing

Design

Depending on the company, the design process can be done in house or at the manufacturing facility. We already discussed the design process in-depth in Chapter 11, but it is important to know that all design details need to be clearly outlined before the shoes go into the manufacturing process. All problems need to be identified during the prototyping and fitting stage. Once the shoe style is in production, it is too late to correct any mistakes. By this time, all lasts are produced, the leather and all other components are in the factory, and deadlines are fast approaching. Any delay can be fatal for the brand.

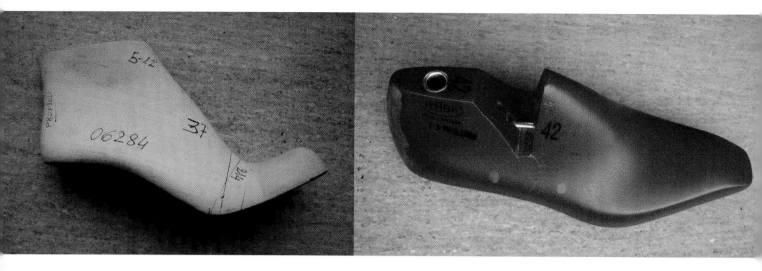

FIGURE 13.14
Wooden last (left) for a high heel shoe, marked with European size 37, and a plastic last (right) for shoe production, marked with a European size 42. This is a two-part hinged last. The heel part folds up for easy removal from the finished shoe. The metal-lined hole is used to attach the shoe last to the lasting machine. Courtesy of Aneta Genova.

Prototyping

This is the time to try out ideas and make changes. Design ideas are coming to life, and it is the first time the designer sees them come into reality. The designer gets to evaluate the look and the feel of the finished shoe and how it fits in the overall concept and collection. During this process the designer has time to present the finished proto (short for prototype) in front of the design director or VP of the company and get feedback on the overall direction of the brand. This is the perfect time to evaluate the workmanship, the quality of the leather and all the little details like stitching, color combinations, and hardware. All of those decisions should be finalized in this stage.

Last-Making for Production

The first last is handcrafted from a block of wood, but the high-quantity shoe production requires multiple plastic lasts (Figure 13.14, right) in all sizes that will be manufactured. This is usually done in a factory that specializes in this process. Depending on the particular construction of the shoe, lasts are created with different hinges so they can be taken out of the shoe once it is completely finished. Some shoes have a very wide opening and the production lasts are very simple. Other shoes have a tight or small opening and require a last that can be taken apart or folded out of the shoe.

Procuring All Components

Each shoe requires a variety of components in order to be completed. Naturally there is a difference between the components of athletic, dressy, and casual shoes, and the process will take longer or shorter, depending on the particular components. A designer would not normally be involved in actually collecting the components unless he or she works for a smaller design company or works within the factory. But it is important to understand what components are needed in order to complete the shoes as designed, so that a realistic timeline can be established.

The following components may come from different factories and thus require special arrangements: outsoles, insoles, leather board, toe puffs, fillers, stiffeners, shanks, heels, etc.

Cutting Pattern Pieces for Production

The first pattern piece for the shoe upper is cut by the patternmaker, using the last as a guide. After adjustments from the first prototype fittings, the pattern gets finalized and ready for production. In the next step, the pattern is graded according to the sizes that will be produced and the materials to be used.

Cutting multiple pieces of the upper can be an automated process or a manual process. In most cases it is a combination of both. The larger pattern pieces are cut with a machine, while the more delicate pieces can be cut by hand.

In Figure 13.15, you see the first step of a computerized process in an Italian factory. To begin the process, each skin is designated a number, and the computer takes a photograph of the shape of the skin and matches it to the corresponding number. The actual pattern layout is created without marking or drawing on the skin. It consists of a process in which the shapes of the pattern pieces are positioned with the click of a mouse and can be rotated to any angle. The operator places a laser outline of each pattern piece on top of the skin by clicking with the mouse and then arranges as many pieces as the skin allows. Each skin is given a number and the computer memorizes the layout for that number. A skilled technician knows how to avoid skin defects and which part of the skin is better for the front, side, or back of the shoe upper. Once the skin is filled with pattern pieces it is folded and transferred to the cutting table.

On the cutting table, each skin is recognized by the computer from its corresponding number. The computer recalls the pattern piece layout for that skin and the machine cuts the pattern pieces according to the layout designated by the operator in the previous step. This means that each skin has a unique layout and can fit a different number of pattern pieces and is cut differently (Figure 13.16). This allows for maximum use of surface and labor with minimal waste of leather.

Factories that do not have the high-end computerized technology use a heavy weight press and premade dies to cut each pattern piece. This process still requires the skillful eye of a technician, who positions each die on the leather, avoiding defects and determining the best place. More than one die can be placed at the same time, but each die is expensive, and normally there is only one

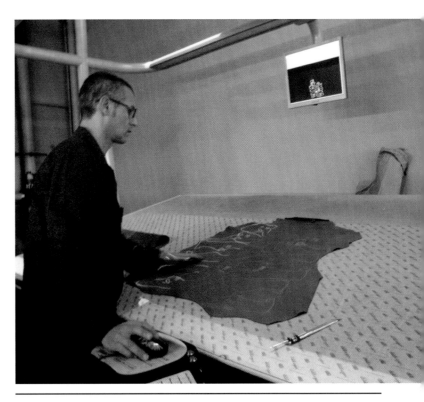

FIGURE 13.15 Automated pattern cutting starts with a technician, marking each skin and arranging the pattern outlines with computerized technology. Courtesy of Aneta Genova.

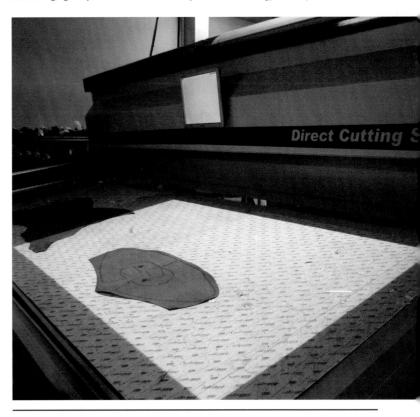

FIGURE 13.16 An automated direct cutting system. Courtesy of Aneta Genova.

FIGURE 13.17 A complicated upper like this one with thin cutouts cannot be cut with a blade by hand; it requires a die. Courtesy of Aneta Genova.

FIGURE 13.18 Pattern cutting with a metal die and handheld press. The technician carefully selects where each pattern would be cut from, places the die, and then activates the press. Courtesy of Aneta Genova.

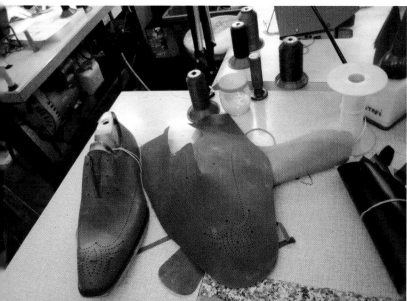

per pattern piece made. Figure 13.17 shows an example of a men's dressy upper, which would require a die made for it. In Figure 13.18, you can see how the technician has positioned the die over the leather skin and is bringing the press over it. Once the press is positioned correctly, he presses a button, the machine applies pressure and the blades of the die cut into the leather to create an evenly cut pattern piece.

Applying Design Details

Each shoe design has specific design details, and so the operations for the upper sewing vary from style to style. But it is important to execute as many operations as possible on the flat upper pattern pieces before they are sewn together. Once the uppers are sewn or lasted into a three-dimensional shape it becomes difficult to work on it and add details. For example, the operation of creating a punched design on wingtips should be completed on the flat pattern piece for the upper (Figure 13.19). If the shoe has a simple upper with one seam and no design details, a plain women's pump for example, the manufacturing process is much shorter and the shoe goes straight to lasting.

Marking

Each upper has identification marks, which align with markings on the sole and are essential for a proper closing of the shoes. Marks can be permanent or washable. Permanent markings can identify size, brand name, style, and place of manufacturing and can be stamped with permanent ink or metallic foil. A metal die is made for each stamp. Temporary marks identify stitch lines or alignment (Figure 13.20) and are usually applied by hand with a template. They are meant to be visible during

FIGURE 13.19 Upper with a punched design and finished shoe with that design. Courtesy of Aneta Genova.

the stitching operation and disappear before the shoe is finished and boxed for shipping. These can be made with chalk-based ink, or a silver ballpoint pen that can be erased or cleaned with solvents. Fluorescent ink, visible only under UV lamp, is another option often employed.

Edge Treatment

The edges of the upper are usually **skived**, a process in which a thin layer of the skin is removed to reduce the thickness. After that the edges can be burnished, bound, folded, or left raw to give a clean finish for the desired design.

Upper Closing/Sewing

The upper components for each shoe are stitched together on a sewing machine, unless, of course, the upper is molded from plastic or rubber. Before the pieces can be sewn together, they are usually glued together at the edges to maintain an easier and faster sewing process. This is usually a separate step performed by an operator before the sewing process (Figure 13.21). The glue is carefully applied only at the seam allowance to hold the separate pieces together. Some factories avoid gluing any parts because the glue binds the leather and stops it from breathing, but it speeds the manufacturing process and allows seamstresses to work faster.

Stiffeners (Figure 13.22), toe puffs, and reinforcements are applied to the upper pieces before stitching. Once all reinforcements are applied, the uppers are ready to go to the sewing machine operators for the next step of the process.

The machines for each sewing operation can vary from flat bed to post bed to cylinder bed and are designed for different functions.

FIGURE 13.22 In this factory, stiffeners are applied to a men's shoe upper with a spray glue gun. Courtesy of Aneta Genova.

FIGURE 13.20 A men's upper marked with bright silver ink markings, which will be covered by the trim. Courtesy of Aneta Genova.

FIGURE 13.21 A menswear shoe seamstress preparing uppers for sewing. Courtesy of Aneta Genova.

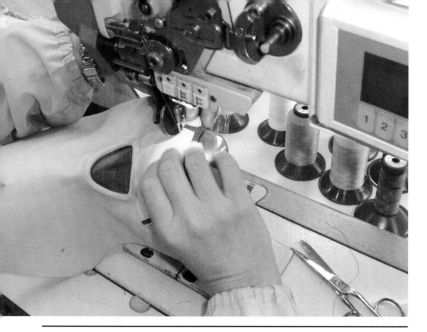

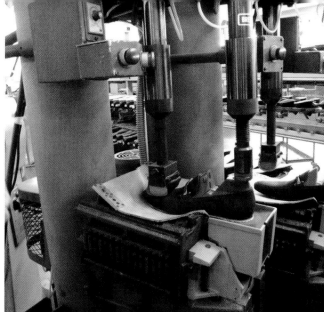

FIGURE 13.23 Sewing the uppers of fashionable high heels requires utmost precision. Seamstresses usually specialize in performing a particular part of the process. Courtesy of Cesare Paciotti.

FIGURE 13.24 A machine performing a step of the lasting process. Courtesy of Aneta Genova.

This operation can be done manually (Figure 13.23) or with a computer-aided machine. The auto-stitching machine can be preprogrammed to execute various movements under a fixed sewing head. The upper components are preloaded and the machine executes specific stitch pattern. (Each machine performs different plain or decorative stitches depending on the design. Some of the decorative stitches typical for shoe design are lock stitch and chain stitch.)

Lasting

The closed upper gets shaped to its design and fit in a process called **lasting** (Figure 13.24). In this process, the finished upper is molded onto the last and attached to the sole by a specific method. This is when the shoe design determines the construction method. There are two methods most often used: flat lasting or force lasting.

In the **flat lasting,** the upper is placed on the last, pulled down, and then attached to the insole at the toe, side, and seat of the last. In the forced lasting the upper is preshaped into a shoe form and then the last is forced into it. In the **force lasting,** the upper is closed with allowances and shaped into a baglike structure with California or moccasin construction (see Chapter 10). The last is then pushed into the

bag, or the bag is slipped over the last and finished. This requires an accurate pattern that will fit the last precisely and works very well with light, soft, and flexible upper materials.

Finishing

The shoe is finished at the bottom and the upper. The bottom finishing involves mechanical and chemical operations on the soles and heels, while the upper finishing involves chemical finishes and shoe dressing.

For the bottom finishing, the soles and heels are shaped to the correct dimensions. Excess material is removed as well as scratches and marks. Soles are polished with a fine grade abrasive, and can be stained before wax is applied to give them a shiny finish. Exposed edges of the soles are painted with ink to give them the desired look of matching or contrasting color. For the upper finishing, steps include cleaning to remove dirt, scratches, and marks and filling any micro cracks; conditioning the leather; buffing; brushing; and polishing.

Shoes go through a testing process before they are shipped to the stores, and for every style there are different testing procedures. Some high-end factories put their high heel shoes through an X-ray machine to make sure all pins and staples are correctly placed and the heel will not lose shape or collapse. Other shoes need to be tested for tear strength, extension break, stitching strength, breaking stress, and fastness of finish to rubbing.

The last steps of the process are adding labels and tags and wrapping and packing the shoes.

Communicating with Factories

Designers and assistants are usually required to communicate with the factories on a daily basis. At each stage of the process, from creating a prototype to actual production, many questions arise, and designers need to be available and ready to answer them. Be prepared to work on a few different seasons at the same time. Usually there are multiple collections from different seasons and at different stages that you need to be aware of. It is extremely important to employ your best organizational efforts and keep your records in excellent order. You should have labeled binders with sketches and paperwork, including the tech pack, for each style that is in the making. Keep detailed notes of each meeting and file them in the proper binder under the right style.

Factories and designers communicate through e-mail and phone on a daily basis. Working with overseas teams, spread around the globe from the Far East to Europe makes it a bit harder to follow up with the answers on time. While you might be just getting to work, your factory contacts might already be nearing the end of the day and could have pressing issues that need your immediate attention.

If you are well organized, you will be able to find your references quickly and resolve problems immediately. If you have to look through a pile of paperwork and have somebody on the phone from around the globe waiting for you, it might be wise to rethink your efficiency and work on creating an organized environment. You need to have a system in place and file all sketches and paperwork as soon as you are finished with them. Having all the needed information readily available at your fingertips will ensure accurate communication with manufacturers and sample makers and enable them to produce the design you intend with minimal problems.

Drawing Flat Sketches

GOALS

To give you practical experience in creating flat sketches and tech packs.

ASSIGNMENT

Draw a black-and-white flat sketch for every design you created in the project for Chapter 12.

Draw multiple views for complicated designs and close-ups where necessary to show details.

Add measurements and notes for all shapes and design details.

DESIGNING

Other Accessories

Part Four

14

VARIOUS
ACCESSORIES

CHAPTER FOURTEEN provides an overview of the design and manufacturing process for hats, gloves, belts, neckwear, and pocket squares. After reading this chapter, you will be able to identify and describe the materials, components, and styles that are common to each category.

THE WORLD OF ACCESSORIES consists of a lot more items than just shoes and bags. For both function and decoration over the past few centuries, we have accumulated an amazing array of additional items to carry or adorn ourselves with. Some have improved our daily life, some just look good, but either way they are needed, desired, and even coveted at any price level. In modern times, designing and manufacturing various accessories is a multibillion-dollar global industry with new items added every season. In this chapter, we investigate the categories of hats, gloves, belts, neckwear, and pocket squares.

Hats

Hats can be fashionable items that flatter the wearer and bring style to an outfit, or they can protect against heat or cold, rain or sun, and most certainly they can be both decorative and functional. Our heads haven't changed much since the beginning of the human race, and most hat shapes were created centuries ago. The scale and decorations keep changing, but the basic two styles can be simplified to brimmed and unbrimmed. Gone are the times when only felt or straw was used as the basic building material for a hat. Nowadays, with the advancement of technology in textiles, we have hats made out of high-tech materials for the avid outdoors adventurer, made with completely different techniques from the process for the high-end couture creations featuring exotic feathers.

Decorative hats are some of the easiest and most powerful tools of transformation in style (Figure 14.1). Using them just for protection throughout the centuries was mostly a mark of a lower class. Otherwise they were a symbol of power and status within society and involved strict etiquette. Crowns distinguish royalty from ordinary people, and hats differentiate a Catholic priest from his parishioners. Cardinals were appointed to wear a red hat during the thirteenth century, and continue to do so, but the laity are required to remove any headwear in a sign of respect. Conversely, Orthodox Jewish men and married women are expected to cover their heads while in a synagogue or even at home. In Islamic cultures, wearing hats is permissible while saying prayers at a mosque, and women are required to cover their hair in public. Either way, strict etiquette is observed by everybody within each religious group, and hats have a significant role and a specific use for power and honor in each social and religious group throughout the world.

The Millinery Workroom

A single milliner might work on his or her designs on his own or with an assistant, while an established millinery house usually has a workroom full of specialists who physically create each and every hat. A workroom is often in the back or directly below the actual shop so

clients can be easily fitted for a quick change. Different skills are required for every shape and material. Some milliners might specialize in sculpting a three-dimensional shape, while others work with fur or straw. Fine fabrics and trimmings require a delicate touch and someone who works only with straw might not handle them properly. With the variety of styles today, milliners also need some clothing or even shoe and handbag making techniques. Leathers and heavy fabrics used in other accessories are great for creating hats too. The overall success of a millinery studio relies on the talents of the team as a whole.

The Client

Every client is unique in his or her needs and approach to buying and wearing hats. A client could be faithful to one milliner or follow the trend. Throughout the last few centuries, hats have been a crucial element in one's outfit and required at particular occasions. Books were dedicated to advice on how a woman should choose the right hat in order to make the right impression. Nowadays fewer clients choose custom-made hats but when they do, the emphasis is more on trend rather than etiquette. Many iconic figures and fashionable women use hats to define their personality and stand out. Practicality is another important reason why a customer may become a client in search of the perfect protection against the elements.

A design house could also be a client of a milliner. A clothing designer might collaborate with a famous milliner to create a collection of hats within the concept of the existing collection. Philip Treacy has been known to collaborate with Karl Lagerfeld, designing hats for the Chanel haute couture collection; milliner Stephen Jones has created some

Having a well-researched concept with plenty of visual references for color, shape, and trims, construction makes all the difference in creating a hat. If you are creating hats to complement an existing clothing collection, then you need to look for innovative ideas that fit the concept and allow for experimentation. A touch of whimsy or a serious trim can transform an idea into a complete piece ready to adorn the most exquisite outfit.

Initial Ideas

Once an idea is formulated, the hat design can be sketched from different angles. This drawing usually represents the hat on a head to show the proper scale, shape, and angle to the wearer. A quick sketch should show the basic shape and form while a more detailed one needs to elaborate on specific details and trims and their proportion within the overall design. A sketch is not always the best and easiest way to work out the idea within the concept. Some milliners like to start working directly with the actual materials. Manipulating the actual felt or straw and just holding different trims to the headpiece gives an instant idea of what the final piece might look like. This quick experimentation with the real trims and materials feels more inspirational to many professional milliners and is often used with better success than sketching.

Materials

Hats can be made from various materials, including natural and man-made ones. Some of the most popular ones are felt, fabric, straw braids, leather, crinoline, veiling, lace, netting, wire, and various trims like feathers, flowers, and ribbons. Nowadays hat makers can buy most supplies like **fascinators** (bases on which to build hats), felt, and braids already premade and create their designs quickly and easily. True creators prefer to make their designs from scratch and thus have more control over the fine details of every element. Milliners making

FIGURE 14.2

Milliner Steven Jones is famous for using a mix of traditional and unusual materials to create extravagant shapes. Courtesy of WWD.

fantastical designs for John Galliano's runways (Figure 14.2). Such collaborations allow for the addition of a milliner's talent to an already developed concept and the creation of a new dimension to the collection.

Inspiration

Just like designing other accessories, inspiration is the beginning of the creative process for hats, and it can come from anywhere: art, photographs, movies, daily life. Since hats can be used purely for decoration, architecture can have a significant influence on their shape and construction. For functional hats designed to protect a wearer from the elements, it is important to look at the latest trends and materials, but for the milliners creating a unique piece, a great concept is the leading factor. Hats can be created in any shape and from such an amazing range of materials that inspiration can be taken quite literally and reinterpreted with great success.

PHILIP TREACY

Milliner Philip Treacy regularly collaborates with famous design houses. The hat sculpture at left was created for an Alexander McQueen runway show, making the design house a client for Mr. Treacy. Courtesy of WWD.

One of the most famous contemporary hatters is Philip Treacy. Born in 1967 in a tiny village in the west of Ireland, he started making hats for his sister's dolls from the feathers shed by his mother's chickens. "My mother had chickens, geese, pheasant, and ducks, so all the ingredients of the hat were in my house," he recalled. He was lucky to receive the moral support of his family, and by 1985 Treacy left school and went to Dublin to study fashion.

In the time-consuming fashion courses where nobody else cared about hats, he made them "as a hobby" to go with the required outfits. "Nobody really had much time for the hats because it was a fashion school, but there did come a point when I was more interested in making the hat than the outfits."

He apprenticed for six weeks with the London hat designer Stephen Jones, and when he got accepted to the Royal College of Art in London in 1988, he "became their guinea pig" for their new hat course. While he was a student, Treacy made Ascot hats for Harrods department store. He was named "the next great British hat maker" in the

Sunday Times by its fashion director, Claire Stubbs. Soon after, Treacy took his hats to *Tattler* magazine, and its style editor, Isabella Blow, fell in love with his creations. Blow commissioned him to create a hat for her wedding, and thus began a prolific relationship between the two of them. Isabella Blow took him under her wing; invited him to stay in the basement of her house, where he set up a studio; and introduced him to established designers like Manolo Blahnik and Karl Lagerfeld and editors like *Vogue*'s André Leon Talley.

Treacy ended up working with Lagerfeld and designing hats for the Chanel haute couture collection, all at the age of 23. At a time when hats were out of fashion, Philip Treacy set out to change that trend. He made fantastical creations ranging from a replica of an eighteenth-century sailing ship with full rigging, a castle based on Blow's ancestral home, and a surreal concoction of pink and green lacquered ostrich feathers and a mortar board so wide that Isabella couldn't fit through the door of the charity event she had ordered it for.

He continued to make hats for famed couture houses like Valentino, Gianni Versace, Alexander McQueen at Givenchy, and Ralph Lauren in 2008. "Having studied fashion design, it helped me greatly when I started working with designers because I understood how the clothes draped or moved and the proportions. What I didn't understand as a student was that fashion isn't clothes; fashion is much more interesting than that; it's a feeling and a mood—not dressmaking."

Treacy opened his first shop in 1994 next door to Isabella Blow and a studio a few doors along that side of the street

and found an apartment opposite. "My world," he once said, "doesn't go much beyond my own street." He has designed a ready-to-wear hat collection since 1991 and has developed ranges for high street chains including Debenhams and Marks & Spencer, but the heart of his business remains his couture hats.

He begins by mocking up the shape in straw "which I bend and stitch, pin and press, until the shape and the proportion fit my vision." Once satisfied with the shape, he has a sleek wooden block specially made in Paris on which the hat is steamed and molded. He works with a team of 15 people and his Jack Russell terrier, Mr. Pig. "I spend a lot of my time torturing normal farmyard feathers until they look extraordinary. Next to all the technological advances in the world, nothing is quite so impressive as a feather. People often ask: 'Where's the machinery?' My hands are the machinery. . . . I only feel dressed in the morning when I've got my thimble on my middle finger. It stays there all day."

Isabella Blow was as famous for wearing hats as she was for being a magazine editor. She was the muse and most regular client of Philip Treacy. Richard Saker/REX USA.

a hat from scratch might need some of these foundation materials:

- **Buckram** Pliable when wet, buckram can be shaped over a hat block or any other frame. It's covered with heavy water-based sizing.
- **Flexie** Loosely woven, very light and flexible, this lightly sized, soft foundation material is often applied on a bias.
- **French elastic** Closely woven, unsized, light fabric is used for light and firm support base. It is lighter than flexie.
- **Cape net** This lightweight mesh material is used for blocking soft cap frames. It is covered with a heavy water-based sizing.

FELT

Felt is traditionally the oldest and most common material used to make hats. It is a nonwoven cloth, created by pressing or matting wool fibers or fur together in a process called **wet felting**. It is extremely strong because every fiber interlocks with other fibers around it in every direction. The resulting felt can be molded into any shape or size with the help of a wet solution. From the mid-seventeenth century through the twentieth century, this process was done with mercuric nitrate, a compound of diluted mercury. The toxic vapors that were produced caused widespread mercury poisoning among hatters and in 1941, the United States Public Health Service banned the use of mercury in the felt industry.

The main types of felt used for hat making are wool felt, fur felt, beaver felt, and artificial felt, which is used for less expensive hats.

- **Wool felt** hats are made from sheep's wool and feel considerably coarser in comparison to the luxuriously soft fur felt. Their popularity is due primarily to their lower price, but they do not wear as well as fur felts. They tend to lose their shape with wear and shrink if exposed to rain. The hat making processes for a wool felt

hat is very similar to the fur felt hat making process and can easily be done by hand with soapy water. **Hand felting** with sheep's wool has been practiced for centuries, and various techniques have been developed by felt makers all over the world.

- **Fur felt** hats are made mostly from rabbit fur. Better quality hats can be made from hare, beaver, or nutria, and medium priced ones from a combination with rabbit and other fur. Fur is the soft and fluffy, downlike undercoat under the coarse hair of these animals, and it has the ability to lock the fibers together to create felt strong enough for a hat.
- **Beaver felt** feels luxurious, soft, and resilient and can easily be manipulated into a variety of shapes. Beaver felt hats date back as far as the fourteenth century, with Europe as the main supplier until the early mid-seventeenth century, when the European beaver breeding became exhausted, and North America became an important supplier of skins and hat manufacturing. Hats made of felted beaver fur were extremely fashionable from 1550 to 1850 throughout most of Europe.

The demand for beaver pelts in Europe ultimately drove the animal to near extinction and fueled colonial expansion as more people sought the fortunes of the trade. In the eighteenth century, beaver felt was still the preferred material for headwear, but a mixture of beaver and wool, or beaver and fur felt were used for less expensive hats.

FUR FELT HAT MAKING

Each manufacturer closely guards his exact felt making process and formula and you as a milliner would probably not get involved in the felt making, but would just block premade felt. From the mid-seventeenth to the mid-twentieth century, hatters used a process called **carroting** to create a good quality felt for men's hats. The first step in making a beaver felt was removing the coarse guard hairs from the beaver pelt, and then brushing it with a solution of mercury nitrate. This raised the scales on the fur shafts and they locked together. Similar processing was done for rabbit or hare. The skins were then dried in an oven and the delicate fur at the edges often turned orange, hence the term *carroting*. The fibers were then cut from the skin and placed on a bench in a workroom called the "hurdle." A hatter's bow was suspended over it. Vibrations of the bow were controlled by the craftsmen, and the fibers responded to them by separating and evenly distributing until they formed into a thick, loosely structured material called **batt**. Several batts would then be shaped into a cone and reduced in size by boiling and then rolled to create a firm dense felt. After the carroting process using mercury nitrate was banned, manufacturers started using safe solutions for the mixing and refining processes.

There are two main steps in making fur into a felt hat. First, the fur is made into a large, loose cone, and second, the resulting cone is shrunk and shaped into a finished hat. The first step, forming the cone, is the key to felt hat making. A cone is produced by placing an exact quantity of fur onto the top of an upright cylindrical compartment, called the forming chamber. Inside it is housed a slowly revolving perforated copper cone about three feet tall. An exhaust fan beneath it sucks the air and the loose fur in the chamber onto the revolving cone, creating a layer of loosely interwoven fibers. The cone is then immersed in very hot water, which shrinks the fibers and starts the felting process. The fur, which has formed into a loose layer of felt, is then removed from the cone.

The resulting hood is several times bigger than the final hat and must be reduced in size through a rapid process of multiple folding, dipping in hot water, and then putting through rollers, which squeeze out any of the excess fluid. A large part of this painstaking process is done by hand. The hood would then be sent onto the hatter who would mold it to the required shape by stretching and blocking the crown, flanging the brim, and then finishing it.

HOOD BLOCKING

Felt hoods are blocked on wooden blocks. The original block is made by hand and the rest by machines, which duplicate the original form. A hat manufacturer must create a set of blocks for each style and every head size in which the style is to be made. A large factory has a number of sets of each style block so that multiples can be created at the same time. The most common wood used for these blocks comes from the American poplar tree. Its advantage is that it has no grain or streaks, which would show on the felt during the blocking process.

The first rough shape is obtained by stretching the crown over a cone. It is done on a machine, which places the cone over a frame and massages the tip of the cone, with metal fingers, pressing the felt and stretching it. The brim stretcher grips the brim with metal fingers and works on the same principle. For a custom order handmade hat, the same process can be done by hand by wetting the felt and pulling it over a wooden block. Blocking to final size is done with steam and an iron and then flanging the brim.

FLANGING

Setting the brim in the hat is called **flanging**. First the brim is cut to desired size and specified width then ironed flat. Then it is laid on a wooden flange of the preferred roll, ironed again, and finally dried and pressed on the flange. Before the hat is complete, there could be other intermediate steps like dyeing or adding design details. The brim is usually impregnated with a stiffening shellac to make it hold up, and the entire felt hat is rubbed with sandpaper to the desired smoothness. Finally the felt hat is trimmed and the lining and band, if needed, are sewn on.

A Visual Review of the Creation of a Felt Hat

The process of making a felt hat at Makins Hats studio in New York City starts with selecting the wooden blocks of the desired shape for the crown and brim.

The felt hood (a general felt shape) is fitted onto the wooden block.

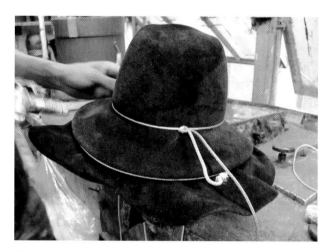

Thin ropes are tightened around the crown and below the brim edge to keep it in place and fit onto the block.

The felt hat is exposed to steam and then pulled tight onto the block.

FIGURE 14.3 Steps in the creation of a felt hat. Courtesy of Aneta Genova.

MODERN FELT HAT MAKING

The modern milliner doesn't have to create the actual felt and has a lot more choices that are not so labor intensive. You can buy a felt hood (the basic hat body), block it into any desired shape through application of steam and heat, and trim the excess. Felt can also be bought in flat sheets and blocked or cut and sewn into any number of different shapes. Premade felt comes in various colors and is widely available at millinery shops along with matching felt trims, embellishments, and various premade shapes. Thus the process of creating a felt hat is a lot more accessible to anybody who would like to create his or her own masterpiece. The secret is in practicing this unique craft. The more hats you make the better you will become (Figure 14.3).

Short bursts of steam through a handheld steamer are used for hard to reach creases and folds.

When the final shape is achieved, the rough hat is removed from the block.

The shaped hat has a lot of excess material.

A seamstress trims the excess.

A sweatband is sewn on the inner part of the crown.

Some hats are left with a raw edge. The brim for this one is turned under and stitched.

Trims and labels are carefully stitched and added by hand.

The hat is once again put on a wooden block for final steam and shaping.

Some elements like the crown pinch and the brim bend and balance can be done only by the hands of skillful, experienced masters.

The hat is brushed to remove any lint or minor smudges and to improve the texture and feel of the felt.

The hat receives a final check for any hanging threads or uneven seams.

The hat is heated one more time to set the sweatband and finalize the shape.

Soft Hats

Creating a soft hat out of fabric is a completely different process from working with felt. Technically it involves different steps because of the materials used in the process. Fabric cannot be steamed and reshaped like felt and needs to be cut into predetermined specific pattern pieces, which are then sewn into the final hat shape. The process might contain some or all of the following steps:

- Concept development
- Sketching ideas
- Pattern development
- Cutting
- Sewing
- Adding lining
- Attaching sweatband
- Adding trims
- Finishing touches may include steaming and resizing

Soft hats can be made in any shape. The name implies that the hats have been made from a soft fabric rather than felt or straw. Some of the most popular shapes include: berets, cloche hats, visors, baseball caps, and turbans.

Hand knit or machine knit hats also fall in the soft hat category. For those hats, the pattern will consist of the knit stitches to be executed by hand or machine. With those, the interest lies not only in the overall design shape but also in the surface texture created by the stitches and the figurative patterns created by different color yarns.

Straw Hats

Straw hat making is one of the oldest and simplest crafts. Straw hats can be handmade from single strands of rye straw or from ready braids utilizing simple techniques of twisting, braiding, and sewing. In modern times, straw hats are developed for the summer season or for particular concepts in a collection that might include nautical influence, for example. Because straw comes in different weights and braids, a finer gauge weave might even be used for an evening or cocktail hat with sophisticated trim or decorative elements.

There is a wide range of ready braids for hat making available in countless colors and various lengths at supply stores. They range from very fine to thicker, coarser ones and can be made from wheat straw, raffia, Coburg straw, twisted grasses, or other vegetable fibers. You can choose thinner braids or wider panels and create a wide range of structures for any design.

If you desire to work with raw straw, the first step is to soak the straw strands overnight, then flatten them and weave a braid with multiple strands. Then the braid can be built in a spiraling manner to fit the desired shape of a hat and stitched together with a curved upholstery needle. A flat or curved brim can be created with a similar technique and stitched onto the crown of the hat.

A straw hat can be a wonderful addition to any summer outfit. A classic boater hat can bring a nostalgic feel while a more innovative shape could bring a sophisticated touch for a complete look as in Figure 14.4.

FIGURE 14.4 Straw hats can be inexpensive or very high-end accessories. Pictured here is a couture large-brimmed hat on the Oscar de la Renta runway. Courtesy of WWD/John Aquino.

FIGURE 14.5

Unusual shapes and innovative materials make for a perfect statement in a cocktail hat like this one shown at a John Galliano fashion show.

Courtesy of WWD/ Giovanni Giannoni.

Rigid Frame Hats

Rigid frame hats include pillbox hats, boaters, top hats, and bonnets, among others. The process starts with buying a premade frame or creating one from buckram or flexie. Making your own frame is like creating a sculpture. With a bit of wire you can turn flat buckram into a fantastical sculpture. The next step is to cover the stiff foundation with fashionable fabric and trims. This requires the development of precise patterns according to the shape of the hat. The fabric is pulled tight or draped and carefully hand stitched onto the frame. Lining is then added and finished with a sweatband inside the crown or trims on the outside. After light steaming, the hat is ready for wear.

A rigid frame hat can be covered with any material or objects you can imagine. Flexible light straw braid is an excellent substitute for fabric and can be used with equal success. Flowers, leaves, or feathers are another great option to cover a frame for a fun hat.

Special Occasion Hats

Stylish little headpieces make an amazing fashion statement. They can be designed to complement an existing outfit by matching the color, fabric, or trims to it or created to stand on their own. These special hats are usually worn on the front top part of the head and are often kept in place by a comb, elastic cord, or a figure-eight wire.

The process of making a special occasion hat, also called cocktail cap starts with a small premade or custom-made foundation, created from cape net or heavily sized buckram. Then, according to the design, the foundation can be covered with fabric, lace or any other material that fits the concept. Colored feathers, ribbons, and flowers are usually the choice decoration for a statement piece. The most important element in cocktail caps is the proportion and balance of the structure. A thoughtful, stable structure with a great concept makes a perfect occasion hat (Figure 14.5).

Modern Manufacturing of Hats

The modern millinery world consists of the haute couture designers, who create fabulous one-of-a-kind structures based on dreams and high-quality materials, and the mass manufacturers, who produce affordable fashionable items every season. Since the late 1800s, the traditional and independent hatters who made and sold hats in their shops were replaced by large hat-making factories that use steam and combine the felt-making process with the production of the finished hat. Nowadays, a wide range of materials are used to create hat supplies, and various machines can create almost any model in a speedy process. There are customers for every price point, and while couture fashion houses rely on exquisite hats to add a touch of elegance

to a collection, the mass market experiences a changing demand as hats go in and out of fashion. There are, of course, some styles like baseball caps, for example, that are always in demand. They are accepted as uniform for some sports and signify a belonging to a certain team or cause through a branded logo, and as such, they are sold all year long.

Gloves

Today more than ever, gloves are functional accessories rather than a show of status or social rank. With the advancement of technology and fabric development, what started as simple animal skin covering for the hands has evolved into highly specialized gloves for every occupation, including firemen and astronauts. Gloves have been seen on the hands of pharaohs and mentioned in the Old Testament and have carried great symbolism throughout the centuries. Members of nobility would be depicted in their portraits, glove in hand among their riches. Knights carried or tied their lover's perfumed glove into battle for good luck. A duel could be provoked with a slap in the face by a glove.

Gloves, like any other accessory, went through dramatic transformations through the ages. Long cuffs with detailed embroideries and multiple buttons were typical of the fashionable men's gloves during the thirteenth century. Gold and precious stones revealed the riches of the wearer and were a clear indication of one's status in society. By the seventeenth century, leather from deer, goats, lambs, and sheep was widely used for the making of gloves. It wasn't until the eighteenth and nineteenth centuries that gloves were matched in style and color to shoes. They still played a significant role in social etiquette and were a must for a well-bred woman or man. It was twentieth century fashion that finally broke all rules, and gloves were somewhat abandoned as symbols of archaic manners. Women still enhanced their outfits with opera gloves during the early 1920s, but the rationing system of World War II included gloves, and women didn't use them as much. In the 1950s and 1960s, women and men wore mostly short gloves ending around the wrist, and after the 1970s, they became a much more functional item, used through the cold months and for sport-specific purposes. In the twenty-first century, gloves are a common fashion accessory appreciated both for their functional qualities and used as a trendy item to complement an outfit (Figure 14.6).

FIGURE 14.6
These gloves by Minna Parikka are two-button length for the grey pair, and four-button length for the red and white gloves. Minna Parikka.

Materials

Silk and leather have traditionally been some of the most common materials for glove making and are still widely used, but, we now also have gloves in waterproof and breathable fabrics. Gore-Tex® fabrics can keep moisture away from the skin and at the same time let the skin breathe. Seams, which used to be stitched, are now seam-sealed, so gloves can be fully waterproof when required. **Seam sealing** is the process of treating the stitch holes and seams in gear made from waterproof fabric to achieve maximum waterproofing and to prevent them from leaking when it rains or snows. Bike gloves can integrate carbon fiber knuckle plate parts for protection, Teflon® can be used as coating for extra protection, and Kevlar can be integrated for protection against cuts. Gloves and gauntlets are integral components of pressure suits and spacesuits going in outer space and combine toughness and protection with sensitivity and flexibility. More simple winter gloves can be made from fleece, acrylic, wool, and polyester, and common function-specific gloves are made from latex, vinyl, and rubber. Lining for fine gloves can be made of fine grade cashmere knit or cheaper cotton knit or woven fabric, flannel, or fleece.

Glove Components and Measurements

Gloves range in sizes from XS to XXL and a size can be measured by placing a tape measure around the knuckles of the hand and then making a fist with the tape still around. The recorded circumference is the correct glove size. The length of a glove is specified in buttons. One button equals one French inch, which is about 1/2" longer than an American inch. The measurement starts at the base of the thumb and follows up the forearm. A two-button glove is wrist length, a six-button glove is halfway to the elbow, and a sixteen-button glove reaches halfway between the elbow and the shoulder (See Figure 14.7).

FIGURE 14.7

The most common glove lengths defined by button lengths.

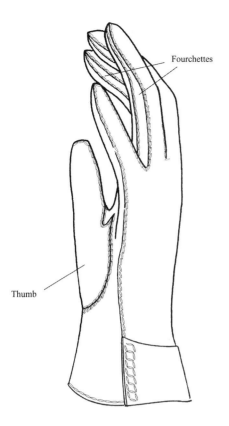

Fourchettes

Thumb

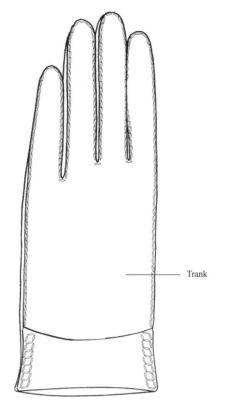

Trank

FIGURE 14.8
This sketch shows
the main parts of
a glove. It could be
as simple as just
having a trank and
a thumb or it could
be quite complicated
and contain yokes,
padding, closures,
trims, and many
other parts. Courtesy
of Aneta Genova.

Gloves usually have fewer than ten parts. The more pieces in a glove the better the fit, although knitted or stretch fabrics can provide a good fit with fewer parts. The major components of a glove are as follows (Figure 14.8):

- **Trank** The square piece of leather from which the main front and back pieces of the glove are cut
- **Fourchettes** Narrow, long pieces, which are inset between the fingers and form the sides of each finger
- **Gusset** or **Quirks** Triangular or irregular diamond shaped pieces fitted at the base of the fingers and thumb allowing for more flexibility and movement
- **Thumb** A separate piece in the shape of a thumb attached to the trank
- **Cuff** An extension of fabric above the palm, protecting the wrist and forearm
- **Lining** Fabric or knit in the shape of the glove, attached and secured inside to add extra warmth and prevent the glove from stretching

- **Hearts** or **Stays** Reinforcing sections on the palm of the glove
- **Pointing** or **Silking** Three rows of decorative topstitching on the back of the glove

Glove Styles

Gloves can be knitted, cut and sewn, or molded from manmade materials. Various gloves have been defined throughout the centuries depending on function and style. Here are the styles defined:

- **Baseball** A reinforced glove made specifically for the players in the field to help them catch the ball and prevent injury to their hands.
- **Cycling** Short knitted mesh glove with a padded leather palm part and exposed fingers.
- **Driving** Leather or knitted short glove with steering wheel palm grips and often with cut-out vents and button or snap closure on top.

- **Fingerless (Waif)** The fingertips are exposed above the center joint of the fingers. Usually made for sports activities or driving.
- **Medical gloves** Safety accessories that limit patients' exposure to infectious diseases and protect health professionals by preventing contact with bodily fluids. Close fitting and usually made out of latex, but for allergy prone people they can be made of vinyl or nitrite rubber.
- **Rubber gloves** Invented by William Stewart Halsted in the 1960s, household latex or rubber gloves are used for washing dishes and cleaning.
- **Chainmail** These armor gloves consist of small metal rings linked together in a mesh pattern and are used by butchers, scuba divers, woodcutters, or for oyster shucking.
- **Mitten** A glove with one thumb and one compartment housing the rest of the hand.
- **Biarritz** Short, slip-on glove with no vent.
- **Wrist length** Short glove, ending at the wrist bone.
- **Mousquetaire** Long cuffed glove, extending several inches up the forearm. Length varies from 8 to 16 buttons.
- **Opera glove** Long length, close fitting glove.
- **Finger free** Created by Merry Hull, an American accessory designer, in 1938 for better flexibility. Representing the first new glove construction in more than 300 years. Made with one long strip, forming the fourchettes between fingers.
- **Gauntlet** A wide flaring cuff extends above the wrist of this glove and protects the forearm.

FIGURE 14.9 A Fendi wood and Plexiglas belt and a rope belt demonstrate the variety of materials that can be used in a belt. Courtesy of WWD; © Conde Nast Digital Studio.

Belts

Belts, like all other accessories discussed so far, serve decorative and practical functions. They can be used to hold a garment, like a pair of pants in its place or to make a silhouette look slimmer. They can be worn in matching or contrasting colors to enhance the look of a garment and can also play up proportion by their width or the placement on, below, or above the natural waistline of the wearer. A belt can be a simple piece of fabric—a scarf could be used as a belt—or or it can be specifically designed and created from treated leather, with custom-made hardware like a buckle, grommets, an end tip, or any other trims. Belts are equally appreciated by men and women as an important and necessary item in any wardrobe (Figure 14.9).

Design Process for Belts

The process of creating a belt starts with a well-thought-out concept that might be a part of a bigger collection including various other accessories, or it might be a part of a belts-only seasonal collection. For both of these scenarios, the first step is to research and find the perfect

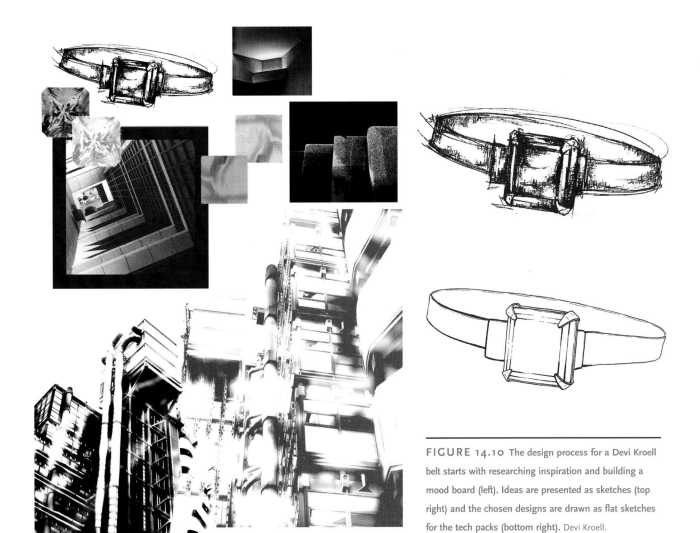

Angular   Cube   Wrapped

FIGURE 14.10 The design process for a Devi Kroell belt starts with researching inspiration and building a mood board (left). Ideas are presented as sketches (top right) and the chosen designs are drawn as flat sketches for the tech packs (bottom right). Devi Kroell.

design direction (Figure 14.10) and then look for appropriate materials. If the belt is designed for a specific garment and will be worn only with that item, then it should fit in the already developed concept for the dress, coat, skirt, or pant it was designated for. In this case, colors and materials are already designated and there isn't much to look for apart from hardware.

The second step in the design process involves sketching the ideas and narrowing them down to the most useful and appropriate ones (Figure 14.10). At this stage, you should also be thinking about merchandising the collection. Sketching the initial ideas, as with any other accessory, can be done in any media on paper or with a computer. The most important part is expressing the finalized ideas with clear flats with exact proportions and measurements. These will be used to create the patterns for each final belt.

All the technical information, color references, swatches, the flat sketches with all measurements, and any reference photographs should be included in a technical package or a spec page (Figure 14.10). This document is handed to the patternmaker to create the patterns, then to the sample maker, and finally to the manufacturer who will produce the belt.

Buckle Development

One of the most crucial parts in a belt design is developing the hardware. A beautiful buckle that fits the design concept is usually an integral part of the overall look and feel of the belt. There are classic designs that require the use

FIGURE 14.11
Each of these
buckles requires
the development
of a separate mold,
created to the exact
shape indicated
by the designer's
specifications and
sketches. Devi Kroell;
Courtesy of WWD/
Robert Mitra; © Conde
Nast Digital Studio/Tory
Williams; © Conde Nast
Digital Studio/Tim Hout.

of the same buckle season after season, but a designer belt normally needs new custom-made buckles for every new collection.

A buckle can be made out of plastic, metal, or any other material that can withstand the pressure of constant wear and tear associated with buckling and unbuckling and the actual wear. Before a buckle is made the shape must be drawn out in a precise flat sketch with a view from every side. The designer must represent every detail as realistically as possible. The next step is to create a model in actual size. Some skilled designers carve their own wax model; others designate that task to a work studio that specializes in that process. Once the model is made, a mold can be created in the shape of the buckle, which is used over and over to duplicate the original design (Figure 14.11).

A metal buckle can have any of the following finishes: shiny, matte, bronzed, antiqued, or brushed, or it could be covered altogether in fabric or leather, depending on the concept. Having a unique hardware design is an opportunity not only to demonstrate the concept through shape and surface finish, but also is a great way to brand the accessory. Many companies create buckles with the initials of the brand as the centerpiece of the design: an RL for Ralph Lauren or intertwined G's for Gucci.

Belt Development

A belt can be as skinny as half an inch wide or as wide as a few inches. It could consist of very fine single or multiple chains, or it could be made out of a single piece of leather. In

FIGURE 14.12
Fit and width of
a belt dictate the
shape of the pattern.
Some corsetlike belts
are shaped at the
waist for a better fit
(top); others need
complicated pattern
work (bottom) that
can be done as a flat
pattern or draped on a
mannequin. © Conde
Nast Digital Studio/John
Manno; © Conde Nast
Digital Studio/Marko
Macpherson.

order to get the right look and fit, a designer needs to determine the drape and position of the belt and estimate the appropriate length for all sizes. For a skinny belt, the fit is entirely determined by the actual width of the belt, but for a wider piece, which sits on a particular position of the body, that could be on, above, or below the natural waistline, the width and shape will affect the overall design. Some belts are designed to fit better around the body and are shaped or curved instead of just being straight (Figure 14.12). This allows a better contour of the body shape around the waistline. A complicated design might require complicated pattern work or the use of a mannequin or a live model in order to achieve the right fit (Figure 14.12). This can

be done with muslin or material similar to the actual leather or fabric to be used in the final design.

When the belt's shape is finalized a patternmaker develops patterns for every piece and traces the shapes onto the finalized material, interfacing and lining. All parts get glued and stitched together and any hardware and trims are added in the appropriate order. As a final step, the belt might be buffed, polished or steamed to achieve its best look.

Neckwear

Men's neckties and scarves for both men and women are both decorative accessories to be worn around the neck, but there are some differences in the way they are designed.

Neckties

Today a necktie is a common accessory used to enhance a business look for men. The easiest way to introduce color or pattern to a conservative business look is through a necktie. Ties have gone through many variations and changes through the ages and can be traced back to the cravat. Neckties can be associated with certain uniforms as well as fashion fads, and most men have worn them at some point in their lives (Figure 14.13).

ORIGINS AND EVOLUTION OF THE NECKTIE

The necktie in the form of cravat can be traced back to the mid-seventeenth century. The name cravat originated from the Croatian mercenaries, who sparked the interest of the Parisians with their traditional small, knotted kerchiefs tied around their necks. The fashionable King Louis XIV was impressed and quickly adopted the style calling it: *la croate*, which means "like the Croats," which turned into cravat. By the end of the century, this tie morphed into the Steinkirk, named after the battle of Steenkerque in 1692 (see Chapter 1).

Neckties were so popular during the period from 1800 to 1850, and there was so much interest in the proper way of tying them that there was a series of publications devoted to them. *Neckclothitania* was the first book that contained instructions and illustrations on how to tie 14 different cravats. It was also the first book to use the word tie in association with neckwear. The scarf was the next thing that appeared around 1850. This neckerchief or bandanna was held in place by slipping the ends through a scarf ring at the neck instead

FIGURE 14.13 Nowadays ties are worn with business attire or as a fashion statement in a more casual outfit. These examples are from Ben Sherman (top) and Tom Ford (bottom). Courtesy of WWD/Thomas Iannaccone; Courtesy of WWD/Arnaldo Anaya-Lucca.

of using a knot. This is known as the classic sailor neckwear and may have been adopted from them.

With the industrial revolution of 1860–1920s, there was a need for a comfortable and easy to put on neckwear, and so the modern necktie was born. It was long, thin, and easy to knot, and it didn't come undone. In 1926, a New York tie maker, Jesse Langsdorf, came up with a method of cutting the fabric on bias and sewing it in three segments. This technique improved elasticity and facilitated the fabric's return to its original shape. The next development was the method of securing the lining and interlining once the tie had been folded into shape, with Richard Atkinson and Company of Belfast introducing the slipstitch for this purpose in the late 1920s.

After World War I, wide, flamboyant, hand-painted ties became extremely popular in the United States and remained so through the 1950s. The more conservative British used Regimental stripes since the 1920s. Traditionally, English stripes ran diagonally from the left shoulder down toward the right side, but when Brooks Brothers introduced the striped ties in the United States around the first decade of the 1900s, they had theirs cut in the opposite direction (Figure 14.14).

Until World War II, men used to wear their trousers at the natural waist and used three-piece suits, which made ties much shorter than they are today. It was considered a faux pas to let the tie stick out below the vest, and they usually ended at or above the navel. The year 1944 marked the beginning of the **Bold Look**, which lasted until about 1951. Ties became wilder and wider, reaching 5 inches, reflecting the returning GIs' desire to break from the monotone wartime uniforms. Designs included Art Deco, hunting scenes, flora and fauna, tropical themes, and girlie prints, and the typical length reached 48 inches.

The next new style, characterized by tapered suits and slimmer lapels, also included thinner,

FIGURE 14.14

Brooks Brothers tie with diagonal stripes running from wearer's right shoulder to bottom left side.

Courtesy Brooks Brothers.

tamer ties. They slimmed down to 3 inches by 1953 and continued to get thinner until the mid-1960s. Men started wearing their pants lower, and tie length increased to about 52 inches. By the early 1960s, ties had slimmed down to as little as 1 inch, and colors became darker until the 1960s pop art brought an abundance of abstract expressionism. The exuberance of the late 1960s and early 1970s tie designs gradually gave way to more restrained designs and wider ties, returning to about 4½ inches wide. Ties were now sold next to shirts, and designers slowly started to experiment with bolder colors and patterns. Narrow ties appeared again around the eighties and can still be seen worn as a fashion statement. The classic tie worn today is about 4 inches at the widest point and about 57 inches long. Neckties can feature a wide variety of designs from traditional stripes, paisley, and abstract shapes to humorous cartoons and company logos.

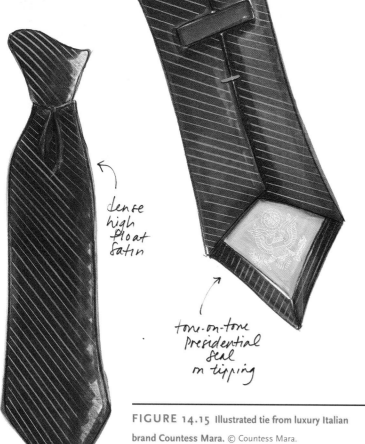

dense high float satin

tone-on-tone Presidential Seal on tipping

FIGURE 14.15 Illustrated tie from luxury Italian brand Countess Mara. © Countess Mara.

DESIGN

Nowadays, there isn't much change in the shape of a necktie, so most of the design is concentrated in the design of the pattern (Figure 14.15). Inspiration comes from vintage objects and patterns, flora, fauna, and traditional stripes and paisley. Various stripes, small objects, and insignia are developed by pattern designers and carefully woven at factories around the world that specialize in silks. Once the fabric is developed, the tie pattern is laid on bias and cut into two or three pieces. The best quality ties are constructed from three pieces and are cut and stitched by hand. They usually have buckram or another interfacing to retain their shape and a lining of the same fabric as the main body. High-quality Italian handmade ties have a thread running down the center back, called a spine, which holds the overall shape together. A loop at the end of it can be pulled to recover the shape of the tie even if it has been crumpled (see Figure 14.15). Knit ties

can be produced flat and seamed at the center back or knitted tubular.

A necktie consists of a shell with an apron (or the front blade), a tail (or the back blade), a connecting neck gusset, an interlining, and facing. The back has a loop label, and a visible bar tack stitch. The slip stitch with which the tie is sewn is hidden.

Scarves

The origins of scarves can be traced to the Chinese Emperor Cheng (Shih Huang Ti) and his warriors, who wore different cloth scarves to mark their rank. During the Ancient Roman Empire, men used a sudarium (Latin term for "sweat cloth") which was worn around their necks or knotted to a belt and used to wipe sweat from their faces. Roman women also adopted the idea of sudarium and started wearing it, too. Ever since then, the scarf has become a women's fashionable accessory. Around the seventeenth century, scarves were seen worn by Croatian Mercenaries. Soldiers wore ordinary cotton ones, while the officers wore silk. During the eighteenth century, French men began to wear a modified scarf as a necktie, called cravat (see "Origins and Evolution of Neckties"), and the color of a man's scarf was a popular way to demonstrate his political inclination.

Today's long rectangular scarves (Figure 14.16) are available in a multitude of fabrications, colors, and designs to complement the outfits of men, women, and children around the world. Scarves can be made from any fiber imaginable from wool and cashmere to fleece. A scarf could be crocheted or knitted by machine or hand, and it could be left with raw edges. Scarves usually have a decorative pattern or trim but can be one color, too. Fringe is the most popular edge trim found on scarves. Scarves have a simple construction: a rectangular or square piece of fabric or knit is finished in an attractive manner and then worn around the neck in various fashions.

The making of a scarf can be as simple as cutting a rectangle of a knit fabric and draping it around your neck or it can involve multiple steps of weaving a fine fabric and hand screen-printing every color of a complicated pattern. A scarf can be made in a couple of minutes or months, depending on those steps.

Some of the most popular modern types of scarves include the following:

- **Babushka** (grandmother in Russian) A triangular-shaped scarf or a square folded in half diagonally to form a triangle, worn over the head and tied under the chin. Can also be worn on the shoulders with the triangle point toward the lower back. Usually has long decorative fringe around the edges. This scarf is a traditional Russian scarf and usually has a flower pattern on a black or white background.

- **Bandanna** A bandanna is a square light woven cotton piece of fabric with a particular print design in black and white and a distinctive border. The classic background colors for this scarf are blue or red, but sold as a fashion item it comes in all colors of the rainbow and slight variations on the pattern.

- **Boa** A long and narrow scarf made out of feathers or fur. It usually appears round instead of flat because of the material it's made of.

- **Neckerchief** A small triangular scarf worn around the neck by men and women. Usually seen on cowboys worn with a denim shirt.

Shawls

The shawl is very similar to a scarf but is wider and worn around the shoulders, draping down

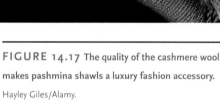

FIGURE 14.17 The quality of the cashmere wool makes pashmina shawls a luxury fashion accessory. Hayley Giles/Alamy.

FIGURE 14.18 The general shape of a poncho is a square, but there are many variations, such as this one from Nina Ricci. Courtesy of WWD/Giovanni Giannoni.

the back and arms rather than the neck and even used as outerwear. The first shawls were worn by men and women in Achaemenid Persia. They were so finely woven that each one could pass through a ring. The shawls were made in one color or with an intricate design in a rich multitude of colors.

The Kashmiri shawls, also known as pashminas are some of the most popular ones used today. They are made from the wool of a special goat, indigenous to the high altitudes of the Himalayas. The name **pashmina** refers to the wool and the textiles made from it, but it has become synonymous with the long rectangular shawls woven from the cashmere fiber. Some cheaper versions of these scarves are made from a cashmere blend with wool or silk.

The scarf usually has fringe on the two shorter sides (Figure 14.17).

Silk shawls with colorful embroidery and fringe, made in China, were popular in Europe and the Americas in the beginning of the nineteenth century. They were called China crepe shawls or just China shawls. The paisley patterned shawls are another popular design, which features an ornate drop-like design. Originating in Persia, this pattern was popularized by the weavers in the Scottish town of Paisley.

Another popular variation of the shawl is the **poncho** (Figure 14.18). A poncho is shaped more like a square or has oblong sides with a hole in the center for the head. It might include a hood and some kind of front closure.

Handkerchiefs and Pocket Squares

Sometime between 1200 and 1500, the modern term of handkerchief came into use in England, and the earliest written record of the English term "handkerchief" is from 1530. The Anglo/French "courchief" was used at least as early as 1223. In Old French, *couvrechief* was derived from *covrir* (to cover) and *chief* (head). A *couvrechief*, or *cuevrechief* was used to cover a woman's head. "Kerchifle" originated in Brittany and literally meant an old piece of cloth used at home for cleaning.

A square piece of fabric or a handkerchief used as an accessory in a pocket, namely a suit in modern times, is known as a **pocket square**. Some of the first linen fabrics used for ceremonial pocket squares were found at Hierakonpolis in the fourth millennium BCE. The linen had been colored with a red oxide powder, which is nonpermanent and would have easily been removed by washing. This seems to support the theory that these linens were the first ornamental pocket squares. By 2000 BCE, wealthy Egyptians were carrying the first true pocket squares made of bleached white linen. Some silk was imported from China in very limited quantities, and only the highest ranked nobles had handkerchiefs made from silk. There is evidence that in classical Greece, perfumed cotton handkerchiefs known as a mouth, or *perspirator cloth* were used by wealthy citizens. About 250 BCE, the Roman emperor had a magistrate drop a handkerchief called an orarium to signal the beginning of the gladiator games in the Colosseum.

In 271 CE, the emperor Aurelian further popularized handkerchiefs by introducing the practice of giving to the Roman people small handkerchiefs made of silk or linen, which were waved by the common people as a token of applause at the games. These were extremely expensive and certainly not an affordable item for common people. A *blatta serica* (raw silk dyed purple) pocket square cost 130,000 denarii, probably about a $1,000 in today's conversion rate. By the fourth century CE, the Roman clergy were wearing a white linen ceremonial handkerchief (*pallium linostinum*) over the left arm, which evolved into a strip of silk known as a *mappula* (from *mappa*, cloth) carried in the left hand by Christian priests.

Through the ninth century, Italian nobles were carrying handkerchiefs in their left hands. In the tenth century Egyptians were weaving luxurious pocket squares of linen, silk brocade, and tissue-thin wool and silk called *khazz*. In the Middle Ages, a handkerchief was worn by knights in tournaments as a symbol of a lady's favor. During the Renaissance, the handkerchief was widely used and made from silk, thin cotton, or woven grass. Handkerchiefs were lavishly embroidered or trimmed with lace. In Italy the handkerchief was called a *fazzoletto*. They were used by women for various signals, like declaring one's love or despise by drawing it across her cheek or through her hands. In England, King Richard II is said to have popularized handkerchiefs circa 1390. He used heavily embroidered handkerchiefs with a Holbein or Assisi stitch in red or black silk, with occasional fringes of silver and gold thread. Popular during the Tudor and Stuart reigns in England, printed limited edition pocket squares became collectors' items but eventually lost ground to the fan about 1700, and in the Victorian era, silk pocket squares were hung out of back pockets.

The nobles of France began using beautiful handkerchiefs in the fourteenth century. Made of silk, they were often heavily embroidered and came in many shapes, including circles and triangles. They were often scented in hopes to mask the smells resulting from a lack of regular baths and clean toilets. Legend has it that Marie Antoinette complained to her husband, Louis XVI, that handkerchiefs were too large to be fashionable. So he in 1785 ordered that handkerchiefs should have lengths equal to their width.

FIGURE 14.19
A bright pattern
pocket square is a
way to add a bit of
color to a business
suit. Courtesy of Aneta
Genova.

Handkerchiefs or *mendil* were used in Ottoman society and were woven from linen or cotton with an embroidered pattern. These early pocket squares were of solid colors and had a contrasting color on the edges. Those were the predecessors of the modern pocket squares. Around 1845, nobles and the wealthy in Germany began to use pocket squares made out of cotton, linen, and silk, and the Irish produced some of the finest linen, which has been made into both pocket squares and fine handkerchiefs. An old Irish proverb illustrates their philosophy regarding pocket squares: "Always carry a pocket square to show, and a handkerchief to blow."

By the 1900s, no fashionable man left home without a pocket square made of silk, linen, or cotton in his suit jacket's left breast pocket. Even the invention of the modern brassiere is connected to handkerchiefs. Legend has it that one evening in 1910, New York poet, publisher, and peace activist Mary Phelps Jacob was putting on a sheer evening gown and noticed that whalebones were visible beneath the fabric and were poking out of her corset. With the help of her maid she created a brassiere from two silk handkerchiefs and some pink ribbon. Her creation complemented the newest fashions of the times, and her family and friends started asking her to make more of these contraptions; on November 3, 1914, she got a patent from the U.S. Patent Office for the "Backless Brassiere."

Modern pocket squares are usually from 10 to 18 inch squares or circles and are made from silk, linen, or cotton fabric (Figure 14.19). The edges in inexpensive pocket squares are machine hemmed or cheaply hand-rolled with loose irregular stitches, and cheaper, mass-produced fabric with no special characteristics. Midrange pocket squares have better hand workmanship for their hand-rolled edges and nicer fabrics with interesting patterns. The finest pocket squares have tightly hand-rolled edges with approximately five to six regularly spaced stitches per inch, which are hidden inside the roll (Figure 14.20).

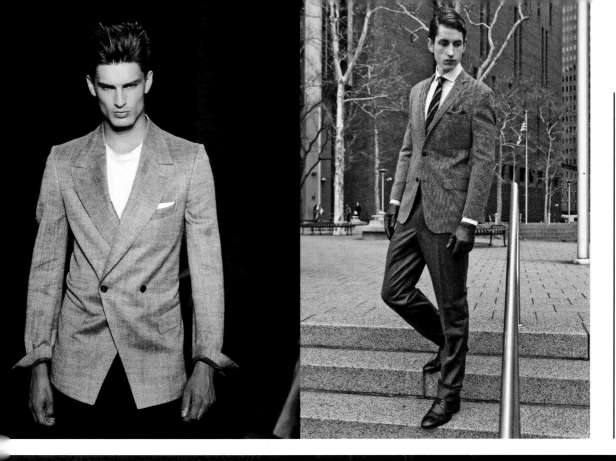

FIGURE 14.20
Pocket squares are usually worn in the left chest pocket of dressy suits and represent elegance and style. They can be shaped in a variety of ways. The most conservative way is to show just the edge of it parallel to the pocket edge (left). Another way is to fold it showing different heights of peaks (right).
Courtesy of WWD/ Giovanni Giannoni; Courtesy of WWD/ Thomas Iannaccone.

PROJECT

Design an Accessory Collection

GOALS

To give you practical experience in designing a unique group of a specific accessory.

ASSIGNMENT

Design a unique accessory collection. For this project, you will dive into a complete design process from concept and inspiration to designing and sketching the whole group. Choose one particular accessory and follow through all steps as outlined below.

1. Choose a theme or a concept.

2. Define the customer who will be buying the products and create a customer profile in the form of a collage. (For more details see the project for Chapter 5.)

3. Find sources of inspiration and compile research materials.

4. Create a mood board with select inspiration.

5. Choose colors, fabrics, textiles, or leathers, and hardware and create a color story and a materials page. (For more details see the project for Chapter 6.)

6. Sketch all design ideas as a finished presentation in a technique of your choice.

7. Select pieces to be made and create detailed flats with precise measurements.

8. Determine any additional trim and stitch details, and create the piece.

GLOSSARY

A

ANKLE BOOT A boot that just about reaches the ankle. (p 185)

ANKLE STRAP Women's shoe with a strap that wraps around the ankle. It can be a sandal or pump, and the straps can be tied or closed with buckles. (p 182)

B

BABUSHKA (grandmother in Russian) Triangular-shaped scarf or a square scarf folded in half diagonally to form a triangle, worn over the head and tied under the chin. (p 281)

BACKPACK A bag of varying shapes and sizes carried on one's back and secured with two straps that go over the shoulders. (p 102)

BAGGES Pockets made of leather that were worn inside men's breeches. (p 14)

BALLERINA FLAT Inspired by ballet slippers, a pump with a flat sole and no heel or a very low flat heel, closed toe, and a slipper-style construction. (p 181)

BALTEUS (CINGULUM) A Roman military belt. (p 9)

BANDANNA A square, light cotton piece of woven fabric with a particular print design in black and white and a distinctive border. (p 281)

BARBETTE A linen band which passed from temple to temple under the chin and worn with a fillet much like a crown over which a veil was often draped. (p 10)

BASEBALL GLOVE A reinforced glove made specifically for the players in the field to help catch the ball and prevent injury to their hands. (p 273)

BATT A loosely structured material that results from vibrations of a hatter's bow being suspended over beaver pelt that separates and evenly distributes the fibers. (p 265)

BEAVER FELT Luxurious, soft, resilient felt that can be easily manipulated into a variety of shapes. (p 264)

BELT *See* girdle.

BIARRITZ A short, slip-on glove with no vent. (p 274)

BIGGINS Close-fitting coifs that covered the ears and tied under the chin. (p 14)

BIRKIN BAG A handbag made by the design firm Hermès and named after model and actress Jane Birkin, for whom the bag was created. This bag has the longest waiting list of any accessory. (p 40)

BOA A long, narrow scarf that usually appears round, not flat, and is made out of feathers or fur. (p 281)

BOAT SHOE (DECK SHOE, TOP-SIDER) Shoe made of leather and usually having a white rubber sole that has a specific siping pattern (thin slits across the surface), which is specifically designed to provide traction on the wet deck of a boat. (p 178)

BOATER HATS Worn by women for yachting and other nautical adventures, made of flat straw. (p 19)

BOLD LOOK Period from 1944 to 1951; neckties were created in a wider fashion (up to 5 inches) to break away from the monotone wartime uniforms. (p 279)

BONNET The most common type of headwear for women throughout most of the nineteenth century. Bonnets were shaped with the help of wire and were covered with the most fashionable fabrics of the time. (p 19)

BOURRELET A padded, crownlike roll worn by men and women atop the head and internally supported. (p 11)

BOWLER Hat for daytime wear, invented in 1850 but remaining a working-class accessory. (p 19)

BREAST The part of the heel of a shoe that sits under the sole; when the shoe is being worn this part is facing the wearer's front. (p 174)

BRIEFCASE Often a flat and rectangular leather case that has a single carrying handle. It is used to carry items like a wallet, files, electronics, and personal items. (p 100)

BROGUE Often called wing-tips, men's low-heeled shoes, usually made from coarse leather with a punched design. (p 176)

BROGUING The hole-punching process used to create decorative patterns, emphasizing the design and seams of the shoe. (p 176)

BUCKRAM A material that is pliable when wet and used in hat making. (p 264)

BUTTON A measurement equal to one French inch (approximately ½ inch longer than an American inch) that describes the length of a glove from the base of the thumb to the forearm. (p 272)

C

CALASH A folding hood/brimless head covering that tied under the chin. (p 17)

CALIGAE Sandals, the classic Roman military army boots. (p 9)

CAPE NET A lightweight mesh material used in hat making for blocking soft cap frames. It is covered with a heavy water-based sizing. (p 264)

CAPOTAIN (COPOTAIN) A conical felt hat with a rounded crown. (p 13, 15)

CARROTING Process in making felt from the mid-seventeenth century to the mid-twentieth century wherein the skins of a beaver were dried in an oven after a solution of mercury nitrate was brushed into the pelt, turning the edges of the fur orange. (p 265)

CAUL A netting, sometimes lined in silk, that covered the pinned-up hair, worn during the Middle Ages. (p 11)

CHAINMAIL GLOVE Armor glove consisting of small metal rings linked together in a mesh pattern used by butchers, scuba divers, woodcutters, and policemen. (p 274)

CHAPERON Began as a form of hood with a short cape and later evolved into a highly versatile hat worn in all parts of Western Europe in the Middle Ages. (p 11)

CHATELAINE A clasp or chain to suspend keys. (p 12)

CHECKBOOK CASE A small rectangular case used to hold and protect a checkbook, sometimes containing slots or pockets for credit cards and ID, and sometimes containing a pen attachment. (p 104)

CHELSEA BOOT A men's boot that has a low-heel and is fitted right around the ankle. It has a plain leather upper and elasticized insets on both sides. (p 178)

CHOPINE A platform-soled mule that raised the wearer sometimes as high as two feet off the ground. Worn during the Renaissance. (p 14)

CLOCHE A small, round, close fitting hat with a very short, soft brim, resembling a helmet. It was the most popular women's hat during the 1920s and was worn over the popular short bob haircut. (p 23)

CLOG Open- back shoe with predominantly closed toe. The heel is usually a thick wood or cork platform with or without some height. (p 183)

CLUTCH A small purse for women that can usually be carried in the hand without a strap. (p 100)

COIF A close-fitting cap made of a light fabric, usually white or natural colored linen (or silk, for the nobility), which was worn by men and women for warmth and protection from the elements and to keep hair out of the face. (p 11)

COIN PURSE A small, one compartment purse used to carry coins, bills, and cards. (p 104)

COLETTE A cap or caul. (p 13)

COLOR STORY The palette of colors for materials, prints, and hardware used in an accessory collection driven by the concept, season, and overall trend direction. (p 81)

CONCEPT RIGS A life-size sample of all accessories and clothing that would be worn within the concept, showing a complete picture of the customers and their lifestyle and how they would wear the accessories. (p 128)

CONSTANCE BAG A handbag made by the design firm Hermès and named after the designer's daughter who was born the same day the bag debuted. This bag is often referred to as the "Jackie O bag" because she wore it so regularly. (p 40)

CORDWAINER Shoemaker. (p 16)

COSMETIC BAG A small bag with zipper closure usually lined in plastic, which holds cosmetics. (p 104)

COWBOY BOOT Boot that has a pointy toe and a Cuban heel and extends to mid-calf. It is traditionally made with calfskin but can be constructed from pigskin, horse, or kangaroo. (p 178)

CRAVAT The first recognizable necktie, made popular by King Louis XIV of France after seeing Croatian mercenaries wearing their traditional small knotted kerchiefs around their necks. Derived from the term "la croate" meaning "like the Croats." (p 16, 278)

CREDIT CARD HOLDER A flat smaller version of a wallet, designed to carry only a small number of credit cards and an ID card. (p 104)

CRESPINE Originally a thick hairnet or snood, it evolved into a mesh of jeweler's work that confined the hair on the sides of the head. (p 11)

CROSS-BODY BAG Usually a small handbag that is designed to be carried over one shoulder and across the chest. (p 98)

CUBAN HEEL A heel style with a slightly tapered back and straight front; this style is typically found on cowboy boots for both men and women. (p 175)

CUFF An extension of the fabric above the palm, protecting the wrist and forearm. (p 273)

CYCLING GLOVE A short, knitted mesh glove with a padded leather palm part and exposed fingers. (p 273)

D

DERBY A men's shoe that is low-cut and closed with lacing. The tongue is part of the vamp, and the quarters are topstitched on top of the vamp. They are usually kept apart at the tongue. (p 176)

DERBY BOOT Men's boot that has the construction of a Derby shoe but extends to right above the ankle. (p 178)

DRAWSTRING BAG Any bag that can be closed or cinched with a drawstring on the top. (p 98)

DOCTOR'S BAG A large handbag shaped like the traditional doctor's bag, often made with leather and having two handles. (p 100)

D'ORSAY PUMP A high heel shoe with the sides of the vamp cut out, revealing the arch of the foot. (p 181)

DRIVING GLOVE A leather or knitted short glove with steering wheel palm grips and often cut-out vents and button or strap closure on top. (p 273)

DUFFEL BAG A large, cylindrical bag with a zipper opening on top, originally used by military personnel, and usually made of canvas or leather for carrying personal belongings. (p 102)

E

EAST-WEST BAG A term used by designers to describe any bag that is wider than it is tall. (p 98)

ESPADRILLE Slip-on shoes with a canvas upper and a woven sole, usually from rope or grass. (p 178, 184)

EYEGLASS CASE A case to hold sunglasses and reading glasses and protect them in a bag or pocket; the shape resembles and closely fits the eyewear. (p 104)

F

FANNY PACK A small zippered pouch suspended from a belt around the waist. (p 102)

FASCINATOR A base that is used to build hats. (p 262)

FILLET A standing linen band. (p 10)

FINGER FREE GLOVE Glove made with one long strip forming the fourchettes between the fingers; the first new glove construction in more than 300 years. Created by Merry Hull, an American accessory designer, in 1938. (p 274)

FINGERLESS (WAIF) GLOVE Glove on which the fingertips are exposed above the center joint of the fingers. Usually made for sports activities or driving. (p 274)

FLANGING The process of setting the brim of the hat. (p 265)

FLAT LASTING Process where the upper of a shoe is placed on the last, pulled down, then attached to the insole at the toe, side, and seat of the last. (p 254)

FLEXIE A loosely woven, very light, flexible, lightly sized, soft foundation material that is often applied on a bias and used in hat making. (p 264)

FOLD-OVER BAG A zippered-top bag, usually flat, that may be folded over (doubled up) and carried under the arm or in the hand. (p 100)

FONTANGE A woman's headdress used to further heighten and elongate the silhouette. (p 15)

FORCED LASTING Process where the upper is pre-shaped into a shoe form and then the lasting is forced into it. (p 254)

FOURCHETTES Narrow, long pieces which are inset between the fingers of a glove and form the sides of each finger. (p 273)

FOUR-IN-HAND NECKTIE A rectangular cloth tied around the neck; popular as a men's accessory in the mid-nineteenth century. (p 20)

FRENCH ELASTIC Closely woven, unsized, light fabric used for light and firm support base used in hat making. It is lighter than flexie. (p 264)

FRENCH HEEL (LOUIS HEEL, CURVED HEEL, POMPADOUR HEEL) A curved, medium-sized heel originally created for King Louis XIV of France. (p 174)

FRONT AND BACK STIFFENERS (COUNTERS) Thin nonwoven shaped pieces attached in-between the upper and the lining at the heel or toe area of a shoe to add some stiffness and structure. (p 172)

FUR FELT Type of felt mostly made of rabbit fur but can be made of beaver, nutria, or hare. (p 264)

G

GABLE HOOD A wired headdress shaped like the gable of a house. (p 13)

GAITERS (SPATS) Cloth or leather accessories for shoes, designed to cover the instep and the ankle and protect during the winter or bad weather. (p 22)

GALEA Protective helmets for Roman soldiers. (p 8)

GAUNTLET Glove with a wide, flaring cuff extending above the wrist to protect the forearm. (p 274)

GIRDLE As used by costume scholars, a women's belt. (p 10, 14)

GUSSET (QUIRK) Triangular or irregular diamond shaped piece fitted at the base of the fingers and thumb allowing for more flexibility and movement. (p 273)

H

HAMONDEY (TASQUE) Ornate drawstring purse. (p 12)

HAND FELTING The process of creating a nonwoven cloth (felt) out of wool by pressing or matting the fibers or fur together by hand. (p 264)

HEARTS (STAYS) Reinforcing sections on the palm of a glove. (p 273)

HEEL The outer part of a shoe that is placed under the heel of the foot. Shoe heels come in varying heights, shapes, and materials. (p 173, 174)

HENNIN One of the most extravagant hats worn during the Middle Ages in Burgundy, France, and Northern Europe. It was in the shape of a cone or a steeple and often had a veil hanging from the top. (p 11)

HESSIAN BOOT A shiny black leather boot with the top finished with a gold or silver braid and a silk tassel hanging from center front. It was one of the most fashionable men's boots of the eighteenth century. (p 18)

HOBO Single strap women's bag with a curved crescent shape and slouchy look, usually with a zipper closure on top. (p 100)

HOMBURG A daytime soft felt hat. (p 22)

I

INSOLE The inside part of the shoe, positioned above the outsole on the inside of the shoe. (p 173)

J

JELLY Any style of shoe made of PVC through injection molding but usually made as a flat sandal or waterproof low shoe. (p 184)

K

KELLY BAG A handbag made by the design firm Hermès and named after the actress Grace Kelly because she was often photographed with it. (p 40)

KEY HOLDER An item resembling either a wallet or coin purse and containing a ring(s) for keys. (p 104)

KITTEN HEEL A thin-based, low heel (usually 1.5 inches or less) that is set in from the back of the shoe and has a little curve. It starts as almost the full width of the foot and tapers towards the bottom into a very thin base cap. (p 174)

KNEE BOOT Boot that reaches the knee. (p 185)

L

LAST Wood or plastic mold made for every style and size of shoe used as a form to shape the shoe. (p 190)

LASTING The assembled upper and sole of a shoe. (p 192)

LATCHET TIE A narrow strap, thong, or lace that fastens a shoe or sandal to the foot. (p 18)

LINE SHEET A grid chart that contains all the pieces of the accessory collection with their names, colors, logos, fabric, leather, trim, and hardware information. (p 88)

LINING Fabric or knit material in the shape of a glove, attached and secured inside to add extra warmth and prevent the glove from stretching. (p 273)

LIRIPIPE A long tail. (p 11)

LOAFER Low-cut, lace-less, slip-on shoes with very low heels. (p 176, 183)

LOW BOOT Boot ending anywhere below the knee but above the ankle. (p 185)

M

MARY JANE Traditionally a shoe with a short, rounded toe box and very flat heel as well as the defining strap that crosses the middle top of the foot. They are low cut and look like the kind of shoes little girls would wear. (p 181)

MEDICAL GLOVE Safety accessory invented by William Stewart Halsted in the 1860s that limits patients' exposure to infectious diseases and protects health professionals by preventing contact with bodily fluids; close fitting and usually made out of latex, but for allergy-prone people, it can be made out of vinyl or nitrite rubber. (p 274)

MESSENGER BAG A rectangular bag with a single flap closure and an adjustable long shoulder strap. (p 102)

MITTEN Glove with one thumb and one compartment housing the rest of the hand. (p 274)

MOCCASIN A soft leather shoe constructed of two pieces of hide: a bottom piece which comes around and up the sides, stitched to a vamp, which also serves as a tongue. (p 176, 183)

MODELLISTA A skilled technician who makes patterns based off a sketch of a shoe made by a designer or a last made by a lastmaker. This term is used more often in Europe in place of "patternmaker." (p 190)

MOOD BOARD A refined and collaged presentation of research using images, fabric references, prints, trims, hardware, and logos that reflects the finalized concept and represents the compiled research for a collection. After seeing this, the viewer should have no questions about the direction of the collection. (p 83)

MOUSQUETAIRE A long cuffed glove, extending several inches up the forearm. Length varies from 8 to 16 buttons. (p 274)

MULE (SABOT) A backless shoe with any kind of fashion heel. (p 183)

N

NECK The back of the heel; when the shoe is being worn this part can be seen from the wearer's back. (p 174)

NECKERCHIEF A small triangular scarf worn around the neck by men and women. (p 281)

NEMES A striped headcloth, extending low down the back, worn by pharaohs and their families. (p 7)

NORTH-SOUTH BAG A term used by designers to describe any bag that is taller than it is wide. (p 98)

O

OPERA GLOVE A long, close fitting glove. (p 274)

OUTSOLE The bottom-most outer part of the shoe, which is in direct contact with the ground. (p 173)

OXFORD A men's or women's shoe that typically has a plain front, is low-cut, and closed with lacing. The quarters are placed under the vamp and topstitched on the vamp. Oxfords are considered formal. Normally they have a plain front, but they can be decorated with cap-toes. (p 176)

P

PASHMINA A long rectangular shawl traditionally made from the wool of a special goat native to the high altitudes of the Himalayas; can be made of cashmere or cashmere blends with either wool or silk. (p 282)

PATTEN Thick-soled overshoe worn over the thin-soled soft shoes of the day for outdoors. Popular from the Middle Ages through the seventeenth century and worn as late as the early nineteenth century. (p 12)

PDA OR CELL PHONE CASE Case made to protect mobile devices, varying in shape, size, and closure. (p 104)

PEEP-TOE (OPEN-TOE) SHOE Women's shoe with a small, generally rounded opening at the front that shows only part of the big toe and the second one. (p 182)

PETASOS A closely fitted Greek cap with a wide brim. (p 8)

PHRYGIAN BONNET High brimless Greek cap with the peak folding towards the front. (p 8)

PILLBOX HAT A circular, flat-topped, rigid-framed women's hat popularized in the 1960s by First Lady Jacqueline Kennedy. (p 29)

PILOS A brimless or very narrow brimmed Greek cap with a pointy crown. (p 8)

PLATFORM SHOE Shoe defined by the thick sole under the front of the foot, not the heel. This sole is usually an inch thick or more and can be combined with a variety of heels. (p 184)

PLATFORM WEDGE HEEL A combination of the platform and the wedge heel adds height to a shoe. (p 175)

POCHETTE A type of handle-less small clutch, usually decorated with dazzling geometric and jazz motifs. (p 24)

POCKET SQUARE A square piece of fabric or a handkerchief used as an accessory in a pocket. (p 283)

POINTING (SILKING) Three rows of decorative topstitching on the back of a glove. (p 273)

PONCHO A type of shawl that can be shaped like a square or have oblong sides with a hole in the center for the head. (p 282)

POUCH A relatively small bag of soft fabric or leather gathered with a drawstring as a means of closure, which usually extend as handles. (p 100)

POULAINE (CRACKOWE) Extreme shoe style of the Middle Ages that had long pointed toes, sometimes held up with strings or chains attached to garters at the knees. Named after Poland and the Polish capital city of Krakow, where this style originated. (p 12)

PROTO (PROTOTYPE) A mock-up made to provide an example of what the accessory will look like when completed. (p 91)

PUDDING HAT A protective head covering that toddlers in seventeenth-century Europe wore when just learning to walk. (p 16)

PUMP The simplest looking shoe; the upper hugs the foot and forms one line. There are no straps or laces to keep the shape. (p 181)

PURSE Synonym for a women's handbag; the term originates from a small container used to hold coins. (p 98)

Q

QUARTER Part of a shoe's upper that covers the sides and the back of the foot. It can be a separate piece sewn onto the vamp of the shoe. (p 172)

R

RETICULE A small simple bag with ribbon or cord drawstrings, intricately decorated with embroidery or feather trims and wrapped in mesh or trimmed with a fringe. (p 20)

RIDING BOOT (EQUESTRIAN BOOT) Traditionally this boot was made to be worn while riding horseback. It is made of stiff calfskin or cowhide leather in brown or black, and has a low heel to prevent the foot from slipping in the stirrup. The shaft ends right below the knee. (p 178)

RUBBER GLOVE Household latex or rubber gloves used for washing dishes and cleaning. (p 274)

S

SABOT A shoe shaped from a single block of wood that was worn by the peasants of France and the Low Countries in the late Middle Ages and Renaissance to keep their feet dry. Precursor to the modern clog. (p 13)

SALPA A material often used to make a prototype handbag because it offers structure and flexibility; it also comes in varying thicknesses. (p 91)

SANDAL Open-toe and -heel shoes that usually have openings on the sides. The upper usually consists of multiple straps, which are attached to the sole and buckle around the ankle. (p 178, 182)

SATCHEL A rigid-bottom bag of varying sizes with one or two handles that is typically carried on the arm rather than the shoulder. (p 100)

SEAM SEALING The process of treating the stitch holes and seams in gear made from waterproof fabric to achieve maximum waterproofing and to prevent the holes from leaking when it rains or snows. (p 272)

SEAT The top part of the heel of a shoe that is directly under the foot. (p 174)

SHANK A metal piece positioned in between the heel and the outsole of a shoe, sitting under the arch of the foot. The shank supports the whole foot and helps the overall structure. (p 173)

SHOE ROSE Elaborate lace or ribbon rosette tie over the instep of a shoe. (p 16)

SHOULDER BAG Any handbag with a long shoulder strap. (p 98)

SIPING PATTERN Thin slits across the surface of the sole of a shoe specifically designed to provide traction; used on boat shoes. (p 178)

SKIVING A process in which a thin layer of leather skin is removed to reduce the upper's thickness. (p 253)

SLIDE Shoes with an open toe and open back; can have single or multiple straps; a true "slide" has no toe or ankle straps. Slides are easy to slip on and off. (p 183)

SLING-BACK SHOE Shoe with a strap that wraps around the back part of the foot that can come from the sides of the vamp or can be tucked in between the insole and sole. It can be open or close toed and can be casual or dressy. (p 182)

SMALL LEATHER GOODS (SLGS) A variety of small containers that women typically carry in their handbags and men in their briefcases or pockets. Despite the term, these are not always made of leather. (p 104)

SNOOD A type of a close fitting hood or hairnet worn over long hair by Medieval women. It was revived centuries later in the 1860s and again in the 1940s. (p 11)

SOCCUS Slipperlike Roman shoes reaching to the ankle. (p 9)

SOCK A lining inserted in the finished shoe. (p 173)

SOLAE (SANDALIS) Roman sandals. (p 9)

SPEC PAGE (SPEC SHEET) A document used to describe to the manufacturer in great detail what an accessory looks like, how it is made, and what it should be made of; it also contains sketches and notes on design, stitching details, colors, materials, hardware, closures, and so on. It can also have pictures of any references for any of the design components. (p 89, 152)

SPECTATOR SHOE Shoe that features two contrast colors and comes in varying designs. The most common color combinations are black and white and brown and white. (p 26, 184)

SPOON BONNET A high-brimmed, elaborately trimmed bonnet of the mid-eighteenth century. (p 19)

STEINKERK A lace cravat tied very loosely, with the ends passed through a buttonhole in the coat. (p 16)

STILETTO HEEL A thin, high heel, named after the stiletto dagger. (p 174)

SUITCASE A rectangular large bag with solid structure and reinforced corners, used to carry luggage on trips. (p 102)

T

T-BAR SHOE Women's shoe with the distinguishing characteristic of a T-strap at the front, connecting the upper to the ankle strap. (p 182)

TECH PACK Black-and-white flat sketch of the design and all technical information needed to make the accessory. (p 88)

THIGH-HIGH BOOT Boot that goes above the knee and has a flexible shaft that opens with a zipper along its full length. It can also be made in part or completely from a stretch material. (p 185)

THUMB A separate piece in the shape of a thumb attached to the trank of a glove. (p 273)

TOE PUFF (TOE CAP) A thick, shaped, nonwoven or metal reinforcement, added to the inside of the upper of a shoe to provide stability, protection, and stiffness to the toe area. (p 172)

TONGUE Part of the upper of a shoe that extends under the laces or other closures to protect the foot. (p 172)

TOP LIFT The bottom part of the heel that comes in direct contact with the ground. (p 174)

TOTE BAG A large handheld bag with two handles, an open top, and a simple structure; this bag is often made from canvas. (p 100)

TRANK Square piece of leather from which the main front and back pieces of the glove are cut. (p 273)

TRAVEL BAG Generally a rectangular bag with multiple compartments and pockets, used as carry-on luggage on airplanes or short trips. (p 102)

U

UPPER Everything above the sole on a shoe—vamp, quarter, back, toe, box, tongue, laces, and lining. This can be cut from a single piece or composed of many. (p 172)

V

VAMP Part of the upper of a shoe that covers the top part of the foot between the toes and the ankle area or the instep. (p 172)

VITA A woolen band that bounded Roman matrons' hairdos. (p 8)

W

WALLET Small flat case, usually with multiple compartments and a zippered coin section, used to carry credit cards, coins, and other personal items like ID and checks. (p 104)

WEDGE HEEL Heel formed by a triangular or wedgelike piece that extends from the front or middle to the back of the sole; it is used on women's shoes. (p 175)

WELLINGTON BOOT (WELLIE) A very plain straight cut boot traditionally made of calfskin but now usually made of PVC to protect the wearer from wet weather. They are named after the Duke of Wellington and were first worn by the military during the eighteenth century as Hessian boots. (p 21, 178)

WET FELTING The process of creating a nonwoven cloth (felt) out of wool by pressing or matting the fibers or fur together. (p 264)

WIMPLE A fine white linen or silk scarf that covered the neck, with ends pulled and tied above the ears or temples. First appeared during the Middle Ages, it was usually worn with a veil and became a part of the dress for many orders of the Roman Catholic nuns until the 1960s. (p 10)

WING TIP The toe cap of a men's shoe. It takes its name from its resemblance to the spread-out wings of a bird. This toe cap is usually applied to coarse leather, low-cut, low-heeled, closed shoes with laces or loafers. (p 176)

WOOL FELT Felt made of sheep's wool; feels considerably coarser in comparison to the luxuriously soft fur felt. This is also more cost effective but wears more over time. (p 264)

WRISTLET A small, usually flat bag with a very short strap that only fits around the wrist. (p 104)

REFERENCES

Websites

http://www.CFDA.com

http://www.cesare-paciotti.com/

http://www.manoloblahnik.com

http://designmuseum.org

http://www.fashion-era.com

http://www.mademoisellerobot.com/2009/03/
mademoiselle-robot-loves-minna-parikka.html

http://www.purseblog.com/meet-monica-botkier/

http://www.fundinguniverse.com/company-histories/
Coach-Inc-Company-History.html

http://www.museoferragamo.it/en

http://www.ninewest.com/Fred-Allard/
designingNine-FredAllard,default,pg.html

http://www.rafe.com/aboutrafe.html

http://en.wikipedia.org/wiki/Rafe_Totengco

http://www.nytimes.com/2009/10/29/
fashion/29FALCHI.html

http://en.wikipedia.org/wiki/Carlos_Falchi

http://www.christianlouboutin.com

http://www.high-heels-fashionista.com/roger-vivier.php

http://en.wikipedia.org/wiki/Roger_Vivier

http://www.jimmychoo.com/The-story-of-Jimmy-
Choo/The-History/stry/thehistory

http://www.jimmychoo.com/The-story-of-Jimmy-
Choo/Tamara-Mellon/stry/tmbiography

http://dazeddigital.com/Fashion/article/4508/1/
Running_in_Art_Nouveau_Heels

http://www.katespade.com

http://en.wikipedia.org/wiki/Stiletto

http://theglassmagazine.com/forum/feature.
asp?tid=628#title

http://www.vogue.co.uk/news/daily/091214-lulu-
guinness-uk-fashion-and-textil.aspx

http://www.luluguinness.com/bio.php

http://www.luluguinness.com/history.php

http://www.vogue.co.uk/video/voguetv/player.aspx/
exclusives/video,9118/

http://www.reshafim.org.il/ad/egypt/timelines/
topics/clothing.htm

http://www.reshafim.org.il/ad/egypt/timelines/
topics/hair.htm#wigs

http://en.wikipedia.org/wiki/Baldric#Roman_balteus

http://en.wikipedia.org/wiki/Cingulum

http://www.nytimes.com/1982/10/03/travel/lock-s-of-
london-gentlemen-s-hatters.html

http://www.lockhatters.co.uk/historyfull.aspx

http://www.torbandreiner.com/index.htm

http://www.wtifelt.com/pressedfelt.html

http://www.hathistory.org/

http://millerhats.com/hatcare_index/felthatsinfo.html

http://lynnmcmasters.com/strawlinks.html

http://neck-ties.com/index.html

http://www.krawattenknoten.info/krawatten/necktie/
neckclothitania.html

http://www.robbreport.com/Style-Turning-the-Tie-1.aspx

Books

McDowell, Colin. *Manolo Blahnik.* London: Orion
Publishing, 2003.

———. *Hats—Status, Style and Glamour.* London:
Thames & Hudson, 1997.

Stall-Meadows, Celia. *Know Your Fashion Accessories.*
New York: Fairchild Publications, Inc., 2004.

Seivewright, Simon. *Basics Fashion: Research and
Design.* Worthing, UK: Ava Publishing, 2007.

Tortora, Phyllis, and Keith Eubanks. *Survey of Historic
Costume.* 5th ed. New York: Fairchild Books, 2010.

ART CREDITS

INDEX

Page numbers in italics refer to images.